Also by Danielle Steel

ANSWERED PRAYERS
SUNSET IN ST TROPEZ
THE COTTAGE
THE KISS
LEAP OF FAITH
LONE EAGLE
JOURNEY
THE HOUSE ON HOPE
   STREET
THE WEDDING
IRRESISTIBLE FORCES
GRANNY DAN
BITTERSWEET
MIRROR IMAGE
THE KLONE AND I
THE LONG ROAD HOME
THE GHOST
SPECIAL DELIVERY
THE RANCH
SILENT HONOUR
MALICE
FIVE DAYS IN PARIS
LIGHTNING
WINGS
THE GIFT
ACCIDENT
VANISHED
MIXED BLESSINGS
JEWELS

NO GREATER LOVE
HEARTBEAT
MESSAGE FROM NAM
DADDY
STAR
ZOYA
KALEIDOSCOPE
FINE THINGS
WANDERLUST
SECRETS
FAMILY ALBUM
FULL CIRCLE
CHANGES
THURSTON HOUSE
CROSSINGS
ONCE IN A LIFETIME
A PERFECT STRANGER
REMEMBRANCE
PALOMINO
LOVE: POEMS
THE RING
LOVING
TO LOVE AGAIN
SUMMER'S END
SEASON OF PASSION
THE PROMISE
NOW AND FOREVER
GOLDEN MOMENTS*
GOING HOME

* Published outside the U.K. under the title *Passion's Promise*.

HIS BRIGHT LIGHT

THE STORY OF MY SON, NICK TRAINA

Photo Credits

Page 4		Roger Ressmeyer
Page 39		Danielle Steel
Page 47		Danielle Steel
Page 48		Danielle Steel
Page 51		Danielle Steel
Page 65	*Top*	Danielle Steel, *Bottom* Roger Ressmeyer
Page 79	*Top*	Roger Ressmeyer, *Bottom* Danielle Steel
Page 81		
	Top and middle	John J. Capistrant – Lifetouch, Hawyard, Ca.
	Bottom and right	Roger Ressmeyer
Page 83	*Top*	Tilly Abbe, *Bottom* Lucy Brown
Page 84	*Top*	Tilly Abbe, *Bottom* Danielle Steel
Page 93		Danielle Steel
Page 109		Roger Ressmeyer
Page 154		Danielle Steel
Page 171		Danielle Steel
Page 178		Harry Langdon
Pages 249-50		Tilly Abbe
Page 281	*Middle left*	Debbi Paine, *All others* Sam Ewing
Page 295		Debbi Paine
Page 301		Danielle Steel/Family
Page 302		Harry Langdon
Page 331	*Bottom*	Bert D. Bautista, *All others* Danielle Steel
Pages 337-9		© Eliot Holtzman
Page 343		Mara Passetti
Page 344	*Top and right*	Mara Passetti
	Bottom left	Tiare Orth
Page 359	*Top and bottom right*	Olivia Sargeant
	Middle	Vikki Anderson
	Bottom left	Samantha Traina
Page 360		
	Top right and bottom	Olivia Sargeant
	Top left	Samantha Traina
Page 401		Tim Kao/*San Francisco Chronicle*

HIS BRIGHT LIGHT

THE STORY OF MY SON, NICK TRAINA

Danielle Steel

CORGI BOOKS

HIS BRIGHT LIGHT
A CORGI BOOK : 0 552 54654 2

Originally published in Great Britain by Bantam Press,
a division of Transworld Publishers

PRINTING HISTORY
Bantam Press edition published 1998
Corgi edition published 1999

11 13 15 17 19 20 18 16 14 12

Set in 11/12pt Sabon by
Phoenix Typesetting, Ilkley, West Yorkshire.

Corgi Books are published by Transworld Publishers,
61–63 Uxbridge Road, London W5 5SA,
a division of The Random House Group Ltd,
in Australia by Random House Australia (Pty) Ltd,
20 Alfred Street, Milsons Point, Sydney, NSW 2061, Australia,
in New Zealand by Random House New Zealand Ltd,
18 Poland Road, Glenfield, Auckland 10, New Zealand
and in South Africa by Random House (Pty) Ltd,
Endulini, 5a Jubilee Road, Parktown 2193, South Africa.

Printed and bound in Great Britain by
Clays Ltd, St Ives plc.

To Nick, first and foremost, who had been asking me for a while to dedicate another book to him. This wasn't the one I had in mind. But this one's for you, Nick. For the lessons you taught me, the gifts that you gave me, the heart that you gave me, and all the love that we shared. Wider than the ocean, bigger than the sky. Fly well, my darling boy, until we meet again. With all my love, Mom.

To Julie, who gave him a life he never would have had otherwise. She gave him joy, and freedom, and respect, and safety, and wisdom, and most of all, love. She gave him the adulthood he wanted and deserved. To her husband, Bill, for being his friend. And to Serena and Chris, for opening their hearts and lives to Nick.

To Paul and Cody, for giving so tirelessly, from their hearts . . . and going to all those concerts!!!

To Dr Seifried, for keeping him going for so long, and caring about him so much.

To Max Leavitt, Sammy (the Mick) Ewing, and Thea Anderson for giving their hearts forever, and beyond.

To Chuck (Erin Mason), for being there when it really counted.

To Jo Schuman Silver, who was his special friend, whom he adored, and who adored him.

To Camilla and Lucy, for years and years and years of loving.

To Mort Janklow, for believing in this book, me, and Nicky.

To Carole Baron, for asking me to write it.

To John, for our lost dreams, and all you did for Nick. The doctors, the solutions, the medicines, and the loving father you were to him.

To Tom, for being there for me, and because Nick loved you. And for encouraging me to write this book, and getting me through it.

To Bill, for giving me Nicky, and being there for me when we lost him and being my friend.

To all the people who cared so much about him, rejoiced for him, laughed with him, cried for him. To all those who worked so hard to make his life as good as it could be, secretaries and nurses and doctors, people in the music world, and all our friends, all the people who were there for him, and made a difference.

And to my beloved children, Beatrix, Trevor, Todd, Samantha, Victoria, Vanessa, Maxx and Zara, for being the best brothers and sisters in the world, and the most precious gifts in my life, just as Nick was, and is, and always will be. For the love and strength and laughter that we share, that you gave Nick, and that he gave us. May you be forever blessed, and may you never again know a sorrow and loss like this one.

With all my love,
d.s.

It is not growing like a tree
In bulk, doth make men better be;
Or standing long an oak, three hundred year,
To fall a log at last, dry, bald and sere:
A lily of the day,
Is fairer far in May,
Although it fall and die that night;
It was the plant and flower of light.

Ben Jonson

'No matter how much I put in the bank every day, I wake up broke every morning.'

Nick Traina

August 1997

Mom . . .

I have known a million people
But never one like you
Many of my friends are special
But I still don't have a clue
How you got to be so wonderful
The world's most perfect mom
You've always loved and helped me
Even when I was wrong
I'm sorry that I've hurt you
I'm sorry I've made you cry
I'll do my best to make you proud
I promise I will try
Everyone sees hardship
And everyone feels pain
And if anyone knows it's you and me
That sun will shine through rain
You've given me so much
That words are not enough
To say how much I love you
I'm trying and it's tough
Without you I'd be nowhere
You believed in me no matter what
My arms are always open
I promise you they'll never shut
I have more respect for you
Than any woman alive
And my shoulder is always here
If you ever need to cry
Everything will turn out fine
Because I will always love you
Until the day I die

Nick Traina
August 1996

Prologue

This will not be an easy book to write, but there is much to say, in my own words, and my son's. And as hard as it may be to write, it's worth doing, if it helps someone.

It is hard to encapsulate a being, a very special being, a soul, a smile, a boy, a huge talent, an enormous heart, a child, a man, in however many pages. Yet I must try, for him, for myself, for you. And I hope that as I do, you will come to understand who he was, and what he meant to all those who knew him.

This is the story of an extraordinary boy, with a brilliant mind, a heart of gold, and a tortured soul. It is the story of an illness, a fight to live, and a race against death. It is early days for me yet, as I write this. He has been gone a short time. My heart still aches. The days seem endless. I still cry at the sound of his name. I wander into his room and can still smell his familiar smell. His words still echo in my ears. He was alive only days, weeks ago . . . so little time, and yet he is gone. It is still impossible to absorb or understand. Harder still to accept. I look at his photographs, and cannot imagine that all that life and love and energy has vanished. That funny, handsome face, that brilliant smile, the heart I knew better than my own, the best friend he became to me, can they truly be gone? Do they live only in memory? Even now, it remains beyond my comprehension, and is sometimes beyond bearing. How did it all happen? How did we lose him? How could we have tried so hard, and cared so much, and loved him so enormously, and still have lost him? If love alone could have kept him alive, he would have lived to be three hundred years old. But sometimes, even loving with all your heart and soul and all your mind and will just doesn't do it. Sadly, it didn't do it for Nick.

If I had three wishes, one would be that he had never suffered from mental illness, the other would be of course that he were alive today, but the third would be that someone had warned me, at some point, that his illness – manic depression – could kill him. Perhaps they did. Perhaps they told me in some subtle way. Maybe the inference was there, and I didn't want to hear it. But I listened carefully to everything that was said to me over the years, I examined every nuance, and to the best of my knowledge and abilities, heeded every warning. My recollection is that no one told me. Certainly not clearly. And it was a piece of information that I desperately needed. I'm not sure we would have done things any differently, but at least I would have known, been warned, of what the worst case could be.

His illness killed him as surely as if it had been a cancer. I wish I had known that, that I had been warned how great the risk was. Perhaps then I would have been better prepared for what came later. I'm not sure that in the minds of the public it is clear that bipolar disease, manic depression as it's more commonly called, is potentially fatal. Not always certainly, but in far too many cases. Suicide and accidents appear to be the greatest cause of death for manic-depressives. Neither are uncommon. If I had been told that he had cancer of a major organ, I would have known with certainty how great the risk was. I might have understood how short his life could be, how tragic the implication. I'm sure I would have fought just as hard, just as long, just as ingeniously, but I would have been better prepared for what came later. The defeat might not have been quite as startling or as stunning, though it would surely have been just as devastating.

The purpose of this book is to pay tribute to him, and to what he accomplished in his short life. Nick was an extraordinary human being, with joy and wisdom, and remarkably profound and astute perceptions about himself and others. He faced life with courage and panache and passion and humor. He did everything 'more' and better and harder. He loved harder and more, he laughed a lot, and made us laugh, and cry, and try so hard to save him. No one who met him was left unimpressed or unaffected. You couldn't meet him and not give a damn. He made you care and feel and want to be as big as he was. He was very big. The biggest.

I have written this book to honor and remember him. But there is yet another purpose in writing this book. I want to share the story, and the pain, the courage, the love, and what I learned in living through it. I want Nick's life to be not only a tender memory for us, but a gift to others. There is much to learn here, not only about one life, but about a disease that afflicts between two and three million Americans, one third of whom, it is believed, die from it, possibly as many as two thirds. That is a terrifying statistic. The statistics are somewhat 'soft' on the issue of fatalities, because often death is attributed to other things, for instance 'accidental overdose' rather than suicide, which is determined by the actual amount of fatal substances ingested, rather than by clear motive.

It is debatable as to whether or not those who have died could have been saved, or if those who will die can be. But what of those who will live, and have lived, and are still living? How do we help them? What can we do? Sadly, no one, and certainly not I, has the magic answers to solve the problem. There are different options, different solutions, a variety of ways of coping. But first, you have to see the problem. You have to understand what you're dealing with, to accept that what you're dealing with is the equivalent of not just a bellyache, but liver cancer. You have to know that what you're facing is serious, important, dangerous, and potentially fatal.

Somewhere out there, in apartments, and homes, and hospitals, in ordinary jobs and lives, and not just psychiatric wards, are people coping with a terrible struggle within them. And alongside them are the people who know and love them. I would like to reach out here, and to offer hope and the realities we lived with. I want to make a difference.

My hope is that someone will be able to use what we learned, and save a life with it. Maybe you can make a difference, even if I couldn't. If it is true that one third of manic-depressives die of this disease, and its related burdens, then two thirds will live. Two thirds can be helped, and can live a useful existence. And if possible, I would like Nick's story, and Nick's life, to help them, to serve them, perhaps to learn from our mistakes, and our victories.

The greatest lessons I learned were of courage, and love, energy, ingenuity, and persistence. We never gave up, never turned away, never turned on him, never let him go, until he let us go, because he couldn't fight the fight any longer. We not only gave him CPR when he attempted suicide, but we tried to keep his soul alive in every way we could, so that he could keep fighting the fight along with us. And the real victory for him, and for us, was that we gave him a quality of life he might otherwise never have had. He was able to pursue a career he loved, in music. He saw victories that few people do, at twice his age, or who live a great deal longer. He knew the joy and excitement of success, and also knew better than most the price he paid for it. He had friends, a life, a family, a career, he had fun and happiness and sorrow. He moved through the last few years of his life with surprising grace, despite the handicaps he was born with. And we were incredibly proud of him, as a man, a musician, and a human being. He was a talented, brilliant young man with a disease. But the disease did not stop him from being who he was, or us from loving him as he was. In retrospect, I think it was one of the best gifts we gave him. Acceptance of who he was, and unconditional love. In our eyes at least, his illness was only one facet of him, not the whole of him.

There is no denying that it is a hard, hard road, loving someone with bipolar disease. There are times when you want to scream, days when you think you can't do it anymore, weeks when you know you haven't made a difference and only wish you could, moments when you want to turn your back on it. It is their problem, not yours, and yet it becomes yours if you love the person suffering from it. You have no choice. You must stand by them. You are trapped, as surely as the patient is. And you will hate that trap at times, hate what it does to your life, your days, your own sanity. But hate it or not, you are there, and whatever it takes, you have to make the best of it.

I can only tell you what we did, what we tried, what worked, and what failed. You can learn from what we tried to accomplish, and develop better avenues that work for you. We tried a lot of things, and flew by the seat of our pants some of the time. There are no rule books, no manuals, no instruction sheets, no norms. You just have to feel your way along in the dark and do the best you can. You can't do more than that. And if you're very lucky, what you're doing works. If you're not, it won't, and then you try something else. You try anything and everything you can until the very end, and then all you have is knowing how hard you tried. Nick knew. He knew how hard we tried for him, and he tried too. We respected each other so much for it. We loved each other incredibly because we had been through so much together, and we cared so much. He and I were very alike actually, more than we realized for many years. He said it in the end. He made me laugh. He made me smile. He was not only my son, but my best friend. And I am doing this for him, to honor him, and to help those who need to know what we learned, what we did, what we should have done, and shouldn't have done. And if it helps someone then it is worth reliving it all, and sharing his joys and his agonies with you. I am not doing it to expose him, or myself, but to help you.

Would I do it all again? Yes. In a minute. I wouldn't give away those nineteen years for anything in the world. I wouldn't give up the pain or the torment or the sheer frustration, or the occasional misery of it, because there was so much joy and happiness that went with it. There was nothing better in life than knowing that things were going well for him. I would not have missed a single instant with him. He taught me more about love and joy and courage and the love of life and wonderful outrageousness than anything or anyone else in my life ever will. He gave me the gifts of love and compassion and understanding and acceptance and tolerance and patience, wrapped in laughter, straight from his heart. And now I share these gifts with you.

Love is meant to be shared, and pain is meant to be soothed. If I can share your pain, and soothe it with the love Nick shared with all of us, then his life will be yet one more gift, not only to me and his family this time, but to you.

It was Nick who made it all worthwhile, and worth fighting for. He did it for us, and for himself, and we for him. It was a dance of love from beginning to end. His was a life worth living, whatever the handicaps and challenges. I think he'd agree with that. And I have no doubt of it. I have no regrets, no matter how hard it was. I wouldn't have given up one second with him. And what happened in the end was his destiny. As his song says, 'Destiny . . . dance with me, my destiny.' And how sweet the music was. The sound of it will forever live on, just like Nick, and our love for him.

He was a priceless gift. He taught me everything worth knowing about life and love. May God bless and keep him, and smile with him, until we meet again.

And may God keep you safe on your journey.

d.s.

HIS BRIGHT LIGHT

THE STORY OF MY SON, NICK TRAINA

1

The Journey Begins

I met Nick's father on his thirty-first birthday, on a sunny day in June. Bill was intelligent, employed, and had a Jean-Paul Belmondo quality to him. He was immensely attractive, well read, well educated, and extremely bright, came from a respectable family, and had nice parents. He had a lot going for him, but also a somewhat checkered past. It was something he touched on but didn't explain in detail.

He was the product of a Jesuit education, had gone to college, played football, and took masters courses in psychology shortly after we met. In his youth he had gotten into drugs, and long since gotten off them. When we met, he neither drugged nor drank. At all. I was impressed by that, as I didn't drink then, and don't now, and all my life have stayed well away from drugs, and people who use them.

There are a number of things that still stand out in my mind about him, other things I've forgotten, or maybe chosen to lose somewhere. I have told myself for two decades that he only spent moments in my life. But now, as I look back over every instant of Nick's life, and the days that led up to it, as I sort through photographs and reach back into the past, I remember things that I had long since chosen to forget. His many qualities. His charm. His appeal to women. We were not in each other's lives for very long, but he made an indelible impression. And our paths having crossed again because of Nick, I realize again now what a good person he was, and is. In some ways, the person he is now not only restored my faith in him, but in myself.

At thirty-one he was a quiet man, he loved the outdoors, loved to fish, and was somewhat shy. He had a great many qualities, some of which I saw in Nick later. I thought he was lucky to have the support of devoted parents who thought he could do no wrong, and, like me, he was an only child. I have no idea if things would ever have worked out between us under normal circumstances. It's hard to say. He was carrying burdens I knew nothing about, and suffering from his own demons. I don't know if the manic-depressive gene came from some branch of his family tree, or mine, there is no way to know that. There has never been mental illness in my family, that I know of. And the only evidence of something awry on Bill's side was his addiction to drugs, which I didn't discover until later.

I have always believed that in many instances, if not all, drug addiction is actually an issue of people medicating themselves, though I don't know if in Bill's case it was. I don't think anyone knows how these things happen, or why.

I knew little of his history in those early days after we met, and was probably not knowledgeable or

I was scared to death, and in one hell of a mess. But I felt I had to make the best of it, for my daughter's sake, and that of the unborn baby. From what I could see, I was looking ahead down a long, hard, lonely road.

And miraculously, within days of making the decision to have the baby, I was offered a writing project that would cover, literally to the penny, what I had figured out it would cost to have the baby: doctor, diapers, hospital, clothes. The sum offered me was exactly what I needed to get by. It was one hurdle I'd made it safely over, but I knew there would be countless more to follow. I had written roughly seven books by then, but only two had sold. And I was making a living, or had been, writing advertising copy, doing translations, teaching English and creative writing, and even taking occasional jobs in stores. The new project meant that I could write full-time. No small miracle to me at the time.

The next hurdle to be overcome was that I had to tell my daughter that I was having a baby, a moral dilemma I agonized over, an outstanding example of 'Do as I say, not as I've done.' I didn't want her making the same mistakes as I when she grew up (and she hasn't). You were supposed to fall in love, get married, then have a baby, not get pregnant and not get married, and be involved with someone you barely knew, whom you only saw from time to time. It was everything I didn't want for her, or myself. And by then, I suspect Bill and I had figured out that we were not a perfect match. He had other pressures in his life, about which I knew nothing yet, we had different interests and lives. Had we been dating, without the pressure of a baby, the romance would probably have already fizzled out, and certainly been less stressful. With a baby coming, the pressure was on us, individually, and together. It was a very tough time.

My daughter was utterly remarkable, and instead of shock or disapproval or embarrassment in the face of the painfully honest confession I made, she embraced my news with excitement, enthusiasm, and open arms. She was thrilled. She had always wanted a sibling, and she was embarrassingly pleased that this was going to be 'our baby,' and we wouldn't have to share it with anyone else. It was, if anything, an optimistic way of looking at the situation, and warmed my heart. It formed an airtight bond between us which has never diminished. Even at nine, she was never critical, and endlessly supportive.

Interestingly, the thought of heredity never crossed my mind at the time. I don't know if I was just naive, or it was simply an era when people didn't worry as much about that. It never dawned on me to question with any real seriousness 'Who is this man? Who is the father of my baby?' I saw the baby as a separate entity from each of us. But even if I had fully understood the potential time bomb of heredity, I wouldn't have done things any differently. I felt I had no choice but to have the child and make the best of it later.

For the next few months Bill and I saw each other, and when I was six months pregnant, he decided to move in with me, and see how it worked out. I agreed, although I was nervous about it, but it seemed we owed the baby at least that much. And by then, we were talking vaguely of marriage, although I don't believe we would have been, had I not been pregnant. (At that point, my parents still did not know that I was pregnant, and I was dreading the announcement to them.)

But within days of moving in, Bill began to vanish. He would disappear for hours and days, behave oddly when he returned, and seemed somehow different than he had been when we met. He was never violent or aggressive, but mostly elusive. His appearance changed from impeccable to disheveled, and his disappearances rapidly became more frequent and longer. I had no idea where he was, with whom, or what he was doing. Sometimes he would come home at one or two A.M. and be gone again before I got up in the morning. His life was more of a mystery to me than ever. His disappearances were a mystery to me as well. In fact, almost everything about him was. The most important thing I knew about him was that I was having his baby. What I didn't know, and didn't understand, was that he had quietly gone back to using drugs, and I had no inkling of it. Being unfamiliar with that world, I did not recognize the signs.

When I was seven months pregnant, he came down with hepatitis, which complicated life further for me and Beatrix, and I took care of him until he recovered. And at eight months, when Bill was back on his feet again, the disappearances resumed, and he got into a car accident, while driving my car. It was at that point that I finally understood what had happened, and the kind of chaos drugs were causing in Bill's life, and would cause in mine, if I let that happen. It was a terrifying dilemma for me. It was a world I wanted no part of, for myself, or my children.

I was eight months pregnant by then, and finally told my parents about the baby over the phone. There was an endless silence, a pause that went on for aeons, and then my father's voice like ice. My father wanted only one thing, for us to get married. Impossible to explain to him that I hadn't seen Bill in days at that point, and when I did he was passing through my house like an express train. I barely had time to say hello before he was gone again, never mind discussing marriage. And how could I marry someone in Bill's situation? On the one hand, I wanted to legitimize the child, and on the other, I was terrified of the problems I would be getting into. I did not tell my family of Bill's history with drugs. But in the end, despite the reservations I had, there seemed to be no other choice but to get married. My divorce was final by then, and marriage was in fact an option. Unfortunately, it was a time fraught with anxiety, and not one I remember fondly.

Bill was gone most of the time, and he never showed up to buy the ring, or get the license. In the end, we were married without one, by 'special license.' And as a result of his disappearances and the stress over what was happening, I literally had hysterics when he finally showed up the night before the wedding. We were married the next day, in a small ceremony, and had lunch with friends at a restaurant. And by that night, he had vanished. It was a week before my due date. The only consolation was that my father was relieved that we had done it, and I hoped that things would settle down with Bill in time.

It was a nightmarish time. My daughter was staying with her father for a couple of weeks until the baby came, and I was alone most of the time. And for some reason, Bill reappeared the night before the baby was born. He spent the night, and got me as far as the hospital, stayed for a while, and then disappeared again. He was in worse shape than I by the time he left. Seriously addicted by then, he had to take care of his own needs, while I remained alone with a friend for long hours of hard labor while Bill came and went.

For the next twelve hours while I was in labor, Bill reappeared and disappeared again. And unfortunately, so did my obstetrician. He was called away for an emergency and left me in the care of his partners, while fate threw me an impossible situation, a few cruel tricks, and a nightmarish labor. The baby weighed over ten pounds, and I am very small-boned and a small person. Bluntly put, he got stuck, which provided an experience of such hideous proportions for me that I wound up with temporary problems with my heart and lungs, asthma, and a number of other complications. I lay in agony for twelve hours, left to residents, and changing shifts of labor nurses and doctors who didn't know me.

To me, it seemed that the only real miracle was that I didn't die, nor did the baby. An emergency cesarean section was finally performed by my own doctor twelve hours after I arrived at the hospital.

And I was surprised that I survived it. It was the hardest delivery of any I've had, mostly due to the baby's size.

The one most remarkable thing about the delivery that everybody was talking about was the fact that when they made the first incision, the baby cried loudly through it, which is very rare. To me, it seemed like a happy sign, a lust for life, and a good omen. It was the first of May, a day for celebration.

The baby, a boy, was so huge at ten pounds one ounce that he was put in an incubator, as apparently overly large babies are sometimes fragile. He looked enormous to me, with huge eyes and dark hair. He looked six months old and so beautiful that every moment of agony seemed worth it for him. He owned my heart from the moment I laid eyes on him. He seemed perfect in every way. And I was so grateful that he seemed to have come to no harm in the delivery that I was more than willing to overlook the fact that the delivery had been agonizing and traumatic for me. It has been suggested since that the long labor may have caused some neurological damage, and learning disabilities that we discovered later on. But there is no way to know that. The problems that Nicholas developed in later life were, for the most part, genetic, we think, as most mental illness is, but the suggested neurological damage and learning disabilities might have been caused or aggravated by birth trauma. It was never a line of thinking we pursued or blamed anyone for later. We had enough to deal with worrying about his being bipolar.

But then, who knew what was to come later on?

All I knew and cared about was that this long-awaited baby had finally come, and he looked like a cherub in my arms. I was grateful to have survived, and to take my baby home with me. His arrival had been extraordinarily traumatic but seemed well worth it to me.

Bill appeared hours late to drive us home from the hospital, and predictably, disappeared again within the hour. I cried a lot. Beatrix came home, and fell instantly in love with the baby. My father died ten days later, having never seen the baby, but relieved that I was married at least. I called my lawyer the day after the delivery and tried to have the marriage annulled, or at least to start the wheels turning towards a divorce, but then dropped it for a while, and finally filed the divorce later, after our problems became too much for me.

Bill came and went for a brief time after Nick was born. He made an unsuccessful attempt to clean up when Nicky was about four weeks old and again later. In the end, his eventual victory over drugs took him long years to achieve, and Nick and I were long since out of his life by the time he did it.

What ensued after Nick's birth, for Bill, was a nineteen-year fall down an abyss from which he did not return until Nick was gone. He disappeared out of our lives as quickly as he had come. No matter how good his intentions, and I believe they were, the pull of his addiction was so powerful it could not be stopped. It was like a tidal wave that nearly drowned him, and fortunately for him, in the end, didn't.

It was sadder for him in the end than it was for us, because we were able to put our lives back together eventually. And he missed so much. He missed it all, an entire life. He never knew his son, although he returned after Nick's death, healthy again, and in recovery, to offer me a hand in friend-ship, and solace both to me and Nick's siblings. And I was, and am, grateful for the support he gave me.

At the time, Beatrix and I were left alone with Nicholas, a miraculous gift in our lives. He was healthy and fat and happy and beautiful, and adored. And Bill was gone to his own life. Beatie and I were on our own, with 'our' baby, our beloved Nicky. And he was the happiest, fattest, sweetest baby we have ever seen.

Nick, Beatie, and Beatie's dolls

2

'I'm Incredible!'

Shortly after Nick was born, I awoke from the anesthetic after the cesarean, and a nurse asked me if I'd seen the baby yet, and I shook my head. 'You haven't?' she asked, looking amazed, and as though I had a great surprise in store. 'Wait till you see him!' She said it the way people talk about a movie star arriving somewhere, whom everyone was anxious to see. She smiled at me and hurried off, and returned minutes later with a bundle in her arms, and put him gently in mine, as I looked down at him in wonder.

I will never forget the sheer beauty of him, the excitement I felt, that round exquisite little face, and the huge eyes looking up thoughtfully into mine. He seemed the perfect child, and he was so huge he looked months old instead of hours. And at the very first instant I looked down at him, I realized that nothing hurt anymore. I held him tenderly as he closed his eyes and drifted off to sleep in my arms, and was overwhelmed with gratitude that he was mine. I had never felt as happy, or as lucky, in my life.

Nicky was the kind of baby people stopped to admire everywhere you went. He was so big and beautiful and healthy-looking that people had to just stop and chat and ask about him. And as Beatie and I pushed him in his pram, we were very proud. We took him everywhere with us, shopping, the grocery store, church, and he even went to show-and-tell at school, and was a huge success with the fourth-grade girls.

He had a ferocious appetite from the first, and I was determined to nurse him. My pediatrician laughingly called him 'the shark,' there was no satisfying him, and however much milk he got, he wanted more. He was insatiable, and within two weeks, I gave up nursing him. It was a battle I couldn't win. We put him on formula, and even that didn't seem to satisfy him, and we had to add cereal to it within the first few days. He ate endlessly, and by the time he was a few weeks old, I cut the top off a nipple and put cereal in a bottle. For some unknown reason, everyone told me it was a bad idea, but it was the only way to satisfy him and get him to sleep. He ate voraciously, which oddly enough, was typical of him for most of his life. It was as though the 'regulators' on his 'fuel tank' didn't register properly, and he himself never knew when he was full. Even as a boy later on, he would eat until he felt sick at times (which was the manic part of him). But he burned it off somehow. Although he was chubby as a baby, and extremely round in his first year, once he started running around, he was always wiry and thin, and remained that way for his entire lifetime. But as a baby, Nick was huge.

He laughed and smiled a lot, slept less than I thought he should, and always woke at night, once, and sometimes twice, to eat. He looked like a little Buddha by the time he was old enough to sit, laughing and chortling, and always anxious to move around, and explore the world around him.

He was not only 'my' baby, but Beatie's. She would dress him up and sit him amongst her dolls, and play with him for hours with her friends. And at night when he'd wake up, he'd barely have time to cry before Beatie and I would rush into his room, separately, and sometimes bump into each other sleepily on the way in. And then we'd argue for a minute about whose turn it was to take care of him. He was the light of our lives, and I loved sitting with him in my arms, in a rocking chair, holding him while he took the bottle, or singing to him afterwards, as I looked out the window at the moon in the night sky. They were wonderful nights, and precious hours, moments of solitude and togetherness, the stuff of which tender memories are made, and I have many of them. I would sit for hours that way, feeling his warmth as I held him close, his head on my shoulder as he drifted back to sleep, his chubby little arms around my neck as I held him.

His first months seemed to rocket by, and I was busy with him, and by the time he was six months old, he was sitting up, laughing constantly, and looked like a one-year-old. He seemed to be on some kind of fast track of his own, he was crawling everywhere, and seemed desperate to walk. We bought a walker on wheels, a little seat with a round tray around it, on casters, which allowed him to touch the floor with his toes and move freely. The moment we put him in it, he took off and all hell broke loose. He zoomed from one end of the house to the other, flirting dangerously with the stairs (we put up gates!), and zipping at full speed around every room. His best trick was heading for the table in the kitchen, which I set nicely occasionally. He would grab a corner of the tablecloth and take off with it, escaping at full speed in his walker, and taking the cloth and everything resting on it with him. The clattering and banging of everything falling to the floor delighted him, considerably more than it amused me.

Nicky was a child who made you laugh. You had to smile looking at him, and he always looked at me as though he wanted to say something to me, and somewhere around seven or eight months, he did. I spoke in Spanish to him most of the time, as Romelia, my Guatemalan housekeeper, did. She doted on him and chatted at him for hours. Beatrix spoke to him in English, and Romelia and I spoke Spanish to him, contrary to everyone's advice. I was told that bringing up a child bilingually, particularly a boy, would delay his speaking enormously. I was warned that he might not speak anything intelligible for years. But that wouldn't have been Nick. Nothing stopped him.

Nick exploded into life typically for him, and began speaking at the same time he started walking. He took his first steps at eight months, careening through the house perilously, and at roughly the same time, he began to talk. And quite sensibly, for him at least, he said words in English to Beatrix, and Spanish to Rome and me. Knowing Nick later on,

44

it made perfect sense. Two languages had done nothing to slow him down. And he never slowed down for a minute after that. He ran all over the house, exploring his world, free of the walker by then, and chattering endlessly, according to his whim, in English or Spanish.

By the time he was a year old, he was speaking in sentences, which seemed utterly remarkable to everyone, although I know now that it was an early danger sign, or could have been. I've been told since that although all babies who talk early do not turn out to be manic-depressive, most manic-depressives do in fact talk early. And he did. But I knew nothing of those symptoms then, and was understandably proud of him. People would meet him and talk to him, and then turn to me and say, 'He's incredible.' They said it so often in fact that I think he got confused and thought it was his name.

When I would take him out in the baby carriage, as I still did then, and people would stop to admire him, he would start talking to them and when they'd ask his name, he would smile broadly at them and say, 'I'm Incredible.' He was of course, undeniably. We would have long conversations as I strolled him around in the pram, and I'm sure that if people saw me from a little distance, they thought I was deranged, chatting with a baby to the extent that I did. But he loved gabbing with me.

There were many things Nick loved, his sister, his toys, riding in the car, and music even then. He had funny taste in music for a child, and developed a passion for disco music, which was still fashionable then, and I was fond of it, too. His favorite was Gloria Gaynor singing 'I Will Survive,' and he would dance endlessly as we played records in my room. He knew the ones he liked and handed them to me imperiously, 'This one, Mommy.' Our first serious argument came while planning his first birthday, when he announced that he wanted a clown and disco music, strange requests for a one-year-old, though he was so large he looked two or three by then, with his blond Dutch Boy haircut, which I did myself, and the excellent coordination that allowed him to move about with ease. And he loved typing on my typewriter, too.

The things he liked were unusual for a child his age, but even more unusual was the fact that he could articulate them, and even defend his point of view. I tried to explain to him that the clown was not a great idea because most of his friends his own age were afraid of them, and they wouldn't find the disco music as appealing as he did. I had envisioned a baby party with several children who had been born to friends at roughly the same time, his sister of course, and a few of my friends, and maybe Bill.

But Nicky and I clashed vehemently about the first birthday plans. He wanted to play my Gloria Gaynor record. And in the end, he did, and we put the clown off for another year.

He was remarkably precocious for a child his age, and exceedingly good company, although we continued to disagree about his choice of music. I put a record on my stereo one night that he didn't like, and he was incensed by it. He wanted me to take it off and put on something else, and when I wouldn't, as he had been on his way to his bath and was running naked through my room, he stopped and peed on my stereo with a look of glee. He made

46

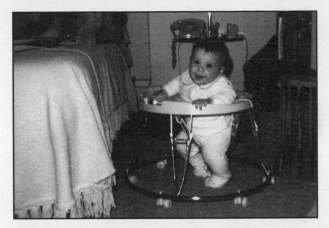

Nick in his walker: five months

Nick at six months

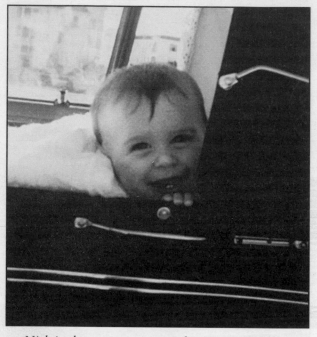

Nick in the pram at six months: 'I'm Incredible!'

his point certainly, and I had to laugh at the outrageousness of it. It was very Nicky.

The other ultimatum he gave me at that time had to do with the crib where he slept. He didn't want to sleep in it anymore when he was exactly a year old, and he made a huge fuss about it. He wanted to sleep in the old twin bed I had put in his room, where I could sleep when he needed me, or when he was sick. But I felt far safer having him sleep in his crib. Because he had walked early, he was extremely independent about roaming around the house, and I was afraid that if I let him sleep in a bed, he'd get into mischief during the night, or before I woke up in the morning. Even then, Nick didn't sleep a lot. He was often awake late at night, and long before dawn. The crib was a source of comfort and security for me, if not him. But as was the case all his life, Nick was anything but easy to convince once he made up his mind. And a nightly battle began. He solved it very simply by backing up like an Olympic athlete in a long jump event or a pole vaulter, and hurling himself neatly over the side of the crib, and then he would sit happily on the floor of his room, catching his breath for a minute before he took off and dashed out of his room. More than anything, I was afraid he'd break his neck leaping out of the crib, and he was so big and so strong that it was an easy feat for him. So he won, of course.

The crib went, and at a year he moved into his bed, and I rather optimistically put a baby gate up at the door to his room, which proved to be no great obstacle to him. He learned rapidly how to remove it as carefully as I had set it up, and just as I had feared before he gave up his crib, he then wandered

49

around the house at night, and more often than not, turned up in my bed by morning.

After the battle over the crib, this was Round Two. It turned out that the bed in his room had only been perceived as a way station of sorts by him, a resting place before he took over my bed, which was the goal he had in mind. He wanted to sleep with me in my room.

But this time I was firm with him. He had to sleep in his own bed. And that was that. What ensued were months of battles and long, sleepless nights. 'Go back to your own bed, Nicky,' I'd say firmly. And he would, looking crestfallen. And he'd stay there for between two and five minutes, and then he'd be back again, begging to sleep with me. I had a big, empty, king-size bed I shared with no one, and it must have seemed ridiculous to him that I wasn't willing to share it with him, and selfish of me. But it dawned on me even then that I might like to share my bed with someone more adult one day, and I didn't think it a good idea to get in the habit of letting Nicky sleep with me.

The point was lost on him. And eventually, we 'compromised,' i.e., Nick won, but he let me save face by going to bed, if not to sleep, in his bed, and allowing me to go decorously to mine, and fall asleep. He no longer argued with me, or woke me up to ask if he could get into bed with me. He just quietly slipped into my bed next to me, while I slept, and when I woke in the morning, he'd be there, beaming at me. It worked for both of us, I guess, and the truth was, I loved having him with me. I loved being with him, and near him, and cuddling him, blowing raspberries on his stomach, and

Nick at one year

Nick at Mom's typewriter: fourteen months old

feeling the silk of his blond bowl cut on my cheek. He was a delicious, irresistible child, full of fun and love, and bright ideas. By the time he was a year and a half old, or in truth, well before, it was obvious that he was extremely bright, and in time we began to suspect he had an IQ of impressive proportions. He did things he just wasn't supposed to know how to do, and said things no eighteen-month-old child said. He said things that made sense, amused, and endeared him to everyone. Everyone was in love with Nick, even then, and especially Beatie and me.

There was one thing about him that worried me then. He never slept, or not enough anyway. Long before he was two, I had come to the realization that I couldn't give him a nap. If I did, it meant he'd be up all night, even long after me, and I worked late at night. But he just didn't seem to need much sleep. Another warning sign. Manic-depressives don't sleep at night, and in time it was to become the bane of his existence for the rest of his life. But at that age, no one picked up on it as anything unusual. I just thought it was a quirk of his, and didn't worry about it. He was different from his sister certainly. At his age, she had been comatose for hours every afternoon, in fact until she was about six. But not Nick. He seemed to need incredibly little sleep. He fell asleep after I did at night, and was awake before dawn, prying my eyes open, peering into them as I groaned. 'Are you awake yet, Mommy?' 'I am now,' I croaked. *Sesame Street* became a vital tool in maintaining my sanity. I would talk to him for a couple of hours, waiting for it to come on, and then plop him in front of the TV so I could get a little more sleep. Getting enough sleep, even as an adult, was challenging around Nicky.

There was another early warning sign then too, although it's not always an indication of danger. His reactions to medication. We would go to a rented house at a beach nearby, but to get there, you had to navigate an unbearably windy road, and invariably Nicky got violently carsick. I tried all the routes available, short ones, long ones, the mountain road, the windy road closer to the beach. Nothing helped, and I finally decided to try Dramamine on him, and just forge ahead and get there as fast as I could. It seemed the only solution.

I was warned by my pediatrician that the medicine would make him drowsy, and probably put him to sleep in fact, but he said it would do Nick no harm, so I gave it a try one weekend before we left for the beach. And rather than put him to sleep, it turned him into a whirling dervish right in front of me. He was going 150 miles an hour, talking as fast as he could, and practically climbing the walls. It had the exact opposite of the effect that had been described, and it worried me. When I called the doctor, I was told that that happened sometimes. And it happened again, later on, with an over-the-counter cough/cold medicine for children this time. The same thing. Instead of slowing down, Nick speeded up unbelievably. It is called a paradoxical reaction, and is again characteristic of people who suffer from bipolar disease. That reaction stayed with him for most of his life, with some medicines. Most cold medications that rendered anyone else near comatose would speed Nick up. Coffee, for several years, until he took medications to balance

53

him, nearly put him to sleep. It made me extremely cautious about what medications I gave him, and needless to say, I gave up on the Dramamine, and eventually on the beach house.

Nick had a strong personality, and extremely definite ideas. Like many children his age, he hated wearing clothes, and loved running around naked. I have a million photographs of him, with his bare, dimpled bottom staring at me as he played on my bed or ran across the room while the camera caught him. And conversely, as a toddler, he absolutely hated being dressed by anyone, or having his clothes changed. It was one of the rare things that made him scream in outrage. You could hear him for miles. There was something very distressing to him about getting dressed, or changed. And more often than not, even at a year and a half, and certainly by two, he had strong opinions about the outfit he was being changed into. 'I *won't* wear that!' he would say with a look of outrage. At twelve or fourteen or fifteen, or maybe at seven, that seems understandable. But at eighteen months, it seemed ridiculous to be arguing with Nicky about a pale blue corduroy jumper. And when he said, 'I won't wear that!', he meant it.

I often dressed Beatie and Nicky alike, in little matching outfits. She was a good sport about it, and would wear almost anything I chose. Not so with Nick. Every outfit was the cause of a major nego-tiation. I was still living a little precariously financially in those days, although things were slowly looking up with my writing. But I loved buying outfits for the two of them, sometimes with little giraffes on them, or flowers or bunnies at

Easter. Nicky always viewed them with horror. 'You expect me to wear *that*, with a *giraffe* on it?!!!' he would scream at me in horror, looking insulted to his core. I would beg him to humor me, and most of the time he would, but not until we had debated the issue for an hour with the utmost passion. Very early on, Nick had definite ideas about everything, his clothes among them, and he wasn't shy about telling me what he thought, on any subject.

By the time Nick was a year and a half old, he was a whole person, with opinions and tastes and desires and quirks, and somewhat entrenched habits. There was no question that he was extraordinary, but he was also very different. Different from other people's children, different even from his own sister. He was smarter than everyone, brighter, faster, had more energy than any child I'd ever seen, and he had a way of looking at me that made me feel he was a grown man in a small child's body. He seemed to be watching me all the time, as though searching for clues to a mystery, and when his eyes met mine, I saw someone wise within them. And although at times it enchanted me, and I was endlessly proud of him because he was so remarkable and brilliant, there were also times when it made me feel uneasy.

I remember a vague feeling of malaise when I looked at him one day. He was wearing a yellow fuzzy sleeper suit with feet in it, and he looked adorable, but something in his eyes worried me terribly as our eyes met, and for the first time, at eighteen months, I wondered if there was something wrong with him, if he was just too different. I felt guilty for even thinking it, and frightened. And

55

when I tried to articulate it to my pediatrician a short time later, he soothed my concerns. Nick was just an unusually bright child with a lot of attention focused on him, which seemed to explain a lot of things. Besides, I thought, how could you be too smart, too cute, too brilliant? In retrospect, it is easier to see that in many ways he had the classic symptoms of attention deficit disorder. But at the time, even his doctors could not see it clearly. I've been told since that 90 percent of children who manifest the same behaviors as Nick grow out of it, which makes pediatricians and psychiatrists loath to make that diagnosis. Most kids do grow out of it. Nick didn't. It seemed ridiculous even to me to worry about him.

Nicky was obviously unusually intelligent, and extremely advanced, and with that kind of intelligence one had to expect a few quirks, and a few things that were different. I felt foolish and ungrateful for questioning gifts like Nicky's, and put it out of my mind with relief. What could possibly be wrong with a child like Nicky?

3

Casanova

Dating with Nicky in residence was a nightmare. I stayed very busy with him for a long time, and he and Beatrix were the focal point of my existence. Between my work and my kids, I didn't have the time or the energy to date much, or the interest. But eventually, I began to make room in my life for other people. Bill was long gone, and I had had a tough time taking care of Beatie and Nick alone. I was ready for some companionship in my life, even if only on an occasional basis.

But Nicky had had me to himself by then, doted on by me and Beatrix, and he saw no particular need for an intruder. And he let me know it in no uncertain terms.

By the time Nick was two, he was extremely articulate, still in both Spanish and English. He remained bilingual all his life, and we often spoke to each other in Spanish. French is my native tongue, and early on I had tried adding it to Nick's repertoire, particularly as Beatrix and I spoke more French than English. She had spent her summers in France all her life, with family, and was completely fluent, and it was more comfortable for me to speak to her in French. But even as a small child, Nick hated French and refused to learn or speak it. Throughout his life, he made fun of me when I spoke it, exaggerating the sound of it, and he did a great double-talk gibberish imitation. I always teased him about it because he had a Spanish accent when he mimicked me in French. He decided early on that, whatever my origins, it was a ridiculous language, and flatly refused to learn it or let me speak it in peace when he was around.

But whatever language my suitors spoke, he outsmarted them with ease, and provided endless entertainment. I would hire baby-sitters for him and Beatrix when I went out at night, and I had a wonderful Salvadorian housekeeper, Lucy, who arrived shortly after Nick's first birthday. She is still with me and adored Nicky. And I would count on the baby-sitters I hired to get the kids to bed at a reasonable hour. My hope and expectation was to find Nicky curled up like a cherub in his bed when I returned. I would look at him lovingly from the doorway. It was an utter fantasy that had no relation to reality during my dating years. When I would come home, Beatie would be sound asleep, the baby-sitter would be passed out in front of the TV, and Nicky would be waiting for me, and would leap to the door the moment he heard my key turn. And I will confess to you that my heart sank more than once, as I opened the door cautiously, and found him looking up at me impishly, with a wicked gleam in his eye, and an appraising glance at my date, who had no idea what Nick had in store for him.

I would shoo Nick off to bed, and usually have to take him up myself and tuck him in, admonishing him to stay there. Then I would wake the sitter, pay her, and watch her go, as my unsuspecting date would pour himself a drink. And as I ushered the sitter out the door, Nick would reappear in his pajamas with feet, and offer to show my date his toys, though he usually tried to make the offer sound both sophisticated and enticing. To one friend who was a connoisseur of rare guns, Nick offered to show him his gun collection, and my date found him so irresistible and adorable that he disappeared upstairs hand in hand with Nick, while I waited on the couch, praying Nicky would release him soon, but of course he didn't. By the time Nick would finally allow him to come downstairs again, like the sitter, I would be sound asleep in front of the TV, and it would be one or two o'clock in the morning. Most of the time, my dates found him enchanting. And sometimes he really annoyed the hell out of me, and I could have sworn he was doing it on purpose.

My love life, with Nick in residence, was nonexistent. He never went to sleep, was impossible to keep in bed, and he acted as though the men in my life were visiting him and not me, and some of the time I think he was right. Those I have remained friendly with and still hear from, still reminisce fondly about their long midnight chats with Nicky.

Nick was also absolutely enamored of women. And just as I had thought early on, he often seemed to me like a grown man in a toddler's body. His passion for pretty women was certainly extreme. He groped, he hugged, he caressed, and who would

59

suspect a two-year-old of anything other than being cuddly? I did. I knew him better. Even at two, Nick was a Don Juan in the making.

He used to sneak up behind my housekeeper, creep under her skirt and pat her bottom, and then laugh outrageously. It was the laugh that gave him away. He always reminded me of my father, who was a real Casanova too, and my grandmother had claimed that even as a child, he had chased pretty women. So did Nick.

When I took him to our neighborhood ice cream store for an ice cream cone, he would invariably stand in line with a look of innocence, and reach up to a comfortable height for him and pat some woman's bottom. I let him go for ice cream with a (male) friend once, who returned looking a little chagrined, as Nick dribbled chocolate mint chip innocently all over his overalls. But apparently, he had done his usual bottom-patting routine, and the woman of his choice had turned around in outrage, thinking that the man who had accompanied Nicky had done it, and she had told him off soundly. He was too embarrassed to even try to blame it on the real perpetrator of the crime, Mr Nicky. Who would believe that a two-year-old child had done it?

And when we went to the beach house we still rented then, he would cheerfully suggest we go down to the beach and 'hug the ladies.' He loved ladies! Always! It was a condition that, with time, grew worse instead of better. He was endlessly charming, cuddly, and adorable, and women flocked to him all his life. He was irresistible, and he had a kind of innocent charm and magnetism that drew females to him like bees to honey. And I have to admit that most of the time, it amused me. (It is a lot different being the mother of a son than of a daughter.)

He used to tell me interesting stories when he was small. He would go on for hours sometimes, just talking about things. We would go for walks, and to the park, or just sit on the little terrace outside his bedroom, or in our garden. And it was during one of these talks that he looked at me pensively one day, and began what he was saying to me with 'When I was big . . .' and then he went on and told me a long story. I couldn't help asking him what he meant by what he had said. 'What do you mean, "when you were big"?' It seemed an odd thing for a child to say, and a little eerie, and it unnerved me, but he explained with a thoughtful look, as though trying to remember something.

'I used to be big a long time ago, and now I'm small again. But when I was big . . .' He went on again then, while I watched him, and then he looked up at me oddly. 'I used to be here before,' he said quietly, 'and I was big then.' It was certainly an odd thing to say, and I didn't question him again. It made me too uncomfortable, and touched on things I didn't want to know. But I never forgot it. I don't know if he was just rambling, in his thoughtful, intelligent way, or talking out a fantasy, or if there was more to it than that. But I was not then, and am not now, ready to know.

In contrast to his extreme intelligence and precociousness, there was of course a childlike side to him as well. He was cuddly and adorable, affectionate and very loving. He was a delicious child, and at two Beatie and I loved him more than ever. He was hungry for male company at times, and would latch on to some of the men I went out with to talk or play, but he never got seriously attached to anyone, nor did I. I think Nicky liked having me and Beatrix all to himself. He had a perfect little world that revolved almost entirely around him. He remained two years and some after his birth the gift that he had been since the beginning. Beatie and I both considered him an enormous blessing in our lives, and when I wasn't spoiling and kissing and cuddling and loving him, she was, or Lucy, my housekeeper. Nick had his own little harem, and we all adored him.

It was difficult toilet training Nicky. As quickly as he learned everything, he seemed to find that concept boring and not worth his notice. At two and a half, he still wet his bed at night, and would have wet mine, except that I was smart enough to put him in diapers at night. And although he used the potty in the daytime, he used it as his sister and I did. There was no man in my life to teach him any other way. And being unable to teach him a skill I had never been able to acquire, I bought something called 'Tinkle-Targets' for him, they were small floating paper bull's eyes and battleships that floated in the toilet. Nick was meant to take aim at them, and sink them. They worked very well, and considering there was no man in the house, Nick learned his lesson well. I still have some put away in a cupboard somewhere, and smile whenever I see them. It was a funny game, but it taught him what he needed to know, and it always made him laugh and squeal with glee while he did it.

He had an absolute passion for certain things. He would become obsessed with a toy or a character or a movie. It was *Sesame Street* for a while, and very soon became Spider-Man. He lived for Spider-Man, and had to have everything made about him. He wore Spider-Man pajamas to bed, Spider-Man sneakers to the park, Spider-Man T-shirts, drank out of a Spider-Man cup, ate on Spider-Man plates, and of course had a Spider-Man doll . . . Spider-Man birthday cake . . . Spider-Man everything. And he pretended to be Spider-Man most of the time. It was a real love affair that went on for a long time, until he replaced it with a new obsession. After Spider-Man came *Star Wars*, and ten million little action figures that he collected for years.

Nick loved games that he could fantasize, where he could be the central character and make things up. He preferred that by far to actual games where he had to follow rules and was constrained by someone else's idea of how to play. Anything set in stone like that annoyed him instantly and he would pay no attention to it. Later on, when we became aware of his learning disabilities, which seemed hard to imagine then, I wondered if he actually couldn't follow rules and directions, so he simply ignored them. But his fantasy life was a rich one.

As he had when he was younger, Nick had very definite ideas when he was two and a half, and if he didn't want to do something, I'd have a hard time trying to get him to do it. He would get belligerent and angry and stubborn. If he didn't like the plan of the hour, it was nearly impossible to get him to go along with it. It made it difficult to take him places, even at that age, because if he didn't like what was happening, he made your life a living hell. It actually worried me at times. It was easy to say he was spoiled, which was what the pediatrician said when I mentioned it to him. Nick was so extremely stubborn sometimes that it made me wonder about him.

My pediatrician was experienced and wise, and I know now how unimportant many of these early differences seem. They all seem so trivial and relatively normal. It is only with hindsight that we can see where they would lead. It is so easy to brush these things off at first, to discount them, or explain them. But I already had a gnawing feeling in my gut by then that Nick was different, and from time to time I would get brave enough to say so to a friend. It was always comforting to me when the warning signs I pointed out were explained away. But despite the reasonable explanations, the gnawing feeling of malaise remained. I just hoped I was wrong, and that he was in fact as normal as I wanted him to be.

Nick lived in a world where he was the constant center of attention. Two women and a young girl doted on him. There was no regular man in evidence to take a firm hand with him, not literally, but just to use a stern voice now and then, or impress him a little. His every whim was our command, and I loved him so much and thought he was so unique and wonderful that I was completely under his spell, as were all those who knew him. He was still 'incredible!' at two and a half, and everyone who saw him said so. It was easy to assume he was spoiled, and the occasional 'difficult' spells were easily attributed to the fact that he was

Nick the warrior *Nick at Christmas 1982*

Nick at four

too greatly loved by too many women, and had no father figure in his world.

Around that time, John Traina came into my life romantically, a handsome, elegant, dashing man, who dazzled me with his kindness, good looks, charm and sophistication and I fell deeply in love with him. He was recently separated after a sixteen-year marriage. He was very social, far more so than I, had two little boys, and during his marriage was obviously a good father to them, as I had seen for years when we were just friends. I had been lonely for a long time, and my life had been a struggle. My previous marriages had been disappointing. My recent forays into the dating world were sporadic and had meant nothing to me. But after the trauma I had experienced with Bill, of touching even peripherally a world which truly frightened me, John's very sane, elegant, wholesome world seemed a safe and wonderful place to me. He was the Prince Charming of whom I had dreamed.

John swept me off my feet, and after we dated for six weeks, he asked me to marry him, on Valentine's Day. It was too soon to know each other as well as we should have, and we paid a price for that eventually. But for long years, we shared a safe, happy world, where dreams seemed to come true.

It was also very important to me that he seemed to like my children, and I loved his two boys, Trevor and Todd, whom I had known for several years through my daughter, and who had come to play often at the house with Beatie and Nicky. They make a perfect foursome. It was a ready-made family, and I loved the fact that John wanted more children. I did too.

John seemed very fond of Nick, although he expressed cautiously once or twice that Nicky wasn't an easy child, which by then was something of an understatement. I remember once when we were dating, John took us out for a hansom carriage ride at the piers, Nick objected to it vehemently. John was making an effort to please him and Nick was so vocal about hating it that he embarrassed me. I wanted to put my hand over his mouth to muffle the awful things he was saying. I figured I'd never see John again, but was relieved when he seemed nonplussed by it. But Nick didn't make it easy for us. Sensing that this was a serious relationship, Nicky was highly suspicious of him, and wasn't embarrassed to say so whenever he chose to.

It was a whirlwind romance. Six weeks after we started dating, we were engaged, and we married exactly four months later. We entered into it with high hopes and loving dreams. John appeared to be the protector I had longed for. I looked forward to a long, happy life with him, surrounded by our children. It was clear to me that it would be good for me, good for my children, and hopefully for John's as well. I was crazy about them, and they were nice enough to welcome me with open arms. And Nicky was more than a little intrigued with the prospect of having two brothers. From his all-female world, he was about to be catapulted into a real family, with two brothers and a father. It seemed to me that all my dreams had come true, and I was happy for all of us. Life had turned around finally. The fates had smiled on us at last. And Nicky had a new daddy.

Right after the wedding, John and I went to New

York for a few days, where we both had business. I laughingly called it a 'business-moon,' and faced it with a little trepidation. In all of Nick's life I had never left him, and felt a real pull in my heart to do so. I worried a bit about being torn between John and my children. For all of their lives, they had been my first love and my primary responsibility and interest. I had never really shared my life with anyone who was a rival for my affections, and I wasn't quite sure how it was going to work, or how my children were going to feel about it, particularly Nicky. I was so used to devoting myself to him, and to his sister, I knew it was going to be an adjustment for them, and for me, to have a husband to share my life with. And in deference to that, we had planned to take our honeymoon five weeks later, and take the three older children to Europe with us. We were going to leave Nicky at home, and I was worried about it.

Interestingly, as it turned out, I never went on our honeymoon. I got sick just before we were to leave, and was suspected of having appendicitis. And convinced that I'd be all right and it was nothing, John left on our honeymoon with the three older children and suggested I catch up with them later, which never happened. Instead, I stayed home with Nicky, which was, in some ways, a relief, because I hated to leave him, though I was disappointed not to join the others on their travels. Not to mention the fact that they went on my honeymoon, and I didn't. I was at home with Nicky.

But just before they left, Nicky appeared in our bedroom one morning, with a very soggy diaper and nothing else. He was just three then. He stood barefoot in our room, hands on hips, looking up at John with a look of displeasure and said, 'Mr Twaina, what you don't understand is that I want her to myself.' Nicky was, even then, and forever after, always honest about his feelings. There was no misunderstanding him. And as he glared at his new father, and turned on his heels to leave the room, he gave John a withering look and closed the door firmly behind him, while we tried very hard not to smile.

4

Siblings and Other Changes

As closely as one can figure it, and I can usually figure it pretty closely, and have often had the opportunity to do so, we conceived Samantha within a week of our wedding. The malaise that kept me from our honeymoon turned out not to be appendicitis, but Samantha. Although we waited a while to tell the children, we were very pleased about it. It was not an accident, we wanted to have a baby, and John was hoping for a little girl.

But within a very short time after we were married, much to my surprise, Nick's father surfaced, and wanted to see Nicky. And I was worried about his continuing lifestyle and its effect on Nicky.

At the same time, I had noticed that Nick was, for some mysterious reason, extremely hospitable to random infections. If someone in the house got a cold, he got a bigger cold, or worse, pneumonia. If he cut himself, it became infected. No one ever figured out why, but for his entire life, he was extremely prone to all kinds of infections. And we thought it was possible that his immune system was less than perfect. In light of that, I was frantic at the thought of his visiting with someone who I believed was a using drug addict. And beyond frantic at the thought of Bill taking him anywhere. In my opinion, he was in no condition to do so.

Pregnant with Samantha, and extremely worried about Nick, we went to court, and the court was sympathetic to my concerns. They agreed to let Bill visit Nick, but in our home, and under my supervision. And to be honest, I wasn't pleased about it. Bill came to the house to see Nick a number of times, and when he did, it was obvious to us that he had not yet resolved his problems. It was very upsetting. His reappearance didn't seem to me like a happy addition to Nick's life, and I worried that it would confuse him. By then, Nick was extremely attached to John.

But at the same time, I had been noticing that Nick seemed wound up a lot of the time, somewhat hyper, and he was extremely unhappy about the baby. He had a kind of evil twinkle in his eye suddenly, and he became increasingly possessive of me, as though to prove that he was mine and I belonged to him, and nothing would ever interfere with us. I tried to reassure him, but I don't think I convinced him.

It was a hard time for Nick. There was a lot of change in his life in a short time. He had a new stepfather, two new brothers to adjust to, a new house, a new baby coming, which he viewed as a major threat, as most three-year-old children would have, and his biological father was back in his life, though he was a virtual stranger to him. If I had been in Nick's shoes, I would have been saying to myself, 'Who are all these people?'

John was extremely cautious and gentle with Nick, and respectful of the relationship I had with him. Later, he said that he hadn't wanted to interfere because he knew, and sensed easily, how much Nicky would resent it. In Nicky's eyes, I belonged to him exclusively, and he did not want to share me, with John, the boys, or the impending baby. And I often felt torn between two factions: Nick, and The Others. I spent a lot of time with Nick, but he became insatiable, wanting more of me than I had to give, as though to make me prove to him how much I loved him. And I loved him as much as ever, but there were other people in my life now, and his.

We made an important decision regarding our family, and decided that we would bring them up as one family: sisters and brothers. Very simple. Not half or step or real, or whatever. They were our children, with no distinction as to who had arrived with whom, or how they were related (and it remains so to this day, not only to us, but to them). And the children were young enough, and loved each other enough for us to do that. Beatrix, Trevor, and Todd had already been good friends for years. And the boys were wonderful with Nicky, and accepted him as their brother from the first.

Beatrix, Trevor, and Todd, when we got married, were respectively thirteen, twelve, and eleven. We didn't deny their other relationships, with Beatie's father, or the boys' mother. In fact, Beatie's father stayed with us several times, and had known John when they were growing up, spent their summers in the same place, and John had dated one of Beatie's father's sisters. It was all very cozy. And as far as the children were concerned, they were a single unit. It was comforting for Beatrix, I think, because her father lived three thousand miles away, and in Europe the rest of the time, and wasn't on hand on a daily basis, and the boys divided their time between us and their mother. In those days certainly, and for a long time after that, a very long time, everyone was very happy. Even Nicky. Although his lot was harder than the others, as he seemed to have more to adjust to.

The visits with Bill stopped eventually. He disappeared from our lives again, but would leave Nick messages on our answering machine, pretending to be Dracula. And it would both frighten and fascinate Nicky. He became obsessed with Dracula, as he had once been with Spider-Man, talking about him constantly, not his father, but Dracula. And at the same time, he began drawing terrible black pictures of people killing each other, swords drawn, and dripping blood from severed limbs. It was a far cry from the drawings of any child I had ever known. I don't think it had anything to do with his father's visits, but the subjects of his drawings concerned me. I discussed it with a psychiatrist, only to be told that he just had a vivid imagination, and the doctor didn't see it as any indication of a problem. But each time he produced one of those drawings, and he did so constantly, I was frightened. I put them in albums to show them to another psychiatrist and, once again, was told not to worry.

Two weeks after Nick turned four, Samantha was born. And Nick was livid. He was irate, incensed, felt betrayed, and was furious with me and the baby, inordinately so, I thought. It went beyond sibling rivalry into something that reminded me of *The Bad Seed*. I was constantly worried about him, and was upset that he was so overtly jealous of Samantha.

The drawings got worse, more plentiful, and blacker. He never ever did any drawings, and hadn't for over a year, in happy colors. Only dark ones. I had hundreds of them. He was still wetting his bed every night, and more difficult than ever. He was becoming a real handful, prone to rages, angry much of the time, and then the sun would burst through the clouds, and he would be suddenly tender and loving, for a while, until another storm hit. He was an angry child a lot of the time, and increasingly hard to handle at home. Yet at nursery school they said he was polite, intelligent, and charming, surprisingly adult (no surprise to me, he always had been), and he still enchanted all who met him. Nicky was always incredibly charismatic and seductive.

It was the people who lived with him who bore the brunt of his anger. I was extremely successful by then, writing by night, and spending time with my children by day. My life was a constant race of school drop-offs and pick-ups, after-school activities, and outings with the older children. I took pride and pleasure in being with my children. I loved being with them.

Four months after Samantha was born, I got pregnant again, but hadn't yet told the children, when I lost it two and a half months later. And got pregnant again, this time with Victoria, less than two weeks after I had lost the last one. My whole focus was still on my children, as it had been for years, there were just more of them. My work was something I did in the midnight hours, while John and the children slept, and never talked much about.

And just around that time, Bill surfaced yet again, once again demanding visitation. We went back to court, citing how unsuccessful the last round of visits had been, how sporadic, and how hard on Nicky. And this time, the court ordered visitation, in a psychiatrist's office, with an additional adult present to observe it.

Nick would often cry and beg not to go. He seemed to be traumatized by the entire process. It was not an easy time for Nicky, and during that time, the court wanted Nick seen by a psychiatrist to evaluate him, and we had him seen by one of our own as well, for an independent evaluation of what the visits were doing to him. But the prevailing belief at the time was that biological fathers, no matter how damaged or damaging, are vital to a child's well-being.

And this seemed an appropriate opportunity to drag out the endless albums I had of Nicky's terrifying black drawings, but no one seemed impressed by them. I was deeply concerned, and convinced that there was everything wrong with them, and possibly something wrong with Nicky. At four he was still wetting his bed, still very angry much of the time, rabidly jealous of Samantha, upset by the forced visits with Bill. And from time to time he defecated in the bathtub. Once on his pillow. And another time, he smeared it across the wall. All of it indicative, I felt sure, of some very deep-seated problem. I continued to believe that there was something wrong with Nick, not due to outside forces, but due to something deep within him. But I was given the same response by the psychiatrists about his brilliance, his genius, my spoiling him, and now the trauma of new siblings. I got nowhere. My albums went back into the cupboard. They had impressed no one. But I was constantly worried about him. I had a nagging gnawing in my gut, a sense that something was wrong, and no one would listen.

The visits stopped with Bill again. It had been a no-win situation for Nick, who didn't want to go in the first place, and seemed upset to have to go to see Bill. And when for some reason Bill failed to show up, as he sometimes did, Nicky would come home feeling that he had done something to upset him. I worried that Nick would feel rejected, anxious, and guilty in those instances. But when Bill disappeared this time, he did not return. He went off to the miseries of his own life, and did not enter Nick's again. The visits were forever over. And however great a loss it may have been for either or both of them at some deep psychological level, I was relieved for Nick's sake. I felt that the visits were just too traumatic for him.

Nick was five and a half when Victoria arrived. I had an easy delivery this time (my only one), spent only one night in the hospital, and came home with her the next morning. Nick had a massive asthma attack that night, and had to be taken to the hospital. It was not the first one he had had (I have asthma, as do five of my seven children), though never to that proportion. He wasn't pleased about Victoria, but as time went on, he ignored her. The full measure of his hatred and resentment was focused on Samantha most of the time.

He was angry, vengeful, and resentful. And it was understandable that he would be jealous of Samantha and Victoria, and upset by the renewed disappearance of Bill, but in spite of those possible causes for his apparent belligerence, his reactions always seemed well beyond measure. I was constantly soothing him and apologizing for him, and trying to make things better for him. I loved him so much, I hated to see him so unhappy. Nick resisted everyone's efforts to draw him out and take him places. I was often the only one who could get behind his walls, and much of the time, he was angry at me too. After all, I was the traitor who had brought home the new babies. But however angry he was, he was still deeply attached to me.

I was fiercely protective of Nicky, always offering excuses for him, and defending him, and he knew it. Nick trusted me, even when he was angry at me. Looking back, it was as though there was a pain raging inside him, a pain he did not know how to soothe or handle. He was not an easy child to love or manage. Just when you thought you had won him over, and won his trust, he would lash out against you. He did it to me too, but somehow I never took it personally, and was always able to see beyond it. Even then, I suspected that there was something eating away at him, more than the obvious provocations for his anger. I knew then, at four, and even more so at five, that there was something wrong with him, but I didn't know how to put words to it, and whenever I tried to, I felt no one was listening to me.

Nick at four at Sammie's christening, 1982

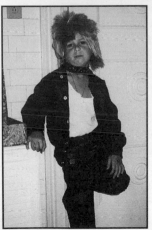

Nick as a rock star on Halloween at five or six

I spoke to one of the psychiatrists he had seen, and he told me that he was fine, all he needed was discipline. But I knew that it was more than that. Like Nicky, I felt trapped behind the walls of silence, imprisoned by what I believed was a case of everyone choosing to remain ignorant. Perhaps knowing that, and seeing it, and feeling it, bound me closer to Nicky. Only we knew of the flame deep within that had already begun to wound him.

Yet another sister, Vanessa, was born when Nick was six and a half. But he seemed unmoved by this one. He was still devoted to torturing Samantha. It was a hatred that burned for several years, like an eternal flame, until suddenly it turned to a love of equal measure several years later, when he was twelve or thirteen, and she became the sibling he was closest to. Once the tides turned, they adored each other. And for every remaining moment of his life, Sam idolized him and adored him and he loved her every bit as much as she did him. I would have felt greatly comforted in those early years, if I had known what would blossom later between them. Theirs was a bond of trust and loyalty and passion that transcended all others.

Six months later, when Nick was seven, we went back to court, to terminate Bill's parental rights this time, so John could adopt him. It was something that Nick wanted, as we all did. The trial started on the day of Nick's seventh birthday. Bill hadn't seen Nick in several years by then, and Nicky was never asked to appear in court, fortunately. And the court ruled that Bill had abandoned him years before, they terminated his parental rights, and John adopted Nicky. It must have been a sad time for Bill.

Nick at about six

*School pictures at six
or seven*

*Nick at his adoption party, with
John, at seven years*

We didn't speak. I hated what he had done with his life, and in those days still felt betrayed by him. He seemed light-years from my life then.

We had an adoption party for Nick at the house, with a vast number of our friends, and Nicky seemed happy to be adopted. The older children were well aware of what was happening, but Nick said that he never wanted the younger ones to know that John wasn't his real father. He had in effect been the father Nick had grown up with, and Nick didn't want to be different from the others. And for several years after that, Nick's adoption by John remained a secret from his younger siblings. It was important to him, and we respected his wishes on the subject.

But despite Nick's obvious happiness over the adoption, he continued to do some very odd things, and to be difficult to manage. The bed-wetting had finally stopped when he was six, and he was doing well in school, but he was an angry, difficult child, who destroyed his toys constantly, and always seemed to be swimming upstream. He was never in harmony with what was going on around him, or what other people were doing. If we were going out, he wanted to stay in. If we were staying home, he wanted to go out. He had no interest in ordinary games, but only in playing war, playing with toys that allowed him to use his imagination, and the fiercely black and bloody drawings continued.

And I can't even tell you why, or the incident that led to it, but when we were in Hawaii on vacation with the family when Nick was seven, I remember watching him, and thinking the situation was hope-less. I had an absolutely clear sense that he was

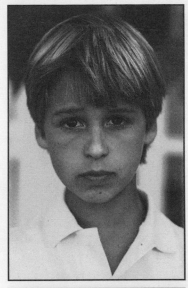

Nick at about eight

Nick at eight years,
Maxx at eight months

Nick at about nine

Nick at ten or eleven

deeply disturbed, no matter how normal he often seemed even to me occasionally and especially to others. But I knew to my very soul that he was all wrong somehow, and feared that it would never be any different. I had absolutely no idea how to help him, or how to change it, or make it better. And I was still, at that point, the only one who could see it. My efforts to expose it to his pediatrician or even his school, and to elicit help from them, had been fruitless. They apparently saw no problem. Only I did. Although John has since told me that he had the same fears I did, but was afraid to voice them to me.

A brother, Maxx, was born when Nick was eight and a half, and this time Nick seemed sometimes pleased, and at other times threatened and jealous. He had a rival, a younger brother, although later, he was immensely proud of him.

Nick's passion by then was baseball. He played it, he watched it, he lived and breathed it, and began obsessively keeping ledgers where he invented imaginary baseball games, with each play written down in elaborate detail, listing every player and all their vital statistics. He even wrote up imaginary World Series. The ledgers, which I still have, are quite remarkable and brilliant, there are stacks of them.

He was also passionate about music by then, and had been since he was about five. He listened to the same music and loved the same groups as his teenage older siblings did, and would often saunter up to their friends and inquire about the groups they listened to. At first, they thought he was being funny, and then realized that he meant it, and knew what he was talking about. He was extraordinarily knowledgeable about their music. It was a lifelong passion for him, and one that never dimmed or diminished. It was what he loved most, and what he was best at, although he was also a gifted writer, and I often said in later years that he wrote better than I do. His sense of pace and timing, and way of unraveling a story, were exquisite.

And when break-dancing became the craze, he somewhat horrified his older siblings by dancing quite expertly in front of their friends. He was six then. And stole the show at Trevor's sixteenth birthday. He also loved to flirt with their girl-friends, who found him adorable and amusing, which understandably often irritated his brothers.

The last baby, Zara, came when Nick was eleven, and this time Nick was enchanted. He was old enough to enjoy her and not be threatened by her (and at that time, he was still tormenting Samantha).

But Nick was beginning to unravel by then. The pain that had driven him from deep within for years was beginning to become more obvious. He was harder still to control, harder to handle. He was destructive of things in his room, yet he never hurt anyone intentionally. He would play with the younger children too roughly at times, but never physically attacked or injured them. But what I was seeing more and more in him worried me constantly. Being with him was like trying to harness a tornado. One moment he would be impossible, the next gentle and loving. And despite the fact that he took more energy and care than all the other eight children put together, I felt an unseverable bond to him, and a constant need to protect him. I knew instinctively that no one else understood him as I did, or knew how much pain he was in. It was like a seed that I knew had grown to frightening proportions, and was continuing to grow, unseen, unchecked, unattended, and there was nothing to stop it. It was like a dragon raging inside him, and my greatest fear was that it would devour him.

And still everyone apparently failed to see it. He continued to make the honor roll at school, despite learning disabilities no one had become aware of yet, and that passed unnoticed. His IQ was so high that it carried him well beyond his limitations, and he was able to compensate as few others could have.

We all had a challenge that year when John had a near fatal accident in the house, a fall that almost killed him. All of the children were frightened and upset by it, as I was. But Nicky was particularly shaken by it, and afraid that he would die, and began wetting the bed again, and defecating in the bathtub, although only for a brief time. But his disturbance got somewhat lost in the crowd, because the others were upset by it too, even the oldest ones who were in their late teens and early twenties. But Nick seemed gripped by real panic. And then he calmed down again as John got better. But at eleven, he was acting out more than he ever had before, and always marching to a different drummer.

When he had been told to wear dark pants and a light shirt to the Christmas show at school, he wore pale chino pants and a black turtleneck instead, and I made him get off the stage and change. Other people found his 'independent ideas' amusing, but I didn't. I knew they were a sign of something much deeper and far more disturbing. And to this day, I do not understand why other people didn't see it. It is hard to fathom why they didn't. Perhaps they didn't want to, or couldn't, or were too frightened by it. But I knew . . . oh, God how I knew . . . and how frightened I was for him. Even then, in my heart, despite all the other children I had, he was my baby . . . the one I knew was wounded . . . and who needed me differently than the others. I would have done anything to protect him, to change it, to will the pain and the dragon away for him, with love if nothing else . . . but even then, I couldn't. And the dragon that was slowly devouring him just got bigger.

5

Sixth Grade:
The demons begin
to let us see them

Nick was eleven, and he had a new passion: his skateboard, although the primary passion in his life, his real love, was always music. He seemed to know every group and song and musician on the planet, and impressed everyone, most of all his older siblings' friends, with his knowledge of them. And for a kid his age, he had fairly sophisticated taste about the rock scene. He was familiar with all the new, upcoming groups along with the obvious, well-known ones. And at first when people in the know talked to him, they always thought he was just 'faking it.' But of course he wasn't. He knew his stuff, usually much better than they did.

At eleven, he had long since been crazy about a good friend of mine, Jo Schuman, who was equally enamored of him. She was one of the few people, and certainly the only one in my world, who knew as much about the music scene as he did, as her cousin was the founder and head of a major record company. And as a special treat, Jo would take him to the big, important concerts, and of course always took him backstage with her. Jo was one of the brightest stars in Nick's Heaven, and they adored each other from the moment they met until he left us.

But along with his true love, music, there was always an additional compulsion. His imaginary (and real) baseball games. He played, and was very good at it. He also collected baseball memorabilia then, and like everything else he loved, it became an obsession. He collected some great stuff, and as always had very adult, sophisticated knowledge, and eventually a fairly important collection of cards, and signed bats and baseballs. And of course earlier, there had been Spider-Man and *Star Wars*. Now there were skateboards. He would skate for hours and hours and hours, and was constantly perfecting his skateboard, buying new parts for it, and changing things on it. At our country house in Napa, he built a huge skateboard ramp himself, and placed it as inconveniently as possible in the driveway. Nicky's world revolved mostly around himself, and by sixth grade, he had become singularly self-involved, and appeared to have no particular interest in other people's needs or problems. Nicky's world revolved exclusively around Nicky. It was not an endearing trait, and did not help him get along with other people. And in the family, he appeared to walk right over everyone to get where and what he wanted. He was singularly obsessive.

At eleven, when Nick was in sixth grade, I had a harder time than ever getting along with him, and worried about him constantly. There was always a gnawing concern for him. He just wasn't like other kids his age, no matter how many excuses I made for him. He was brighter, faster, harder, louder, meaner when he chose, and at other times sweeter. Everything about Nick was more extreme, as though the colors he painted his life with were brighter and sharper than everyone else's. He was relentless when he wanted to do something, or have something, and merciless in his attempts to get it.

And I cannot pretend now to any kind of magic insight or omniscience. All I knew was that Nicky had problems, and I had a constant gnawing in my gut, like some kind of radar or sonar device that told me he was out of kilter. But I had no real words to put to it. I was still inquiring discreetly at his school at regular intervals if they thought he was okay. He was still doing well, and whenever I suggested that something was wrong with him, I felt that they looked at me like I was crazy. Nicky? Of course not. But they didn't live with him. They didn't see the things he broke, the rages that seemed to be getting slightly worse, or have to deal with his frequently obsessive behavior.

I cannot say now that I knew all along what was happening. I didn't. I didn't wake up one day, slap my hand to my head, and say, 'Oh, my God, of course, my baby is manic-depressive.' At that point in time, I knew nothing. What I sensed was that something was wrong with him, but I couldn't have told you what if my life depended on it, and what I hoped more than anything was that he'd outgrow it. I think, in my heart of hearts, I also hoped that no one else would ever really notice. Since everyone always insisted that he was just brilliant and difficult, I prayed that people would continue to perceive him that way forever. I didn't want people to think something was seriously wrong with him, although privately I thought so. I didn't even say as much to my husband. I told no one. It became my own dark secret, and whenever necessary, I made endless excuses for him. 'He's tired, he has a cold, this is hard for him, his sisters annoy him, the older kids are jealous of him and don't understand him, his teachers didn't know what they were doing.' There were a lot of ways to account for his behavior, but only one that would have been accurate, but it was obscured by all of our ignorance, my prayers not to see, and what I believed to be the continuing blindness of the professionals who might have seen it.

Neither my pediatrician nor his school told me that they saw anything unusual about Nicky, and later, for a long time, I resented his school for it. I have since forgiven them, because even if we had known then, I don't think we could have changed it. All we could have done was offer him medication, which might have blunted his sharp edges a little, and made him easier to get along with, but it wouldn't have cured him.

One of the big excitements for Nick in those days was a lip-sync contest they held at his school each year, in February. It was a big event for all the kids, but most of them shuffled into the tryouts for it, grabbed a few friends along the way, and argued for half an hour about what song they would pretend to sing. And when the actual contest came, they would awkwardly get up onstage, scramble around,

Nick as Prince on Halloween

*Nick as 'Rock Star'
at his school lip-sync
talent show*

muff it most of the time, but look sweet and child-like while they did. But not Nicky.

For Nick, this was his moment to shine, his hour of glory, his shot at the gold at the Olympics. He began preparing for it months before, every year, carefully selecting his 'band,' choosing the songs, forcing them to rehearse regularly, and eventually diving into my closets and coming out with wigs and costumes. My favorite cowboy boots disappeared, my sequined T-shirts that I never wore but hung on to anyway, an old disco jacket he had also worn when he dressed up as Prince once on Halloween (Prince was another of his many obsessions, as was Michael Jackson early on, The Police, Sting, Nirvana, Guns and Roses and countless others). For the lip-sync contest, he doled out the wigs I owned but never wore, and of course when I got them back they were beyond recognition. I used to grumble, 'Why do you have to supply the wardrobe and wigs for half of the sixth grade?' But the lip-sync contest was what Nicky lived for. It was his opportunity to be a 'real' rock star for a few hours. And when he did, he dazzled everyone who saw him.

He used strobe lights, real instruments, and by the time his 'group' slid past the tryouts into the real thing, it was like watching a real rock band perform in a real concert. He took everyone's breath away, and of course after months of hard work, he usually won it. It was an early glimpse into who he would be later on, in the music scene, how hard he would work, how creative he would be, and how hard he would drive the other musicians (however young and inexperienced they were) that he worked with. Nicky was brilliant at it, and those lip-sync contests were just a tiny glimpse into the future, as he writhed and rocked and rolled and mesmerized his audience, stage-diving into the crowd, leaping through the air, and imitating every tiny quirk of the band he was emulating. It used to make my heart sing to see him. However much I complained about what he did to my wigs and my favorite cowboy boots, even I knew way back then that it was worth it. I loved it. And it always amused me when I saw him in one of my wigs, to realize that, with the right hairdo, he actually looked a lot like me. Most of the time, I thought he looked like his father. The truth was he looked like neither and both of us, he looked like himself. He was an incredibly handsome boy, even as a child. And his appeal to women only grew over the years, and never diminished. They loved him!

He was still fairly athletic then, although sixth grade may have been the last of it, or the beginning of the end. He was great at baseball and tennis, a powerful and graceful swimmer, but he began to think that outdoor pursuits weren't 'cool,' and preferred to sit in his room, both in the country on weekends and at home, and listen to music. In truth, I realized later, this wasn't about being 'cool,' he was becoming isolated.

He wrote a lot in those days, scarily sophisticated short stories that always showed an adult perception about subtle things. He had an elegant writing style, a sharp command of the language, and an extraordinary sense of timing. I used to read what he wrote, listen to the cadence of it, feel the sharp jolt of the power of his prose, and feel him reel me in and out as he chose. He had a natural, innate, powerful style and a gift that was so natural to him, he never noticed. He loved to write, but preferred his music, and never thought much about his writing. His stories were often violent, and always had a dark twist to them.

And later, when his demons began to get the better of him, he explained to me very simply one day that he couldn't concentrate anymore on long blocks of writing, (his early short stories were pretty long) and it worked better for him to keep it short and write lyrics. They were the extent of his ability to concentrate on writing by then, and served his purpose anyway. And like his early short stories, some of his lyrics were brilliant, wise and perceptive and clever. I ran across some of his short stories the other day, while looking through his room, and I was startled again by how good they are. And along with the short stories, he kept endless diaries and journals. I never invaded them, never read them, until now, save one which I 'borrowed' from him when he was fourteen and I was so deeply concerned about him, and wanted a glimpse into just how serious the problem was that he was facing. The answers I found there were deeply disturbing.

At eleven, as I read through his journals now, he was still in fairly good shape, though angry a lot of the time. But in sixth grade, you could blame his complaints and quirks on the beginning of raging hormones. You could blame it on a lot of things, sunspots, TV, bad parenting, annoying siblings. If you want to find excuses for unusual behavior, if you try hard enough, you can always find them.

There was one very odd thing about his behavior then. Our Tylenol stock in the house began to decline rapidly. I would find empty bottles everywhere, or a few broken tablets left around, and more often than not, the empty Tylenol bottles turned up in his room. He always feigned surprise and innocence when I found them, and even when he was grown up and we talked openly about these things, he denied the Tylenol 'habit' I thought he had developed. Nick was almost always honest about things, astonishingly so, and even as a kid he would admit to things others wouldn't. And later on, he never shied away from the truth, and told me some things with complete candor that made me shudder. But he never admitted to the Tylenol, although I feel sure that he was taking it. I think he was beginning to feel seriously uncomfortable in his own skin by then, and he was seeking relief, anywhere he could find it. It wasn't a dangerous substance, so although I worried about it, and constantly questioned him about the evidence I found, I didn't panic. But we locked up the Tylenol and all our medicines, so he couldn't get to them.

His next step to self-medication was Sudafed. My husband took it for sinus headaches. We kept most medicines locked up, because of the younger children, but if nothing else, John always had a few Sudafed in his pockets. And I would find the little foil wrappers strewn around Nick's bedroom. When I asked him about it, he just said he was getting a cold or had a headache, he didn't deny it. I myself am allergic to it, and along with an adverse reaction, it nearly makes me jump out of my skin. Most people will say that the medication speeds them up, but of course Nick still had his paradoxical reactions to medication, so what would speed up most people would calm him down. I think Sudafed did exactly that for him, and it was his awkward first attempt to buffer, if not still, the demons. Even then, they could not have been easy to silence, judging from the disturbing entries in his journal.

As always, I was worried about him, and the Tylenol and Sudafed he was obviously taking in fairly noticeable quantities set my alarms off. I was seeing a therapist myself then, and I asked him to see Nicky. Nick thought that was a dumb idea, and balked at it at first, but eventually he agreed to talk to him, and would go over once or twice a week to do so. Nicky thought he was cool because he liked baseball. I'm sure they talked about more than that, and although my therapist did not quell all my fears, he said he didn't see anything direly wrong with Nicky. He was an unusual boy with startlingly clear perceptions about adults and the people around him, albeit not very charitable views at times, but he was brilliant and perceptive. He was still deeply jealous of Samantha, and we put down some of his acting out to sibling rivalry, and the fact that he was nearly, or perhaps truly, a genius. Nicky was just Nicky. How else could one describe him? There was certainly no one else like him. Not in my world anyway, or many others.

Even when he ran away Nicky made me laugh, although at the exact moment it happened, I did not find it amusing.

I had asked him to change his shoes for some family event, and Nick refused to do it. He took a great deal of pleasure by then in being oppositional, and one of the best ways to do it was with his clothing. He never wanted to dress appropriately for any occasion, yet when you finally got him to, he looked terrific. But just getting him to dress properly for school was a battle of Olympic proportions. It was always a huge struggle every morning as we argued over a shirt, a pair of pants, his hair, his shoes, and he insisted on wearing something totally inappropriate, sometimes I thought, just to get a reaction. The behavior itself wasn't unusual, but the degree was. Eventually of course he would appear looking angelic and impeccable, and no one would have imagined the agony it took to achieve it.

We are a fairly conservative family. When Nick was young, I loved dressing the little children in pretty clothes, the older children always had a fairly preppy look, and my husband was then an extremely conservative and elegantly dressed man. What Nick liked best was to shock us. I tried to maintain a sense of humor about it, and remain rational, while giving him room to be himself, but at times he tried me sorely, and I lost it and would scream at him to pull himself together and for once get dressed without making a national crisis of it. It was more than a little trying, but certainly not worth getting an ulcer over. Most of the time I kept my perspective, but tried to remain firm about it. I felt that he, like everyone else in our cozy little world, should conform to certain standards. Nick was not of that opinion.

So, on the day in question, the day of the famous runaway, he was meant to wear a blazer and gray flannels, a tie, and respectable shoes to go to a family function. He chose to appear in some wild outfit, with worn-out sneakers. My mother was visiting, as was my stepmother, and I can't remember what it was, but we were going to one of the staid family events that so intensely bored him. Bit by bit, and piece by piece, we argued his outfit together. He went along with all of it, releasing each item of inappropriate clothing like hostages, begrudgingly, but he did it. Except for the shoes. He wouldn't change them. And I will confess that I yelled at him finally. He would drive me to that at times, though I never raised a hand to him, nor him to me or anyone else. Nick wasn't violent, just mouthy. Very! And when he chose to be, extremely insulting. He could rile a grown-up faster than any kid I've ever seen, and regularly reduced adults to tears with his sharp tongue and ability to use it.

The shoes remained an issue. He would *not* change them. And I wouldn't give in on this one. He made everyone late, as he often did. I felt everyone was looking askance at me with the usual silent accusation that said, 'Can't you do anything with him?' The fact was that I could, sometimes, but only if Nick was amenable to it. If not, I was out of luck. You could either give in gracefully or spend the next two days arguing with him. Nick did not give in on anything with ease or grace, unless he chose to, and if he did, he made you pay for it, with an attitude and vehemence that made you wish you'd never gotten into the tug-of-war in the first place.

I went upstairs to his room to check on him to see if he'd changed his shoes, and he was gone. And instantly, I sensed that this time something was different. I don't know how I knew, but I did. Nick had run away, but the funny thing was that he had actually changed into respectable shoes to do it. The torn sneakers had been left in the middle of the room like a message. So he had done what we wanted him to, but he was going to show us. Retribution.

We looked everywhere for him as I panicked. He was, after all, only an eleven-year-old boy, and because of my fame by then, the children weren't allowed to go anywhere alone. I had no idea where to look for him, but we all spread out and ran around the neighborhood looking for him. I called 911 and reported him missing. A friendly policeman came to the house fairly quickly, as I wrung my hands and cried, of course feeling very guilty to have made such a fuss over a miserable pair of sneakers. And then, God only knew why, I glanced out the window.

We lived across the street from a small park that was about four blocks square, and there, directly across the street from the house, sat Nick, with a small brown bag, eating doughnuts and Hostess Twinkies. He looked vastly unconcerned, slightly amused, and was dressed beautifully, not only in shirt, tie, blazer, and proper shoes, but he had put on his fancy little trench coat as it was chilly. He looked like a very small banker or lawyer, sitting in the park and eating lunch, having just left his office. Later, I laughed about it, but at the time, I was livid. Everyone was upset, we had all run all over the place for an hour. My mother was horrified at how little control I had over my children and did not hesitate to say so. 'Does this happen all the time?

How often does he do this? You should put him in reform school.' Thank you, Mom. My mother is of the old school and a rather stern one. And then at least, she thought that children should be seen and not heard and behave the way they used to, or the way I did. But in time of course, as he did with all of us, Nicky taught her that things with him at least were different, and she fell in love with his crazy hair colors, wild outfits, and even his nose ring, because she understood who was behind it. It was hard to resist him.

I walked outside to my little renegade, with the policeman, who gave him a stern lecture and threatened to take him to juvenile hall as a runaway. Nicky looked up at him innocently, stood up respectfully, apologized, shook his hand, and offered him a doughnut. Who could resist him? He thanked the officer, looking deeply mortified, and we took him home and read him the Riot Act. We had been scared stiff about him. And finally, hours late, the rest of us looking disheveled and unnerved, while Nick looked calm, cool, collected, and perfectly dressed, we went off to our family event. It was one of only two times he ran away, and the other was barely more serious than this one. Running away wasn't something Nicky did. He stood his ground, and stayed close to home. The chains of our love for him, and his for us, bound him closely.

6

Seventh Grade: Slowly downwards

As you can see by now, some of the things Nick did were unusual, but none of them was so extreme that you could point a finger and say 'Aha! There is something seriously wrong with this boy!' and then diagnose it. Some of his antics were in fact very funny, many were less so. There was sometimes a meanness to him at that age that upset me deeply, but even that was something you could explain away by virtue of his age, and of course others were quick to say that the shock of acquiring five younger siblings in as many years, and my ever increasing celebrity and fame, were just hard on him. Perhaps the former, but in fact not the latter.

I was careful to keep my career well away from the kids, all my daily activities still centered around them, and my writing was something I did late at night, and seldom discussed with anyone. I did no interviews or publicity tours. I was a fairly ordinary mom to them, and that was how I wanted it, and kept it. But there was no denying that going from being the baby, the star, the focus of all attention, to being the fourth in a group of nine, was stressful for him. He was still hating Sam in those days, and being very vocal about it. She was eight, and he was twelve by then, and I worried a lot about the damage he was doing to her self-esteem. He was constantly critical of her, and at times really cruel about it. It was a full-time job buffering her from his overt meanness. And it was one of the many things that worried me deeply. For Samantha, more than Nicky. But perhaps because he made an about-face eventually, and adored her so completely, she seems to have survived it.

But seventh grade was the beginning of a long, at first slow, downward spiral for Nicky. For the first time in all his years, he began to act out in school noticeably. And believe me, they noticed. The child that I had been discreetly inquiring about for seven years in the same school, and even nursery school before that, and eventually even openly suggesting to them that he wasn't 'normal' – and who they had insisted to me was utterly wonderful – suddenly became a major headache for them.

I began getting calls from the school, and in seventh grade, Nick taught me a new skill, which I was to become an expert at for the remainder of his school years. Groveling. I added it to my repertoire of motherly feats and virtues. Anything to keep Nick in school, and then hope Nick would change. But the calls became increasingly frequent. He was mouthing off in school, and was openly disrespectful of his teachers. He wasn't doing the work regularly and allowed himself liberties of behavior and attitude that they viewed with extreme displeasure. Nicky was no longer 'fitting in,' and they no longer thought him cute, clever, or amusing. Suddenly they turned the tables on me, and began pointing out to me that his behavior was unacceptable and just too 'different.' No news to me, but they seemed both startled and outraged, and expected me to change it, and impress the seriousness of their displeasure on Nicky. Nick found it vastly amusing. Nothing scared him.

The only thing that impressed him was when they threatened to keep him out of the lip-sync contest that year, which filled him with panic, and straightened him out for a while, until the contest. But more than anything, I was aware that he was no longer coloring within the lines of his school life. He was beginning to go over the edges of the picture they were painting.

And what made it even harder for him was that there was a fairly new headmaster at his school, who understandably didn't want Nick creating problems. But torturing teachers seemed like good sport to Nick, and conceding to the headmaster was of no interest to him. I tried to explain to him that this was his show (the head's), not Nicky's, it was 'his house, his rules, his marbles,' and he didn't have to let Nicky play if he didn't want to. But as with other things, and somewhat appropriate to his age and disposition, Nick thought he was invincible. As he said about himself, in one of his journals, in an entry he'd written later, at the time, *'I thought I was charmed. I figured I could handle or do anything because I was special.'* He wrote that when he was twelve, in seventh grade. And he was special. To me certainly, but not necessarily to outsiders, and Nick couldn't seem to understand that. The head of the upper school called me once a week, or every other week, but I felt as though every time I turned around, they were calling me to come to the school and apologize for him, which I did, though I can't honestly say I enjoyed it. They also expected me to change his behavior, which, try as I might, I couldn't.

I tried explaining to them that Nick was different, that he was not your ordinary kid, with ordinary ideas or behaviors. Even in my own family, he did not perfectly fit the norms or the rules the rest of us lived by. Nick was undeniably different, and the rules I had applied so uniformly to his three older siblings were just impossible to apply to Nicky. He wouldn't conform to them, and what's more, by then I had begun to suspect that he couldn't. He was different and special.

The school recommended a new therapist, whom we went to immediately, and who was diligent about delving into the reasons why Nick acted the way he did. The therapist turned his attention to us, and the family, but the clear signs of Nick's disease had not yet surfaced. I suspect it must have been too early to diagnose him.

Nick was like a burning cigarette tossed into the dry grass at the edge of a summer forest. He was a forest fire waiting to happen, and while the conflagration began to burn, and the flames began to devour him, none of us could yet see it.

Things began to go seriously sour for Nick that year. He began to experiment with drugs. Others have tried it at the same age, and come out the other end, but like everything else he did, Nick fell into it with a certain manic passion. He drank a little and tried pot, and along with a group of friends, late in the school year, he tried acid (LSD). That would have terrified me, had I known it. He reported it to me several months later. Nick was usually pretty honest, and even when he didn't volunteer things, if I discovered them myself and questioned him, he was almost always honest about it. But when it happened, I didn't know what he was up to. I only discovered it later, when he told me.

I think he also became sexually active in seventh grade, and was usually drawn to girls slightly older than he was, as he thought he could get further with them. And judging from the long lists of names in his diaries, the varying degrees of stars and ratings he gave them, and the things he claimed they did with him, if any of it is true, he was not mistaken.

I was at least fairly willing to look at that and face it squarely. I gave him assorted lectures about being responsible, not hurting people's feelings, not being casual about sex and only sleeping with people he cared about, which, let's face it, made me feel better, and Nicky must have laughed heartily at my romantic notions. He was a young boy in the grip of raging hormones, and out to enjoy anything he could get away with. But at least he was polite while he listened to me, and indulged me. I also made a rule at our pharmacy that he could charge prophylactics any time he wanted to, but nothing else. And if he did so, I promised not to ask questions, and didn't. Practising safe sex seemed to me more important than grilling him about it, and he got the message and used condoms.

So in the seventh grade came the advent of sex and drugs, and the door to danger began to open. He was a handsome boy, much admired by all, as much for his willingness to be outrageous and take risks, and behave any way he wanted to, as for his good looks and charm. Nick was the boy everyone wanted to be like, or at least be with. And that year, he was asked to model.

He did a little of it, and it didn't go to his head particularly. I think he actually found it boring, and began to think he wanted to do some acting. He went on a couple of interviews in Los Angeles, which my husband took him to, and they fell in love with him at the auditions, but my ground rules were firm. He could only go to Los Angeles to act during school vacations or on weekends, which made it too difficult for them to use him. And he was mad at me for it.

He was on one of those auditions towards the end of the school year, trying out for a part in a TV show that he could have been in that summer. And he was still on the plane, returning from Los Angeles with John, when a terrible tragedy happened. A group of his friends had been dropped off at a friend's house for a party. Among them were Nick's entire group of best friends, the boys he hung out with at school, and the girls whom they liked best. Co-ed parties began that year, and among the girls was a little dazzler he had gone to nursery school with and stayed close

Nick at eleven or twelve

to. She was his closest female friend, and in first grade he wrote for a school project, 'I want to get married to my girlfriend when I grow up. We will work together as an actress and a singer.' What he wrote is still framed on my office wall, where it has been since he first wrote it. Her name was Sarah, and she was a beauty. They were no longer 'girlfriend and boyfriend' by then, but best friends in the nicest senses of the word, confidantes and cohorts. They talked to each other on the phone, daily and nightly, talking about who liked whom, 'fixing up' their friends, and indulging in the little intrigues and romances that were appropriate to their age then.

And apparently the group got to the party a little too early. 'No one was there,' Nick explained afterwards, having heard it from his friends, which meant that the 'cool' people weren't there yet. So they decided to go across the street to the Marina, to hang out for a while, and then go back to the party. It was a practice which, by my rules at least, was strictly forbidden. You didn't go anywhere once you got to a party, you didn't leave, you stayed there, and I never let kids do it when they came to my house. I didn't want to be responsible for what happened to them when I couldn't see them, and the policy was most of all for their own good. But for whatever reason, the 'cool' group of Nick's friends left the party.

The kids dashed across Marina Boulevard, which is a wide, dangerous street that feeds fast-moving traffic onto the Golden Gate Bridge, in this case at sunset. I know myself from having driven there that at certain hours of the day, sunset being one of them, the sun shines in your eyes so blindingly you can't always see danger coming towards you. Perhaps that happened to the driver who hit Sarah. I never heard the precise details of the impact, and couldn't have borne to listen to them.

The group apparently split in two, with half of them crossing at the crosswalk, as they had been taught since they were small children, and the others choosing not to. Sarah was among them, with her long, flying blond hair, her huge eyes, her face like a cameo, her long graceful limbs in all their thirteen-year-old beauty. The driver's vision was supposedly obscured by a passing van, and the kids must have flown at them like a flock of birds, unexpectedly and dangerously crossing their path. One of the other girls was grazed by the car that hit Sarah full on and flung her onto and through their windshield. And the details of the result are anything but pretty.

Sarah lay in the hospital with severe brain damage and assorted other injuries for a week. And all those who knew her were stunned and devastated. It was a tragedy that rocked everyone to the core, and none of the kids knew how to handle it. For many of them it was a shock from which they would not completely recover. And Nick among them. He was even less equipped than most to handle it, and for years, he surrounded himself with photographs of her, memorabilia, things she had given him. He dreamed of her, thought of her, wrote to and about her, and obsessed about her. There must be at least fifty agonized and devastated entries about her in his journals, all the way through high school. He never forgot her, and never got over losing her. She was his best friend and he loved her with all the passion and devotion of childhood.

He first heard about it the next morning when I took him to play baseball. And at first I discounted it, and thought it was just one of those exaggerated rumors that kids pass on and blow up out of proportion with each telling, like a chain letter of disaster. I couldn't believe it, things that terrible just didn't happen. But they did. And they had. We left the game, and Nick insisted on going to the hospital, despite my reservations. She was in a coma, as she had been since the night before, her long blond mane had been shorn, and I didn't want him to see her that way. I somehow sensed that he was too fragile for it, and I wanted to protect him. But for the next week he was beside himself, and I couldn't keep him away from her. And like him, the other kids gathered at the hospital, waiting for a miracle that never came. A week after she was hit, Sarah died, and it was probably the single most devastating event in Nicky's life. Time seemed to stand still for him, and the others. I don't think any of them recovered for a long time. Losing Sarah sent Nick into a spiral of depression, and in his journals, he talked constantly of wanting to die and be with Sarah.

And as little able as the kids were to tolerate the unfairness of it, so was I. It seemed so unfair, such a cruel, terrible blow to her parents. It was one of those mysteries you do not solve, and cannot find the answers to, you simply have to accept it finally and go on. But it was no easy task for Nicky.

There are still photographs of her in his room. And perhaps there is some small consolation now in thinking that he has found her. I think of them running free again, together, their incredibly good looks dazzling everyone in heaven. She was a golden child, and as Nick did for the rest of his life, I still miss her.

7

Eighth Grade:
The beginning of disaster

Summers were always difficult for Nick. We had a house in the Napa Valley where we spent the entire summer with the children. But Nick needed more than that. It was tedious for him. In fact, we used to laugh about it together sometimes, because I disliked it, too. As Nick said much later on, we had a lot in common, we both hated bugs, dirt, and nature. Like Nick, I found Napa incredibly boring. But even if I could not escape it, because John loved it so much, I tried to find other options for Nicky.

We tried three camps, in different years, and as one of the camp directors said, he made it more my experience than his. As usual, he kept me busy. And he turned his fictional abilities to the letters he wrote home, writing me horrifying stories of injuries, abuse, torment, and torture. I was on the phone to the camp every five minutes, to ascertain their veracity and determine his well-being. He terrified me. He also hated camp, and figured it was the best way of talking me out of sending him again, and eventually he convinced me.

But as much as he hated camp, he loved Hawaii. It was paradise for him. We stayed at a luxurious beach resort, which was not only fun for us, but a haven for children of all ages. Even our older kids loved it, and still do. We still go there, and we all love it, as did Nicky. But it presented challenges and dangers for him that it did not for the others. One of the early signs of Nick's illness, which worsened considerably over the years and was only barely kept in check by medication later on, was his lack of impulse control. It is typical, I now know, of his attention deficit disorder. If he got an idea into his head, he acted on it immediately, much to his friends' delight, and our horror. If the flag on the beach was red (indicating dangerous tides) and he wanted to swim, he did, with no concern whatsoever for potential danger. If he wanted to try to do a 'tightrope act' on the edge of the balcony, it seemed like a good idea to him, and he did it. And Hawaii offered him a myriad of opportunities to try daring feats and meet new people. In spite of our constant vigilance, he smoked marijuana there, got drunk with his friends, and cruised the beach endlessly looking for women.

Despite my complaints, and constant monitoring, at twelve and thirteen he wanted to hang out with seventeen- and eighteen-year-olds, and mentally he had more in common with them than he did with his peers. At eleven his friends there were sixteen. And in his teens he openly picked up girls in their twenties, or sometimes even his friends' mothers. And much to my chagrin, they always found him both seductive and amusing. He was so enchanting, so witty, so full of fun, so willing to live on the edge, and at the same time so warm and cuddly, what woman could resist him? Few, from my observations. If any.

I tried to keep my eye on him, particularly in Hawaii, but it was no easy task, and it took the entire family to check on him, round him up, and occasionally make excuses for him. It was typical of Nick when I went to a cocktail party there one night, and the mother of a nineteen-year-old girl told me that it was 'such a shame about Nicky.' She said it with such a tender air that I was immediately suspicious. He was twelve then, and I knew he had been cruising her nineteen-year-old daughter, who looked sensational in a bikini.

'Shame?' I asked innocently, waiting for what would come next. But knowing Nick, I knew it would be a good one. And as usual, he didn't disappoint me.

'About his illness.' I nodded dumbly, innocently munching the hors d'oeuvres, wondering if he had told them he had leukemia and had to get laid before he died the next morning . . . it was the only thing that would save him. He was extremely creative, particularly when on a hunt for sexual favors. 'His glandular problem . . .' the woman went on, as I continued to nod. I have to admit, sometimes he even amused me with his outrageous antics. He was so damned funny.

'Oh, his glandular problem,' I agreed, wondering what he had come up with this time. 'Yes, it is. We worry a lot about him.' Not entirely untrue, but his glands were the least of my worries.

'He explained to us how his illness stunted his growth when he was twelve. But he's such a wonderful boy, and so good-looking. He doesn't look twenty-one of course, but the minute you talk to him, you realize how old he is. What a remarkable son you have, you must be so proud of him.' Ahhh . . . yessss . . . indeed. Twenty-one. Nice going, Nick. I discussed it with him when I went back to the room, and told him this time he was really pushing it. Twenty-one? Give me a break, Nick.

'Awww come on, Mom,' he said, looking five and not twelve, and certainly not twenty-one, no matter how horny he was for the nineteen-year-old in the bikini. 'Be nice, don't tell them.' I made a deal with him not to blow his cover as long as he didn't do anything outrageous. I kept my end of the bargain, but I'm not quite as sure that he kept his. He had even told them where he went to college. I forgot where he said he was at school, but knowing Nick, he would have been capable of telling them he was at Harvard. Oh, Nicky.

Nick slid into the eighth grade quietly. He was sad that year. They all were. Over Sarah. In September, four months after her death, none of them seemed to have recovered. And the year did not go well for him. He seemed depressed to me. Nick talked about Sarah constantly. And even the others seemed sadder than usual. They didn't seem to know how to handle the pain they were feeling or the loss they felt so deeply. Nick was still seeing the same therapist but nothing dramatic had surfaced. The obvious signs of his manic depression were still waiting in the wings then. Although I have learned since that adolescent hormones can begin to bring out the early signs of mental illness.

But what worried me was that nothing was really

helping Nicky, and I didn't know how to help him. Things weren't going well in school for him, the calls complaining about his attitude and his behavior and his lack of seriousness about his work were ever more frequent. He was constantly on probation, and the headmaster had begun to threaten him with expulsion if he didn't shape up soon. I was worried sick about it, and felt helpless. I talked to Nicky endlessly, ad nauseam, for both of us, but I didn't have the tools or the skills I needed to help him.

The eighth-grade parties were wilder that year. More of the boys seemed to be out of control, and the girls who had gone to school with Sarah were still grieving for her too.

Nick was in love with one of Sarah's best friends at the time, and they talked constantly about her. Like Nick, Sarah was one of those kids who affected people deeply, and people were still talking about her. Her loss was a wound that had not healed yet, and it was easy to see that her old friends were having trouble coping with it.

According to Nick's journals, he was continuing to use marijuana and drink, at thirteen, and when I discovered it occasionally, I was none too happy about it. Extremely upset, in fact. He was smart enough not to let me ever catch him, but when I heard about things, I went straight to Nick and raised hell about it. He was even honest about it, which in some ways made it worse, in others better.

But the entries in his journals are disturbing all that winter. Had I seen them then, I'm sure I would have panicked, but I didn't realize the extent of his depression then, although I knew how sad he was about Sarah.

He began isolating himself, staying in his room all the time, avoiding the family, which is never a good sign. But it became harder and harder to pull him out of it, and he was in full thirteen-year-old rebellion. I had become his enemy by then, at least some of the time, although he was grateful every time I went to school to speak up for him. He was always sweet about thanking me for that, but he was constantly in trouble, his grades were slipping badly, and he was in the midst of applying to high school.

Nick kept journals diligently, but in my efforts to respect his privacy, I never read them. As I read them now, he talks about being lonely, sad, scared, and ashamed of it sometimes. In his own words, he says, *'I am always depressed . . . I am always lonely.' 'I don't feel like I belong anywhere. I am a loner now, in groups of people, I don't feel like I fit in. I feel very sad.'* He talks about being miserable, isolated, having low self-esteem. He reproaches himself, at thirteen, for being self-centered, and is very hard on himself. And then says, *'It is hard for me to love other people.'* And again and again and again, he says, *'I miss Sarah . . . She was my best friend . . . I love her so much I don't want to live without her.'*

In January 1992, at thirteen, he wrote:

'I don't see what the future holds for me but more pain. I miss Sarah so much. Life's purpose is gone for me. I'm thinking of suicide.' This is the first mention of suicide in his journals. My heart trembles now as I read it.

In February, he wrote again, '*I just want to end it.*' He talks about missing Sarah, and being '*sick with worry.*' He began writing letters to Sarah then, in his journals, telling her how lonely and unhappy he was. At the end of them, '*Save a seat for me. I'll see you soon enough.*' He says he has tried suicide already once by then, with sleeping pills, which may have just been talk. In fact, probably was, because if he had attempted suicide, I would have known it.

But two weeks later, he writes that he tried to kill himself with a garbage bag tied over his head, and then changed his mind and took it off. And the entries to and about missing Sarah continue.

At the end of February 1992 (still thirteen), he writes: '*I wish I'd die, and it would all be over. I love life and everyone but me.*'

In March, he writes that he is contemplating suicide again, and again in April, he says, '*I'm gonna commit suicide soon,*' and then gets seriously introspective. '*I am so depressed. Maybe I'm manic depressive. I'm bummed about life. Everyone hates me, and I hate everyone.*'

It was obviously a nightmarish time for him, and although I was aware that he was deeply unhappy and slipping away from us, I didn't know the depths of his despair, and I didn't know how to stop it. When I talked to the therapist about how desperately unhappy I thought Nick was, he seemed not to be as concerned as I was, or perhaps he just didn't show it. It seemed as if he wanted to talk about my work, my fame, and my other children. I felt Nick was in crisis, and no one else seemed to see it.

Parenthetically, we had moved into a big new house that fall, and Nick's room was just above my office and bedroom. I would hear him wandering around at night at all hours, and go up to him. He never seemed to sleep, and he looked so desperately unhappy. And I felt helpless. I suggested medication to the doctor for Nick, and he didn't agree with me. Nick was still young to take the kind of drugs I was suggesting. I thought about changing therapists, but worried that changing shrinks again might not be the best thing for him. And the therapist he was seeing was extremely respected.

And things weren't going well in my life either. My success had finally reached such vast proportions, with the success of some TV movies I had done added to that of my books, that I had finally come to the attention of the tabloids. And they were having a field day with me, they had unearthed everything I'd ever done, and a number of things I hadn't.

They had a hard time making anything sensational out of my first marriage. It was quiet and wholesome. We were married for nearly nine years, he was a French banker, and from an extremely illustrious and respectable French banking family. Our life had been circumspect and our divorce clean. But the two youthful 'mistakes' I'd made afterwards were being blazoned around the world in banner headlines. The first 'mistake' was my brief second marriage to a man I lived with only for months in my twenties. He was convicted of rape, and sent to prison. It had been a heartbreak for me. I was young and innocent, and although I had told John of it, it was not something I was happy about or proud of. The experience had been extremely traumatic for me. And having it published for all to read in the tabloids brought back memories of an agonizing time for me, and reports of it had been embellished and distorted, which made it even more humiliating. The second story they reported was my pregnancy and subsequent brief marriage to Nick's father, again sensationally reported. And Nick was as upset as I was when he read about it.

The stories made me look terrible, I thought, humiliated me and my family, and embarrassed my husband although he knew about both marriages and I had no secrets from him. But it was a time I found agonizing, as did my children. Despite the quiet family life I led, and had for years, the price of celebrity had finally come home to haunt us. And although some of the stories were inaccurate, I chose discretion as the wisest course, and said nothing, but was heartbroken over the scandal I had become, in the eyes of my friends, my husband, and children. To say that I was devastated by the stories in the tabloids would be modest. I was nearly destroyed by the way I was portrayed, and the public humiliation of tabloid stories and tabloid TV shows.

In the midst of it all, Bill (Nick's father) had been interviewed in the tabloids, and appeared on TV, talking about me (as had my second husband, still in prison). And Nick had powerful feelings of loyalty for those he loved, and was desperate to do something to defend me. He asked me how to get hold of Bill so he could 'tell him off' for talking about me, and I said I honestly didn't know, but he knew the name of Bill's parents and called them to leave a message for him, I believe, telling them what he thought of him. Nick's lack of impulse control was in full evidence, but so was his good heart and his compassion. I know he must have hated seeing me as devastated as I was then.

And as soon as Bill got the message from Nick, he must have called him, although I didn't know it. I see in Nick's journals that he met with him once briefly, although I don't know how he pulled it off without my knowing.

It was a tough time for all of us, particularly Nick, and he was worried about the tabloid articles, because they referred to him and the trial that had terminated Bill's parental rights, and John's adoption of him. Nick was still adamant then, at only thirteen, about not wanting the younger children to know that John wasn't his natural father. In fact, we adjusted our wedding date when we spoke of it, to accommodate Nick's wishes, and make him 'legal.' When John had adopted him, the state had issued him a new birth certificate, not at our request, but as they apparently always do, which listed John's name as his father, and made it look as though we had been together at the time of his birth. But it created a funny awkwardness for him too, as our actual marriage date was three years after his birth, which once again made him seem 'illegitimate.' The other thing the court also did automatically, not at our request, was seal the entire record of his adoption, for his protection. It was a procedure they told us they followed without exception in the state of California.

But there was nothing I could do to silence the tabloids, and despite the many distortions and cruelties they ran, again and again, for months and months, I refused to sue them. I thought suing them would only make matters worse for all of us, and preferred to suffer in dignity and silence. It seemed the wisest course to me, but meant that no one ever heard the truth, or my side of the stories.

National magazines and other newspapers added fuel to the fire then, picking up the stories that had been run elsewhere and reprinting them, and the tabloids continued to torment us. It was a hard time for me, and Nick was very angry over it. His sense of helplessness, like ours, just added to his depression.

Everything came to a head in May when Nick went to a dance a few weeks before his grammar school graduation, and observed a drug incident of one boy passing drugs to another. The school was very clear that Nick had not been a participant, but only an observer, and the dance was not in any way sponsored by the school, but they had strong codes about behavior on and off campus, 'conduct unbecoming a gentleman,' etc. And for seeing what had passed, allowing it to happen and not reporting it, and also possibly because he had been such a thorn in their side for two years, they expelled him, weeks before graduation. I was heartbroken over it. He had been in the school for nine years, and expelled such a very short time before graduation. But it was certainly their right to do so.

Nick was in shock, and we were devastated. This couldn't happen. We begged, we pleaded, we promised, we crawled, and of course, we groveled. To no avail. They would not allow Nick to finish the year, or graduate. They had to respect their rules, and maintain their standards, and Nick understood that. And the only deal we were able to make with them was that we could have him tutored, and they would in fact give him his diploma, but as a sign of their strong feelings on the subject, he would not be allowed to attend graduation. And funnily enough, I think I felt the blow of it more than Nicky. He was more philosophical about it than I was, and just for the record, I asked for an official letter from them, stating that he had been an observer of, and not participant in, the incident. Several other boys were expelled along with him. It was an enormous statement of warning and principle to any evildoers in the future.

So Nick was at home, and I was scrambling around frantically to find him tutors, so he could finish the school year. He did fine work, and all of his tutors were impressed with him. He received his diploma, as promised, and could not attend graduation, which broke my heart, if not his, after nine years in the school. But there were even greater consequences to contend with. One by one, the schools that had accepted him for high school withdrew their offers. Nick had no high school to go to. More groveling, more begging, more pleading. I called everyone I knew, on the board of every school I could think of, and finally found one boarding school that was willing to take him. It was a miracle, and I was grateful to everyone who had helped me.

Nick seemed mollified by the lesson he'd learned, but still depressed, understandably. But he liked the idea of the boarding school he was going to more than I did. I am not fond of the concept of boarding schools, and think that those midteen years are the most important to be at home in the bosom of one's family. I want to see what my children are doing between fourteen and eighteen, and have some influence on their decisions. Once they reach college age, I figure they're ready to step into the world without me. But before that, no matter how big a pain in the neck they think I am, I want to be there.

But in Nick's case, we had no choice. There wasn't a single school in the city that was willing to take him. Expulsion from eighth grade was hardly an advantage. And his only option was the boarding school I'd found him. I was very grateful that they would take him.

I sent him to visit friends in Germany for two weeks to get him away from his routine and where he seemed to be in better spirits.

And in August, everything got underway to prepare him for his big adventure. Like most fancy boarding schools, they allowed him to bring everything but his own bungalow with him.

We bought linens, towels, a boom box, a stereo, a computer, a bicycle, a refrigerator, framed posters, a bulletin board, packed all his favorite trinkets to remind him of home, and of course, he took half a dozen framed photographs of Sarah. I was beginning to think it would do him good to get away. He needed a new life, a fresh start, and a new location. His bedrooms both at home in the city, and at our country house, had become shrines to Sarah. And he was still facing the aura of disgrace that had fallen on him with his expulsion from school. I was happy he was getting a fresh start, and he was genuinely excited.

We flew down to the school on schedule, and rented a van to carry all his new belongings and treasured old possessions, spent a day settling him in, plugging things in, making the bed, setting up his computer, and left him there, with a great deal of hope, and only a small tremor of trepidation. He was going to be fine, I told myself. He was like any other kid going away to school, I said reassuringly to my own inner voices. Stop worrying. But how could I not? I had worried about him all his life, been there for him, laughed with him, cried for him, made excuses for him, apologized for him. As I drove away, all I could think of was how much I was going to miss him. It was like setting a small bird free in the sky whom you have loved and nurtured and cared for. All I could hope for was that he would fly safely and well, and that the hawks that always hovered over him wouldn't get him.

8

He crashes

Nick's stay at boarding school was alarmingly brief, and what came swiftly on its heels was deeply disturbing. I had no warning of trouble there, and ten days after he had arrived, with his gypsy caravan filled with his belongings, they called me. They were blunt, and they were right. They said that something was seriously wrong with him, and that leaving him there was an invitation to disaster. They didn't want him to have another expulsion on his record, but they were absolutely sure that if he stayed, he would get into trouble. 'He's not capable of being here,' they said. 'He needs treatment.' I knew it, but they were the first ones to say it. They didn't know exactly what was wrong, but they knew something was. He couldn't follow the rules, not so much 'didn't,' as 'couldn't,' which was something I knew about him too. There was no malice about the things he did or didn't do, he just couldn't follow the music and keep in step, and sometimes to cover that fact, he pretended he didn't want to. But they saw through it.

They felt that something was off about him,

they had noticed his lack of impulse control, and the crazy things he did, and I knew as well as they did that we had to do something about it. The problem was that I didn't know what, or who would help me do it. Despite their best efforts, I felt that the two psychiatrists he had seen hadn't really helped him, whatever their good intentions. He seemed to slip right through the cracks, particularly with the last one. I was at a loss as to where to go next, or what to do. But it was obvious that Nick was no longer able to function in an ordinary environment. He couldn't play by the rules anymore. He was slowly losing the ability to control himself, slowly but surely and steadily, and I knew I had to stop the momentum before it destroyed him.

I called everyone I could think of once again, got the name of a counselor who dealt with difficult kids and recommended schools for them, and unorthodox solutions. Perfect. Just what we needed. I called him, and made an appointment for the next morning. I had someone else pick Nick up at the airport, with his mountains of stuff, while I made the calls, and he was sitting in the living room, when I walked into the room, as calmly as I could manage, to see him.

I was determined not to lose my temper. It served no purpose, and I knew he must be feeling rejected by being sent away from the boarding school. All I wanted to do was help him.

But I got a shock when I walked into the room. He was sitting in front of a bank of ferns I had there, and I could see instantly that he had shaved his head. All I could see was his face, and the kind of broad, sheepish smile he wore when he knew he had done something he shouldn't.

'I fucked up again, Mom,' he said somewhat forlornly, as I walked towards him to kiss him.

'No, you didn't. You didn't get kicked out. They said it was the wrong place for you. You wouldn't have been happy there, Nick,' I said, and then got another shock as he stood up to hug me. He hadn't shaved his head, he had been in true camouflage with the ferns. When he stood up, I saw that he had dyed his hair exactly the same shade of green the ferns were. He grinned broadly at me when I saw it.

'You like it?' he asked hopefully.

'Yeah, sure. I love it.' And that was the beginning of Nick and exotic hair colors. We moved from green to blue and back again, from sapphire to turquoise to blonde, a sort of flame concoction at one point that was half red, half blonde, and finally to jet black, which actually suited him, and I came to like it. I would have to say that second only to his passion for music was his obsession with his hair color. I never saw it a natural color again, but to tell you the truth, after a while I got used to it, and wouldn't have recognized his original color if I saw it. But the green was certainly different. (I am innately conservative to my core, and not the sort of person to find green hair 'amusing.' But I had long since accepted about Nick that the standards I apply to myself and the rest of the world, just didn't apply to him.)

He was sad about having left the boarding school. He had met people there he liked, made some friends, and said he was going to miss it. I promised him a better solution, and promised myself I was going to find a school in the city. He had proven that he couldn't handle boarding school, and they couldn't handle him. And somehow, we had to help him deal with his problems, his depressions, his lack of impulse control. I didn't realize then that he had been thinking about suicide for the past nine months, or I would have truly panicked. As it was, I was pretty damn worried.

He was welcomed back into the bosom of the family, and everyone was happy to see him. He cheered up that night, and the next morning bright and early (much to Nick's chagrin), we met with the counselor who had promised to find a school for him. Nick was never happy about morning meetings. All his life, he had been up late at night, and he had trouble sleeping. And he was never at his best in the morning.

The counselor made two suggestions, both of them unacceptable, and Nick and I both looked devastated by what he was saying. He had read what material I had from Nick's grammar school, and knew of him by reputation. (He had called some friends who taught there, apparently.) He had also spoken to the boarding school Nick had just left, and he said without preamble or artifice that no school would take Nick. According to him, we had two choices. One was a school in Utah or Nevada or Colorado or somewhere that was, in effect, or sounded like, a prison for children. It was locked down, cut off, I couldn't visit him for a year. There was no escape and no vacations, no phone calls, no contact with the outside world. Nick looked as though he was going to burst into tears as the counselor told me they would shape him up in no time and that it was what he needed. There was another one similar to it, in Southern California, which was equally out of the question, but he didn't recommend it. His second suggestion was well-known in Europe, where Nick would stay for two to four years, and again be incarcerated, though in a far prettier location. It was full of kids from rich families who didn't know what to do with their problem children. So they shipped them off and let someone else handle their problems. Neither of which was my style. I was not looking to shut Nicky away, to get rid of him. I wanted to help him, at home, hands on, and do whatever it took to do it.

I reassured Nick that this wasn't going to happen to him, he wasn't going anywhere, and I would keep him at home and have him tutored if I had to. And I said as much to the counselor, who continued to try and talk me into his two options. I told him he was wasting his time, and asked him to put his thinking cap on again. We needed a day school for Nick, close to home, and he assured me it would not be an easy project. It would take time, he said, as I nodded.

And within a couple of days, he came up with an interesting suggestion. He said he needed time to find a school that would be willing to take Nick, but he had another option to keep Nick busy in the meantime. It was a wilderness program, modeled on Outward Bound, but specially designed for children that were disturbed or troubled in one way or another. And I have to admit, it sounded intriguing.

I was a little suspicious of it, and wanted to be sure it was safe, but he assured me he had known other kids who had gone through it, and he thought it was a perfect place to put Nick for three weeks, to keep him busy, and build up his self-esteem again, while we found a school for him at home, and got everything ready for him to step right into it the minute he completed the outdoor program.

It made sense certainly, and had some real advantages, the only thing I didn't like was that he told me privately that the element of 'surprise' was an essential part of it. According to him, Nick shouldn't be warned, or allowed to prepare, particularly since a lot of kids ran away when faced with something that different and scary. I didn't think it was a real fear, as Nick had never run anywhere, except the day three years before, sitting on a park bench and eating a Hostess Twinkie. I didn't like the idea of surprising Nick, or frightening him. It felt like a betrayal. But eventually, the counselor convinced me, and I should have known better. I knew my own child, and I rarely, if ever, let other people interfere with the integrity we shared, but Nick was undeniably in a poor frame of mind, he was feeling down, and I let the counselor convince me that he might run away if we told him.

The man from the outdoor program appeared, looking to me like an executioner, early one morning a few days later. He looked about six feet ten to me as I let him in my front door at six in the morning, in my barefeet and nightgown. And he must have looked twice as big to Nicky. Nicky was fourteen then, and if things had turned out right for him at boarding school, he would have been a high school freshman. Instead he was a sleeping boy with tousled hair at six A.M. (I had made him dye the green back to something resembling his natural light brown color, and believe me, it wasn't easy. The hairdresser who did it still talks about it.) But when I saw Nick's face, my heart sank. He looked terrified. Who was this stranger in his bedroom? I suddenly wanted to step in and rescue him, but I knew I shouldn't. Or at least I had been told not to.

John and I had talked about it at length, and I had aired all my misgivings to him, but we had decided it might be the best thing for him. And it was only three weeks, not a lifetime. I was aware of the fact that I had protected Nick too much, and this seemed a good time to let go a little. But I felt like a monster as the man explained to Nick that they were flying to the wilderness program. Nick looked as though he wanted to kill me, and I don't blame him. If someone showed up in my bedroom at six in the morning, threatening to drag me away to the bushes somewhere, I'd want to take out a gun and shoot him. Nick looked as though that concept would have appealed to him immensely. And the wilderness program the man rhapsodized about clearly didn't. But rhapsody or not, the guy looked as though, if Nicky didn't like the idea, he was going to drag him out of bed, throw him over his shoulder, and take him. Nick didn't argue with him.

They left the house half an hour later. I tried to kiss Nick goodbye and he wouldn't kiss me, which was the first time he'd ever done that, and I walked back into the house, sobbing. I felt as though I had totally betrayed him, and perhaps even put him in danger. I had never in my life felt as rotten, or as lonely, or as worried about him. I had confidently put him in the hands of strangers. What if they weren't trustworthy? What if something happened to him? The idea didn't bear thinking about, but it was all I could think of.

His escort allowed him to call me from the airport, and Nick told me how much he hated me and what a monster I was for what I had done to him. I didn't entirely disagree with him, but told him I was trying to do something for his own good. But he was still furious, and hung up on me.

And for the next three weeks, the days were endless. He had a counselor there who sounded like a mountain man, but was kind and wise and gentle. He seemed to have a genuine affection for Nick when he called me. But it was the first time in Nick's entire life that we were out of communication, and it was agony for me. I dreamed of him at night, terrified that something terrible would happen to him. But every few days, his counselor would call, and assure me that he was fine and doing well, and that he would be a new person when he emerged from the wilderness and came home to us. I liked the old person just fine, but I also knew that he had to turn things around, start feeling better about himself, and get control of his life, whatever it took to do that.

But I was extremely discouraged when, close to the end of it, the wilderness counselor told me that I had to start thinking of a school for Nick, and although he had done well, the counselor felt that he couldn't manage to live at home yet. He needed to be put in a 'special school' for a year or two, until he had adequately dealt with his 'problems,' whatever they were. We knew one thing for sure, he had terrible impulse-control, and as time went on, he had ever greater problems of concentration. I still felt certain that we could fix him at home, and everything inside me shrieked that sending him away was wrong. He was still my baby. And all of the schools the counselor recommended were far, far from home. It would be hard for us to visit him, I had five tiny children to take care of at home, and the schools he was suggesting were not anxious for him to have visits anyway. He even suggested one of the places the first counselor had recommended, the one that sounded like a prison for children. Nick was not a bad kid, I reminded him, he was a sick kid. But the counselor insisted it made no difference, he could no longer handle living at home with his family, he needed more 'structure' to control him. He made it sound like a barbed-wire fence they were going to wrap around Nicky.

So as Nick struggled with the elements and the dirt and bugs and nature he had always so desperately hated, I set out to find a school again. So far, despite considerable effort, the counselor in town had turned up nothing. And a doctor I knew finally came up with what sounded like a viable suggestion. It was a tiny boarding school for disturbed kids, in a town I'd never heard of. We could visit him on weekends, and he could even come home from time to time, if he behaved himself. And the doctor sang its praises, one of his closest friends knew the school and loved it. I spoke to his friend who knew the school, and didn't like what I heard.

It sounded like another jail for children, a place where people sent their kids because they couldn't handle them and didn't want to be bothered, or just couldn't, for one reason or another. The doctor's friend apparently had a son who was violent, and had physically attacked him on numerous occasions. This was a far, far cry from Nicky. Nick was a troubled soul, who turned his anger on himself or his belongings, never physically on another person. But it was also obvious that whatever efforts I'd made so far had not been fruitful. So I decided to try it. They had counselors who lived at the school, and a psychiatrist to work with the kids daily. Despite my reservations, it sounded perfect.

Meanwhile, Nick was finishing up his wilderness program, and they let me talk to him on the phone a couple of days before he came home. He had even done a 'solo,' which was one or two days alone in the wilderness, during which he was observed for his safety's sake, although he didn't know it. He had learned first aid and CPR, and rescued another boy who had gotten lost. He sounded absolutely terrific, and all the grief it had caused me, and him, seemed worth it. He was full of hope and promise and was certain he had his life back on track. All he wanted was to come home and prove it. And then I had to break the news to him that he was going to a boarding school for special children. I felt like an axe murderer telling him, and it nearly killed him. He cried, he begged, he pleaded, he swore he'd do well at any school I sent him to, but not to send him away again. I cried as much as he, but begged him to try it. After checking out the school by phone, I had a bad case of the flu and wanted to go up and see the school myself but John offered to go instead. Most of the time, I was the 'front man' for all the creative solutions I came up with for Nicky, but this time John offered to look at the school and make sure it was okay. He flew up, and returned to report that it looked fine to him. John hoped, as I did, that Nick would like it. Nick was due home in two days, and we were going to meet him at the airport, spend a couple of hours with him there, and then send him on to the school we had chosen. We had decided, at the recommendation of the wilderness counselor, that if we let him come home even for a few hours, or a day or two, it would be too hard for him to leave again, so he would leave for the school straight from the airport, after we had lunch with him.

The last few days of waiting to see Nick again seemed endless. I couldn't wait to get my hands on him, to hug him, kiss him, feel him, smell him. He was the cub I had lost somewhere in the jungle, and I was desperate to find him. Either because of the way our life together had begun, or because he had flaws I sensed more than saw, or perhaps simply because we had a special bond and were very similar in some ways, I always had a visceral connection to Nicky. It was as though he was a part of me, and every time he was removed from me, it was painful. I never lost that bond to him, it never dimmed over the years, but only strengthened. I have a similar bond to my other children, and am happiest when I am near them, but as they are healthier, I am better able to let go, for a short time at least, when I have to. With Nick, it was always harder for me.

I wrote him this letter in his last days at the wilderness program, and found it recently among his papers.

Tues 13 Oct 92

Sweet darling Nicky,

The words tumble all over my head, my heart, my tongue . . . I am dying to see you!!! A thousand million bzillion times I've thought all kinds of thoughts and messages, and silly things to you, since you've been gone. I've thought of keeping a journal . . . of keeping count of how many times people say they miss you (the numbers got too high for me to count them). I kept wanting to reach out my heart to yours, and finally just decided to think of you in silence. This imposed silence between us has been near impossible, like a caged lioness I have paced this house at incredible hours, endlessly, aching, prowling, missing you, with you lodged in my heart and mind, like a door that wouldn't close, no way to shut you from my mind for a single moment. No man will ever know the strange but powerful bond one has with one's children. It was an ache for you, a longing, a need to see your face, to touch and hold you and know that you were all right. (I literally feel sick if I am away from Zara or Maxx sometimes. There is a need to check them out, see that they are safe, know that they are nearby.) And you are still tied to my heart just as they are, an unseverable bond which, thank God, you will never feel as I do — because you must grow and have your own life, but it must take a long, long time for those bonds to grow thinner and more reasonable with one's children. I love you. I love you so much. And oh how I have missed you!!!!! I have been in your room a thousand times a day, the straightening of the rug, or a lamp, or a cushion has become all important, the exact positioning of your magazines became crucial, as though you would read them at any moment.

I will never exactly know what you went through, the ache in your soul, the fear, the excruciating process of growing, of changing, of learning things that are painful for us all. We all have our demons to wrestle with, and other people never quite know how hard it is. I think I know. I want to, I will try with all my heart, but if I miss it sometimes, if I fail to understand, if I don't quite get it, please, please, tell me, show me as best you can, and forgive me if I turn out to be stupid. I'll really try not to. And if there are things I need to know, in order to make our relationship work better, tell me that too. I'll try, Nicky, I really will. I promise. It is a growing process for us all.

You have done the hardest, bravest thing in the last 3½ weeks – 24 days. Want to know how many hours or seconds? I'm sure I could count them. But seriously, Sweetheart, you have. As little as I know of it – one thinks one knows, but one doesn't if one isn't there. How can I possibly be fair and imagine, while I lie in a comfortable bed, what it must be like to be on survival conditions in the wilderness, not only fighting for a crumb of food, or some warmth – but trying to readjust your whole notion of emotional survival. I am in awe of what you must have faced, emotionally even more than physically, Nicky. And I am so proud of what you did there.

You'll never know the strength and pain it took to send you there, and all I can tell you is that the only thing that would lead me to send you there was my own desperation. I knew all the signs that you were on a disastrous course, and had no idea how to stop you. It's like watching someone drown, you would throw a piano bench at them if you had to, to save them . . . my only fear was that the cure would be worse than the disease, and if the choice was right, then we have all been blessed with good fortune. I can't claim any great wisdom here. I was clutching at what seemed right-est at the time, but it terrified me.

As I said to Dad, if it turns out all right, sending you there will be the bravest thing I've ever done, and you!! If anything goes wrong, I'll never forgive myself. I did a lot of agonizing, and I think the worst of it was the silence. We had no word at all for the first ten days, and my highly paid imagination went wild with ghastly scenarios that would have made Stephen King pale. When left to my own devices, I can come up with some real lulus!!! Thank God that you're okay, and that you feel it was worth it.

I know that the reentry must be hard for

you. You must have done so much thinking, so much taking stock of yourself, and your life, and those around you . . . my shrink reminded me once a long time ago, that although I had worked hard and gone a long way, the others in my life hadn't gone anywhere. She (the shrink was a woman), reminded me not to expect too much of those around me. They hadn't changed. I had. That's kind of a shock sometimes. Also you are so newborn into your life, you have come so far, the rest of us must seem simpleminded, and dwarfed by your accomplishments. Some will be impressed, some won't know, some won't care, some won't be impressed, and some will expect you to do more. That's got to be frustrating. Try to be patient. Pat yourself on the back constantly for what you did, and keep on trucking up the mountain. You will find, Sweetheart, as one does in life, that one is never completely 'there,' just when you figure the work's all done and you can sit on your ass for a while, life provides a new challenge. Most of them are a pain in the ass, some are worth-while, but that's the way it is. You've got to meet the challenges and solve the problems. You have found some wonderful tools within yourself to do that. Keep using them, keep doing it, keep going!!! You're really on the right track now, and we recognize and acknowledge that 100%.

I know that going to a somewhat restrictive interim school is disappointing, but it's also part of real life. We don't make the rules, you, or Dad, or I. We know where you are and what you've done. But you have to take your steps in the world now. And you will. This place sounded pretty reasonable. If you behave well, and keep your work up, you get the privileges and freedoms. If not, we're not talking San Quentin here. I absolutely could not have lived with one of the schools, which fortunately you do not need. Please keep it that way. I absolutely couldn't stand you ever being in a school like that, i.e. the punitive ones. (Not like this one. This one is not like that – it's nice.) And I truly believe that this is a small step to growth and freedom. But it's a safety net too. It would be a shame to blow all the beautiful work you've done on a bad day, or in a weak moment.

I don't think this is so bad, and you'll tell me if I'm wrong. But I get the feeling it will be pretty mellow. I wouldn't have done it if I thought it was bad. Think of it as an interesting piece of your life, a part of this new growth, it's a bridge from one good spot to the next one, and part of the trip. It will help you get where you want to go. And the better you work with it, the faster you'll get there. I think one day you will look back at all this and realize how lucky you were to learn so much so early. Many, many people screw up their entire lives, or a huge part of it. Many don't figure out what you have until they're a lot older. This vision, this change, this learning process, is a real gift, from the people who helped you make the realizations you made, but also from yourself – you're doing this for you, Nick. And I can't tell you often enough how proud I am of you, and so is Dad.

I don't see this new school as some kind of punitive action, and want you to know that. I don't think it is. I think it is a stepping stone to what you want in life: freedom, home, good values, a good life, and also a good school. I have to tell you, I would like you to get your shit together, please. I've about had it with boarding schools. I have never liked them. And I never will. I would like you at home, making chili in my kitchen, and being reminded regularly to clean up your room. The thrill of your presence is one I would love to have here no end, and so would everyone else. All we want, all of us, me, Dad, the little kids, is to have you reach a point where your life is together enough to come home. I know you think you're there but the schools naturally don't yet. That's only fair. They can't see inside your head. They don't know how clean it is there. If they could plug you into a special light and have your nose turn green, it would be a lot simpler. But this way, they need some time, some proof, some grades, some reasonable behavior. It really does make sense, and you're mature enough to know that.

Also, to have you at home, even faintly wobbly, would be scary for you and for us, so maybe this worked out right again for a while. It's going to take time for your friends, and the world at large, to understand that this is a new

Nick we're dealing with. Some of them are going to relate to the old Nick and it puts a huge burden on you to have to prove that constantly. It may be very comfortable for you for a while at the school. Things work out right usually, and are for the best. If getting kicked out of the last school catapulted you into a place physically and emotionally where, as you put it, 'your life could be saved,' then maybe that brief encounter with the last school was the best thing that ever happened. (And if **you want** boarding school later on, you can, I'd just love to have you home, but it's up to you.)

I'm going to bore you with one more small piece of philosophy. A saying from my church: 'Divine Love always has met, and always will meet every human need.' The key words for me in that have always been 'always,' 'every,' and 'human.' It doesn't say it'll meet some of your needs sometimes. It says **all** your needs, **every** need, always ... and it says '**human**' not lofty, not spiritual, not religious. Divine Love always has met, and always will meet, every human need. I've found it very comforting at times, maybe you will too.

The only important thing in all this is how much we love you. The rest is poopcakes. Sometimes life is poopcakes. But seriously, that's the great part, we love you ... oh how we love you!!!

And hopefully, though at fourteen maybe it's too much to ask, but you've aged in these last three weeks, and then some – but part of

*growing up or being grown-up, is realizing
that all things are passing, nothing difficult or
unpleasant lasts forever. I hope you like the
new school, find it unorthodox but fun, think
it's a gas to be studying with only forty kids,
sitting under a tree, or whatever. They go on
some great ski trips, and a fabulous foreign
spring vacation every year. I'm hoping you
love this, maybe not like the wilderness
program, but as a valuable time in your life.
(It's not the giant challenge the wilderness
program was. It's just rolling along like real
life.) I hope you like it, and I hope that it's fun,
but if it turns out to be dull, or boring, or
tedious, or even irritating at times, try to keep
it in perspective. This is not for the rest of
your life, or even the rest of high school. It's
as long as it needs to be and no longer. Grow
from it, learn from it, use it for you. But don't
get yourself worked up. Think of it as a cruise;
you'll reach your destination soon, so relax.
No school, no place, no person, nothing is
perfect. As Alex Haley used to say, 'Find the
good and praise it!' (The food has to be better
than it was where you are.) And believe me,
the hardships in my life have made me appreciate every comfort, every job, every moment
of health, every beautiful, bright-eyed child or
happy moment. You'll appreciate them all
more now because of what you learned where
you are.*

*And know with every ounce of you how
much I do recognize what you did there.
Nobody is saying that you didn't accomplish*

great things . . . but life is a mountain range, it is not just one mountain . . . like the colored belts in karate . . . you've reached one of those terrific high-middle colors, but the black is yet to be won . . . you're on your way there.

I love you, Sweetheart. I'll go to bed, and when I wake up, it'll be only a few more hours till I see you. A million times a day I have tried to imagine what you were doing, sleeping, eating, walking, thinking . . . that night you were awake most or all of the night. I felt you in my heart all night. I hope you're sleeping now. It must be exciting and scary to be leaving there and coming back.

I am tired of living by other people's rules for you, and for us. Learn some good rules of your own, so we can all be free again, my love. Life is a growing process, and you have grown so much . . . sweet little tree that I love, may God always love and protect you, as I know He will, and may you always know how much I love you.

With all my heart and soul, sweet Nick . . . with all my love,

Your Mommy

P.S. I loved your phone call and all the wonderful things you said about missing and loving us!!! I love you!!! M.

And as I sat, missing him, waiting for him, he wrote in his journal. He wrote these entries while he was at the wilderness program, in a little note-book he carried everywhere with him, and which I found when I went through his journals after we'd lost him (he was fourteen years old when he wrote this.):

I have two identities. Essentially, one is good, one is bad. Right now, all I want is to decide which one I want to be, and be it. There's even a third identity there: the impatient one who wants me to decide.

First identity: I want to go home to my family, be good, be loving, and be loved. I know I am capable of doing it, if I decide I really want to. I believe that I can.

Second identity: I want to get sent to some school, and have my money and stuff and leave. Party for the rest of my life, never look back, and die before I turn twenty-five. But at least I'll have had fun.

My Mission:
I want to be able to change other people's lives and be honest, trustworthy, and caring. All I want to accomplish, I want to do it on my own.

When it comes down to it, the main thing that could screw up my mission is me! No matter what the distraction, I'm the one who let myself be distracted.

Who I'm going to be:
I want to be strong. I'm practicing that now. I don't want to live in my father's shadow. I want to be me. I want to be honest, to not only know right from wrong, but to do right. I want to show my true feelings of love and caring to my family, and I want to be a part of them. I don't want to be living

a facade. I want people to see the new, real me, I don't want to hide him anymore. I want people to know they can believe in me and trust me, so I have to be less mercurial. I want to be good. I want to be Nick.

I really don't like hurting people. If I inadvertently do, it's always followed by huge tidal waves of guilt. And even if by chance it's on purpose, it always makes me feel awful, so I do it as little as I can.

What I want is to be looked upon as a trustworthy and responsible person. I want to be happy with myself and to have others be happy with me. I want to know I completed something challenging and have that to back up my word that I have changed. I no longer want to be the person I was. I was unhappy and couldn't believe my own word anymore. I just want happiness, and respect from myself and others, after I finish what I start.

I have irrepressible feelings about my mother. I love her so much it hurts. I tell her but I don't know if she knows it for real. If I hurt her, the guilt I feel hurts me five times worse afterwards. I hate it. I don't know how to show or tell her how I feel. When I tell her, it feels really good that I'd told her, but then if I do something that inadvertently or even purposely hurts her, I feel like I've disproved myself. My love for her is unconditional, as hers is for me, but I really don't know if she knows. I hope she does. Hopefully, this program will give me the courage to tell her, and to be able to hold my word.

I see a tired confused boy
He's angry, but not too angry.
He's sad . . . sort of.
He's hurting . . . I think.
He loves me . . . I hope.
He needs me . . . but can't or won't admit it.
He doesn't understand me . . . maybe I don't understand him.
He tries to show me how he feels, I see him struggling . . . but it just comes out wrong.
I see a boy who has seen too much.
But like I said, he's still a boy.

If I were to die today, I wouldn't exactly be sad. I would be more disappointed. I am doing this program to try and turn my life around, and I have my friends and family supporting me. This is the final and hardest step in the ladder to a normal and decent life. If I died right in the middle of it, it would be a disappointment. Of course I would be sad that I never said good-bye to my family, and tell them that I love them, or had a chance to tell my friends how I truly felt about them, but disappointment, I think this is the prevailing emotion.

When I do die, I want to be remembered as a strong person who was able to turn their life around without threats or scoldings, who did it on his own accord. I want to be remembered for the person I want to be, not for the person I was.

I'm a very versatile person, but my basic personality is of someone who cares.

When I think of a true friend, I think of someone who really loves and cares about me. They'd make sacrifices for me, just like I would for them. Someone trustworthy, someone who I share beliefs and opinions with, and someone who won't leave my side if I'm down (loyalty). A true friend is someone who won't give up on you, no matter what. Someone who wouldn't put me at risk and would keep me out of trouble, just as I would for them.

NOTHING would make me compromise these qualities in a friend. And I also believe that you never lose a true friend unless you've done something to violate what they expect of you as a friend.

I'm a 'my rules for me, my rules for you' kind of person. I only expect so much from a friend, because I would do all of the above, and more for them too.

Two things come to mind as I read these journal entries of Nick's today. One is that he was sick, he had a rampaging disease that was beginning to control him. He was a good kid with a bad disease. And so often kids like that, and people like that, are treated like bad kids, and punished for what they can't help. I fought desperately for Nicky. I never wanted him to be punished for being sick. It wasn't his fault. It was my responsibility and one I refused to turn my back on for his entire life. I hated the places that shut these people away, removed them from sight, punished them for their peculiarities, and proved to them that no one loved them after all. I always believed that loving Nicky enough would make a difference, or help, or maybe even cure him. It didn't cure him perhaps, but never for a single instant of his life did he ever doubt that he was loved. That was my gift to him, the only gift I really had to give him.

The other thing that struck me when I read his journals is that he had so many friends, really good friends, friends who stuck by him and to whom he was loyal all his life. The friends I saw in the end, and whom I still see at my dinner table now are the ones he grew up with, went to nursery school with, and some he collected along the way in the course of his life. Many of them never left his life. And he added to them over the years, with special people who crossed his path. He was a good friend, and his friends loved him. Although he isolated himself at times, he never lost sight of them, and they hung on to him, and kept him going when he was sad. They never let him down.

In any case, Nick got off the plane from his wilderness program, looking healthy and happy and tall. He told us all about it over pizza at the airport restaurant, and we chatted for a couple of hours before he left for school. He had some real trepidations about it, but he was willing to give it a chance. I promised him that if it wasn't good, or right for him, I'd take him out later. John reminded me that even if he didn't like it, he had to stay. There was no place else to put him. I didn't answer him, but I knew I had given Nick my word that if it wasn't a nice place he didn't have to stay there. And we had promised to visit him on the weekend.

I didn't hear from him all week because I knew he wasn't allowed to call, and on Sunday, the whole family went to visit him, and everyone was excited to see Nicky.

We arrived, and as promised, the school was

Nick and Zara about 1993

Nick and Beatie about 1993

Nick with his friend Max Leavitt

small, and it wasn't unattractive. The boys lived in dorms, and there was kind of a rec hall. But the 'teachers' looked like bouncers in a bar to me, and the students had a dead look on their faces. They looked abandoned, and hopeless, and they stared at us like concentration camp survivors who had somehow lost their grip on life. I didn't like what I saw. We were the only people visiting that day, and when I saw Nick, I felt agony clutch my heart. When I looked into his eyes, I saw a look of panic.

He took me aside and told me how terrible it was. He said the headmaster didn't live on campus as he had said that he did, the monitors were hard on the kids, and most of the students were both violent and crazy there, and there was no shrink at all, contrary to what they'd told us.

'I'm scared, Mom,' he said, and I couldn't help remembering the endless, fabricated tales when he'd gone to camp, of beatings and attacks and torture, just to keep himself amused and see if I would take him out, but I knew that this was different. Nick was begging me for help. And as I looked at him, I knew to my very soul, that he was being honest with me.

We talked about it for a little while, and as I left his dorm with him, I saw human excrement on the stairs. I knew without a doubt that he was telling me the truth, and I couldn't leave him there. I said something to John, and he thought we should try it for a while, at least until we had other options for him. And with a heavy heart, I kissed Nick, waved good-bye, and left with the other children. And I have rarely in my heart felt so strongly that I had betrayed someone I loved.

I paced the house all night, barely slept, and when John woke up, I told him what I was going to do. He was right, we had no other options for him, but that was no excuse to leave him in a place like that. I called the counselor again, to help me find a school for him, and he grudgingly admitted he might have a possibility for us, but he hadn't spoken to them yet. I didn't care. If I had to, I would teach him myself. But I was not going to leave him there.

I called the school he was in and told them that I was pulling him out. Their first response was to tell me that I couldn't have the tuition back. He had been there for exactly five days. I knew I had to get him out. I owed it to him. I told them to keep the money, to just give me back my son. I asked them to put him on a plane that morning, and that afternoon he was home with a grin on his face the size of Texas. Of all the many things I have done in my life, foolish and wise, good and bad, bringing Nick home was possibly one of the best things I have ever done. It restored my faith in myself, my ability to do the right thing, no matter what, and it told Nick more than ever that he could trust me, that I meant it, and would live by it when I gave him my word. He has never hugged me like that in my life, and I have never loved him as much. It was a perfect moment of faith and trust and love. And I never regretted for a minute pulling him out and bringing him home. It was the right thing to do for him, and I knew it.

Many years after that I was called by an attorney, who told me that the school had closed. Children had allegedly been abused, and injured there, and there was a court case. Years before, there had even been criminal charges against the people who ran the school. They stupidly wanted me to testify, to say what a nice place it was, and I gave them an earful they'd not soon forget. I would have happily been a witness for the prosecution, I said, before hanging up, and never heard from them again after that phone call. I had been right all along about the place, but even without that phone call, I'd known it long before.

I think that Nick trusted me totally after I took him out of that school, and I knew without any doubt from that moment on, that I would never send him away again, not to a place that I didn't trust, or feel good about, or any place if I could possibly keep him at home. I made a commitment to myself, and to him, to do everything that I could for him. I didn't want to lock him away, to put him in other hands. We were going to find a solution for him, and we were going to make it work, no matter what it took. And I think for the most part, for the rest of his life, as best I could without endangering him at times, I lived up to that promise.

9

Demons

Once we brought Nick back from the last school, we had to start all over again. Where were we going to put him? And how were we going to help him? I must have made a thousand phone calls, and tapped into every resource I'd ever had for him. We needed a school, and fast. But aside from that, we needed a new shrink, and a competent support system. I called friends, counselors, schools, doctors, psychiatrists, everyone I could think of.

The first thing I did was line up a new psychiatrist, again highly recommended. He said he had time, and agreed to take Nick on as a patient.

Next, the school. I called the counselor again, and he recommended a small school in another county. It meant a commute each way for Nick every day, but that was fairly easy to deal with. Nick, John, and I went to see it together. It seemed like a nice place, run by friendly people with good ideas, and they were willing to take him. We had to get some recommendations from his old school, but that was easily accomplished, and within a day or two, he was accepted.

So we had a school and a psychiatrist, but I knew we needed more than that, and a pediatrician I knew told me about a new drug program for kids that was supposedly run by some very interesting people. I explained that we didn't need a drug program for Nick, but he thought they were worth talking to anyway, in case they could suggest some kind of support group for Nicky.

So I convinced Nick to come with me, to talk to them. He didn't want to, but I asked him to indulge me. And if I remember correctly, I think I bribed him. Either with a movie he wanted to see, or something like a Chinese dinner. I was not above bribery at that point. I would have tried voodoo if it would have helped him. If nothing else, Nick always forced me to be creative.

Off we went to this drug program, to talk to a woman I'd spoken to on the phone. She sounded young and energetic and enthusiastic, and I liked the way she responded when I told her of Nick's recent problems. I did not tell her I thought my son had mental problems, I only said that he had just been kicked out of two schools, or rather expelled by one, and asked to leave by the other. I told her about the wilderness program he'd completed, and she was impressed. And I also told her about the appalling school I'd just taken him out of. And from everything she had said, I was anxious to meet her. Nicky wasn't.

He listened to his Walkman on the way, looked bored, and told me he didn't want to stay long. It was late October by then, on a crisp, cool day, and as we rode along, I thought of all the hoops Nick had had to jump through, and changes he had to adjust to since the previous summer. I knew how hard it had to be on him, but ever since I'd pulled him out of the last school, he seemed in relatively good spirits, and he was looking forward to his new school.

We waited for a few minutes in a waiting room at the drug program. It was a decent-sized house, with the twelve-step creed blown up on a wall, and a handful of teenagers wandered in and out while we waited. And then the woman we had the appointment with appeared. She was young and pretty, had long, dark-blond hair, huge green eyes, and her name was Julie. I remember that she was wearing a long, flowered dress, and a warm smile, as she shook my hand, and introduced herself to Nicky. And instantly, I knew I liked her. I'm not even sure why, except that she seemed bright and quick and warm, she seemed to get the gist of everything we were saying, and she was interested in Nick.

We told her about his new school, and new psychiatrist. The idea was to give Nick a fresh start, and we weren't quite sure why we had come, or what we wanted from her. But one thing I knew with absolute certainty five minutes into the interview was that I wanted this woman in Nick's life. I felt immediately drawn to her. And something about her told me that she could make a difference. Little did I know at that point in time how much she would come to mean to me, and to Nick. How could I possibly have known then that she would become my sister, my partner in Nick's survival, and a friend for life?

We decided that the best way to proceed was for

him to come and visit her once a week for counseling, just to shore up what he was doing with his psychiatrist. There was no point putting him in the drug program, but I liked what she had to give, the spirit, the hope, the life she radiated. She was willing to see him privately once a week as an independent patient, and the drug program she worked for let her do it. Neither she nor I were exactly clear about what her usefulness would be, but I liked her so much, and admired her openness and honesty, and obvious skill with Nick, that I wanted him to see her. And Nick was equally enthusiastic about her. As I had, he really liked her. She seemed like a translator between the world of psychiatry and how Nick applied it to his real life. She was also a terrific translator between Nick's teenage angst and needs, and my more mundane conservative ideas.

All of Julie's expertise, she explained to us, was in the area of chemical dependency, but her real gift was understanding teenagers. She liked them and enjoyed working with them. Problem teenagers were her specialty, usually involving drugs, but not always. She also dealt with behavioral problems, which seemed appropriate for Nick. She said she was in recovery, and had been for close to ten years, and had been counseling teens for most of the time since then. She seemed to me to have a gift for it, but she also let us know that although she had years of experience, she had no formal training. But from what I could see, and her quick, insightful way with Nick, it didn't matter to me.

She was the adolescent program director at the place where we met her, and previously she had been the program director for another well-known drug program. And she told Nick that she had had experience with drugs herself in her youth. But more than anything, she seemed able to listen to Nick, and translate what he was saying into reasonable needs and feelings. It was as though she understood not only his needs and fears, but his language, which at times, I didn't.

It had taken only days since his return, but I was immensely relieved at the resources we'd found, and for once, I felt optimistic about the outlook, as Nick did. He was actually excited about what he was doing. If we were lucky, we were going to help him turn his life around. At fourteen, that would be quite an accomplishment, and I finally felt hopeful about his future, for the first time in a long time.

His life was a bit of a relay race after that, as he traveled across one bridge to school, and back again to see his shrink several times a week, and then across another bridge once a week to see Julie. He was lucky if he got home by dinnertime most days, but he seemed to like what he was doing. For a time at least.

But within a month or two, he was having minor squabbles with the powers-that-be at school. They had a complicated disciplinary system that required you to make points, or chastised you when you lost points. And Nick seemed to have a hard time following it. The rules thing again. But he did his best, and they weren't complaining. And Julie seemed to be helping him, he liked going to her, but the real disappointment was the psychiatrist we'd found him. I had the feeling that he had little interest in, or sympathy for, Nick. And the message I was getting from him was that Nick was a spoiled brat, and his problems were fairly minor. And in return, Nick hated him, and described him as 'an asshole.' I thought of switching shrinks again, but I had tapped into every resource I knew, and Nick seemed to be so resistant to psychiatry. I was beginning to think it was hopeless to find the right shrink for him. And during that time, Julie seemed to meet many of those needs.

Nick went on with the status quo for a few months, did well at school at first, but eventually things slowly began slipping. He was getting depressed about everything again, and dabbling in drugs off and on. I found an empty nitrous oxide canister in his room, which panicked me, and the school thought he'd used one at school, during recess, although Nick vehemently denied it. And this time, I believed the school, and not Nicky.

In reading his journals now, I know that during that winter, before he reached fifteen, at various times he used or tried a veritable smorgasbord of drugs to boost his spirits, everything from marijuana, to LSD, to 'mushrooms,' ecstasy, and speed. I think he must have been using a fair amount of marijuana, which most probably only depressed him further.

He was 'isolating' in his room again, keeping away from the family, and although he wasn't having any serious problems in school, he wasn't happy either. The only thing that seemed to help him was seeing Julie.

I was not aware of his drug use at the time, although I kept a fairly good eye on him. I think he also tried cocaine. He wasn't addicted to anything, but he was definitely self-medicating. I had also been told by then that problems that presented themselves like his, with fairly consistent depression, worsened markedly during adolescence. The constant increase of hormones in his system would be an ever-greater challenge if he truly had serious mental problems. But at that point no one had confirmed, or even admitted, the fact that he had serious problems. He was constantly defined as a very bright, spoiled boy, who was having a tough time with adolescence. All I wish now is that I, and the professionals who had said those things, had seen his journals. They would have given all of us important clues we needed. But I had too great a respect for his privacy to read them.

Julie left the program she was in, in the spring, and began seeing private clients in their homes, to help with teenagers who were having behavioral problems in school, or trouble getting along with their parents, and I asked her to see Nick at home. He was getting harder and harder to manage, more isolated, more depressed, more belligerent, and more hostile. Getting him to come to dinner at night was a daily ordeal, and when he arrived, he was just as likely to show up in his underwear as in his bedspread. Bluntly put, he was starting to act downright crazy. And even Julie said he was different, and more difficult than the other clients she dealt with, but it didn't seem to daunt her. She was tirelessly creative about coming up with solutions to make life more palatable to Nicky. She also seemed to find a way to get through to him, even when we couldn't. And it was obvious to me even then that she was extremely gifted at what she did. She could reach Nick when no one else could.

I spoke to my own therapist about Nick then, as he was a constant worry to me, and she said something to me that no one else had. She said that although she had never seen him, she suspected that he was indeed mentally ill to a serious degree, possibly either schizophrenic or manic-depressive, which shocked me, and she expressed surprise that his own therapist hadn't expressed greater concern about him. And at first, I resisted what she was saying, and insisted he was normal, which I knew he wasn't, but what she said was very threatening to me.

She also said that when I stopped having normal expectations of him, and treated him like 'our crazy aunt in the attic,' things would go better, or at least they would be more realistic. He was fourteen years old and the idea that he was truly mentally ill, and maybe even severely, appalled me, and made my heart ache, but I couldn't deny it. But she was right in what she said. What difference did it make if he came to dinner? In fact, it would be easier for all of us if he didn't. Every night at the dinner table had become a nightmare, he argued about everything, insulted everyone, farted, burped, sneered, screamed at anyone he chose to, and obsessed constantly about things he wanted to do that were months away, like what concert he could go to three months hence, and who would take him. He made conversation impossible, and the other children could never get a word in. I tried to set rules that wouldn't allow him to ruin the meal for everyone, but they were just more rules he either couldn't, or wouldn't follow. And it broke my heart to see him. He had started looking unkempt, refused to comb or brush his hair, and he seemed to take pleasure in torturing everyone, particularly me, by starting arguments and being insulting day and night, and especially at every meal.

In a matter of months despite everything we were trying to do for him, he seemed to have lost both control over and respect for himself, and he had plummeted unchecked into an abyss of depression. But for the first time in his life, he was both abusive and aggressive. He was fourteen years old and he was in love with a girl three years older than he was, and he insisted they were going to get married. His life was a tangle suddenly of irrational behavior of monumental proportions.

Julie started out seeing him once or twice a week at home, and as the end of the school year drew near, and his fifteenth birthday approached, she came to the house to see him daily. I couldn't have survived without her. Her calming influence, scalpel-sharp insights, and wise words not only made his life more bearable, but ours as well. She was like an interpreter between warring factions. Sometimes she would deal with the smallest problems of daily life, like getting him to take a shower, or put on shoes. And sometimes she dealt with issues of far greater proportions.

In addition, like all parents dealing with problem children, John and I had divergent views at times, and the angst of dealing with Nick minute by minute, day by day, put an almost inevitable strain on our marriage. Sometimes Nick would be in our room at two and three and four A.M., arguing about something trivial, and Julie wasn't there at those hours to help us. If nothing else, it was exhausting and painful and sad for all concerned.

Nick's behavior by then was putting a strain on everyone, although we did our best to deal with him separately, and not allow him to disrupt the younger children. But it wasn't always possible, and it surely wasn't easy. In those days particularly, living with Nick was really a nightmare, and John and I were both worried. There were so many things and aspects to think and worry about, his physical well-being, his academic life, his behavior at home, and the example he set, negative or positive, and beyond that, the far greater fear that what was fueling his obstreperousness was actually something far more disturbing than adolescence.

My whole focus seemed to be on Nick on a daily basis, and I was always fighting for time to spend with the other children. Having Julie there to step in for me, and talk to Nick, gave me the time I needed to pay attention to them.

And there were days when I wanted to lie on the floor and scream, or thought I would go crazy. The worst part of it was that I didn't know how to help him. Patience and reason made little or no impression on Nick, threats and consequences didn't sway him. We tried writing contracts with him, which he argued about for hours, negotiated endlessly, eventually signed, and would break minutes or hours later. The contracts were worthless.

I was worried that the time he was spending at the psychiatrist was having little effect on him, and as yet no one had suggested medication. When I mentioned to Nick's therapist what mine had said, about Nick possibly being seriously ill, I got the feeling he was not yet ready to come to that conclusion, and after all, he knew Nick better. Instead, he suggested more 'structure,' and suggested we write up another contract. I could have papered the walls with the ones we'd already written with him, and knew by then that they were useless. No matter how reasonable they sounded at the time we concocted them, or feasible for him, he never lived up to them. Not for a day, or a minute. It was as though the agreements we made with him evaporated the minute we made them. They were of no interest to him.

I know now that his journals would have said it all to us, and to his doctors, certainly, if we could have seen them. Therein lay the key, but the key was in Nick's possession. Only he knew how truly tormented he was, and he told no one. What we saw was a deeply troubled boy, hostile, aggressive, sad, afraid, awake half the night, and wandering the house in uncombed hair, in his bedspread, sometimes sleeping on the floor. And still no one I spoke to seemed to share my concerns.

These are from Nick's journal. These particular entries are from a journal he called 'Monkey Boy,' which was a name he gave himself then. Some of the entries are utterly incoherent. Others, most of them, are quite brilliant, particularly for a boy of fourteen.

'Demons'
Demons kick their way into my head, spinning and laughing. Senses are dead. I cringe at their timing. They giggle and pinch me, their evil nails digging

into my flesh. I twist away, retching, coughing up vomit colored blood, dying. Hanging up here on this hook is no easy task, so here I swing, being tortured, swallowed up by the great escape. I see no other background besides the green steel wall, leering above the piles of destruction left by my tormentors . . .

This journal is still full of stories about Sarah, his little friend who had died nearly two years before, in seventh grade. But he still missed her so acutely, and longed to be with her.

And then on . . . into his private hell, where he must have been so lonely. It makes my heart ache to read what he wrote.

The smell of burnt flesh bites at my nostrils. I'm sitting here, slouched over, sleepy, itchy. They're talking. Everything's soft and fuzzy. Eyes out of focus, blurry, beating their fists at me, faces red. They tell me 'You're bad. You've been a bad boy.' I don't feel like it. I'm not bad. I'm not crazy. I just want everyone to be quiet, leave me alone. I want to be warm and comfy and to tingle all over. I just can't find that place. That small, peaceful place to rest my head, put my feet up. 'Come in, stay awhile, take off your hat, your shoes, make yourself at home.' I want to feel wanted, hugged, looked at. I want to be told I'm beautiful. I'm perfect. But they never tell me those things. It's the endless battle to get where I want to be, away from everyone else, lounging in the smoky lounge of misanthropy. I just want my boots off, my feet resting on the coffee table. I

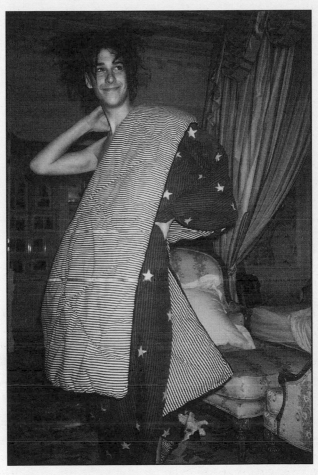

Nick in his bedspread

want to feel this way forever, away from the bad things, the mean people, the endless grey tread-mills filled with suffering grey people, old and mean, stuffed with resentments, and cold sharp hatred for things different from themselves. I don't like them. They all look at me funny, laugh at my back, point their fingers in my face. They make me hurt and not feel wanted. I hate that.

More journal entries.

'Hurt'

I'm sick and tired of it! I do my best all the time. I do what I have to do. No matter how it makes me cry and throb on the inside. I feel like no one cares. No one sees the effort. I do it and do it and do it until I'm sweating and sobbing and shaking. I get so filled with fury and hate that I can't see. Everything starts to spin. I twitch and grope at the rope that will drag me to salvation but every inch closer I crawl, someone pulls it farther away, laughing at my tears, my sweat, my blood. It makes me sick. It's not worth it. I find relief from it. I get up off my knees, brush off my clothes, the blood off my face. And then I go away. I leave your laughter, your joy. All the fighting and trying is pointless. It's like trying to walk through a wall. And your bony pointless hatred still pokes me no matter where I run to get away from it. I can't run, no matter how fast my legs move. Can't hide no matter how dirty I'm willing to get. It's all a game to you, a trick to see how far down the line you can push me. I'm over the line now. What is a game to you is my life.

'Strength'

Did you ever wrap your arms around yourself just
to imagine someone else holding you? Did you ever
wish you could talk to them and hold their hands?
Did you ever feel like you were ugly and worthless
and try to find your flaws, staring in the mirror for
days on end? Did you ever get laughed at? Did you
ever feel strange and foreign? Did you ever get
singled out and fucked with, being burned and
raped in your head? You couldn't see what they
wanted. Couldn't find what they needed. Did you
ever hide your sensitivity, your true feelings,
because you feared getting stepped on? Well, I did.
I did all of that. I lived through it. I am living
through it. I keep myself company and try to
imagine somebody loving my hate-racked body and
soul. I have to be strong to do it. I have to clench
my fists, grit my teeth, pretend to be pure and get
on with my business, despite the consequences.
Despite the pain and fire that will scorch my chest,
I need to put my feelings in check and deal with it.
No food, no laughter, no applause, just survival.
Just the sweaty rotting toothed skeleton that guides
me and scares the shit out of me that I have to deal
with. I have to find my ultimate addiction and take
it to the last page so I can go with a loud smoky
fucking bang.

'Sneaky Lil Fucker'

I am just an angry boy. I am not an imbecile. I sit
on his windowsill and let the rain make by back
wet. I don't know where I will go from here. Every
time I bend over, the black tar spills from my lips.
My lungs collapse and my stomach fills with blood.

When I die, I too will turn to dust. I'll fly my little kite and run in the big wide open field. I'll have friends. I'll have a family. I've had enough of this life. I'm tired of trying to get away with everything, tired of having to get away with everything. I have to do it everyone else's way, and all I want is to not be so filled with the dirty black hatred that rots my insides.

'Explode'

Normal is bad, balance is shit. I want to be angry and fierce and shirtless and sweating, screaming at the top of my lungs and clawing at my own skin for the rest of my life. I want to roll on the dirty carpet, the air raid sirens exploding above me, ripping the air to shreds. I want to be angry and alone, hating the world, hating my parents, hating myself. I don't want to have to call anybody on the phone, and have to pretend to be happy, have to pretend to be everything I'm not. I can't handle all of it anymore. I want to throw myself into the machine and get all tangled up in my own insides and just stay there, panting, being violent and loud. And it is all I have ever dreamt of doing, and all I have ever wanted to do. It's such a simple thing. But they won't let me do it. They hold my arms, laughing evilly at my rationalizations. They ask me why I do the things I do, and why I'm such an evil boy and why I am so bad. But I don't have any answers. I just strain against their wall of psychosis and think I will burst soon if I can't escape, if I can't make it to the other side to scream and pound and follow my heart. They have their fists around my heart, squeezing, constricting and all the while

174

telling me I'm getting better. I'm being healed. I can't see anything through the water and red puffy dragons that are stuffed into my head, barely contained by my bulging eyelids. I have to get away from them, launch myself into safety. Why don't they just go away? I guess it's not that simple anymore.

'Lovely Ugly Brutal World'

Why am I so confused and unhappy and fucking angry all the time? What goes on in my brain that makes everything seem so twisted and shitty? Or is everything really so ugly and bad? It can't be. People say it's not. But if it's not, why is there blood on the ground, and blood on the walls, and blood on my hands? Sex is violent, pain is silent. I stand in the eye of the hurricane with carnage and body parts twisting and flying all around me. And I can't seem to move because I'm afraid to get caught in that whirlpool called Sanity.

Do you ever watch couples on the street? When they are young, they hold hands so they don't kill each other. When they are old, they hold hands so they don't fall down.

> When I am in love
> It is like an ice cube
> tickling its trail of numbness
> behind. I feel queasy but
> content, nervous but excited.
> It is the ultimate feeling
> of fear and hope combined,
> When I am loved
> it is like cold hands touching me.

It is pleasing but frightening.
I feel uncomfortable though I am
sitting on a fluffy pink cloud,
I feel alone.

'Control'

Broken evil sunshine filters through the walls of my cell, I close my eyes to it, I don't need its warmth or its healing light. I want to stay here in darkness, pale, panting and bleeding, wishing for an escape into reality, but I find none. My soul is empty. I am weak, hollow, alone. I pray to the empty black sky at night and ask the Being my parents told me of to save me, but he won't. There is no God watching over me, no Heaven awaiting my arrival. I scream into the echoing abyss and lash out at the darkness, my fists striking out at the air. I wish I could hit something just to know I wasn't alone in here. But I am. Nowhere to go, and nothing to see. I am locked into my cage, like an animal, and I begin to feel like one. All I know is I must spend night after strangled night here in my room alone.

'Dream'

A dream crashed down upon my head this afternoon. It left my skull fractured, my mind ruptured, and my heart torn. I know I can fix it but that might be just as hard as letting it slip through my fingers. I weep at the thought of that and I know I cannot let that happen. I can't let myself slip away from the light I've struggled so hard to reach. I don't want to live in darkness anymore. I have too much to lose. I have more good and happy things in my life than I have ever had or thought I would ever have.

And I no longer have the weapons to beat away reality. I can no longer numb myself away from it, and I'm not sure I even want to anymore. I want happiness more than anything and I've found new tools to help me find it. I need to make life work for me and I can only achieve that if I work for it. I know I can do it, and I know how scary it is to actually try to make myself into anything. I'm sure I can do it. I have love clutching my right hand and she is helping me reach toward life with my left. She is what I need to help make me strong again. I no longer want to be afraid and weak. I've seen the light, and I want to try and get there fast.

This particular journal, though so devastatingly raw and agonized, seems to end on a note of hope, while he was still fourteen. But there was no question in our minds that he was getting sicker then. The demons that raged inside him were slowly getting out of control. Julie and I spent hours talking about it, trying to find ways to drag him back to 'normal.'

He was having more and more trouble in school, as the school year came to an end, and he turned fifteen. They finally called us in and said he needed some kind of treatment before he could return in the fall. Julie and I put our minds to it, as did John, and she researched it for us. He was playing with drugs at the time, though not seriously, but obviously still to find relief. A drug program wasn't appropriate for him, a mental hospital seemed too cruel, and his psychiatrist wouldn't have gone along with it. Not living with Nick, he couldn't see the problem as clearly as we could. I asked about a program or

Nick at fifteen

hospital for Nick and he didn't seem to feel Nick's problems were severe enough to warrant in-patient treatment.

I went to a session with Nick and his psychiatrist that spring, and all Nick did was sit and insult the man, while the doctor spoke patiently to him. But I could see easily that Nick had no respect or affection for him. From a medical/psychiatric standpoint, we seemed to be going nowhere. This had been Nick's third shrink in four years, and Nick had no interest in cooperating with his treatment.

Julie seemed to be the only one who got anywhere with Nick, although she was the first to admit that she had little or no training in the field of mental illness. Her expertise was in the area of drug abuse, and kids with ordinary teenage problems, but she loved Nick by then, and wanted to do everything she could to help him. But the world of the mentally ill was new to her. The beauty of it was she had no preconceptions. She was willing to try anything to help him, as I was. But it was clear to us, if to no one else by then, that Nick was mentally ill, whether or not his 'problem' had a name.

Julie was willing to learn as she went along, as were we, but it was becoming clear to all of us by then that the issues that plagued Nick were mental ones, there were vast psychiatric holes in him, which we struggled desperately to fill, just the three of us, John, Julie, and I, with no one else to help us. It was like trying to stop Nick from bleeding to death. He had cut an artery somewhere, deep in his soul, and all we knew was that we had to find it, and sew it up again. Quickly. Before it killed him.

10

Programs, evaluations, and finally medication. A small hope dawns at last

Just before Nick finished his freshman year of high school, Julie recommended a hospital with an adolescent program in another state for a brief stay over the summer to satisfy his school, and hopefully help him. He had just turned fifteen, and we weren't sure if a hospital was entirely appropriate for him, as their main focus was chemical dependency. These resources were the ones Julie knew best, and she still felt that there were ways for Nick to use them. We figured it couldn't do any harm, as long as there were psychiatrists on hand to talk to him. We didn't know what else to do, and the place had an excellent reputation.

We had to do something, we knew, and it just seemed to us that his psychiatrist was not yet as desperate as we were. He said he had nowhere to recommend for treatment for Nick, although we all recognized the fact that Nick was sinking daily deeper into depression, and there were even times when he no longer made much sense. I see it now more clearly as I read his journals.

Nick agreed to go to the hospital as kind of an experiment, although he wasn't enthused about it. But as his school had required that he get some kind of help before coming back in the fall, he didn't have much choice in the matter. And Nick's psychiatrist approved of the place we were planning to send him.

Nick nearly missed his plane when he locked himself in the bathroom just before he left. He said there was something he *had* to do before he left the house, but I began to panic when someone in the house said he had gone into the bathroom, wearing rubber gloves. I pounded on the door, threatening to have someone break it down. I had a terrible premonition that something awful was happening in there. And when he finally opened the door and I saw him, I knew I hadn't been entirely wrong. He stood there, grinning at me, with blue dye running down his neck and the sides of his face. His hair was still wet, and the hair dye was all over him, the floor, and the bathroom.

'It's a new color. It's called turquoise. How do you like it, Mom?' He looked like a kid who had just done his first finger painting in kindergarten. It was hard not to love him, or forgive him for the crazy things he did. 'Don't you love it?' Yeah, more than life itself, Nick. I hurried him then so he wouldn't miss the plane.

Julie was flying with him to the hospital where he was supposed to stay for a month. I was going to Napa with the kids, and when he was through at the hospital he was going to join us there.

I was hoping, naively and foolishly in spite of experience with him, that this would be a peaceful experience this time. He would do his thirty days, call from time to time, tell us how well things were going, and come back better than he left. Julie was planning to spend the first week with him, at least, leave him there when he felt comfortable, and then return for the last week and bring him home.

But I knew Nick better than to have dreamed it would go smoothly. I must have been nuts to think it could possibly happen like that. Things were fine for the first few days, as his journal entries show. He was at least thinking clearly then.

If you are a nice person, others should be nice to you. If you're an asshole, you deserve the same. I try to treat people with respect, even if I dislike them, so I'll receive the same. If they in turn aren't nice anyway, then they're the asshole, not you. I think it's especially important in here because you can't really avoid anyone. Especially peers in your group because you constantly have to deal with them. It's good practice for the future because in work situations you can't just go off on people at random and expect them to be cool to you.

1. I admire honesty, loyalty, kindness, generosity, creativity, sensitivity, and strength. Not physical strength, but I admire people who went through hard times, and came out a more knowledgeable and smarter person because of it.

2. I admire my mother because she worked for everything she has. She started out poor and went through some very tough times, but came out stronger for it, instead of bitter. She is very kind, loving, generous, and honest. She can express her feelings, and she is extremely loyal to her family.

But something went wrong after the first few days, and things began to get out of hand. I can see it in his journal entries. He says that he thinks he is manic-depressive and crazy, and then writes about death, blood, pain, excrement, all in violent images filled with rage. And then he writes:

I am trapped in a state of boyhood. I've stunned myself with the journey through the wringer. I'm dirty. I lie. I am a chart, a picture of regression. I am the lowest creature in the cycle of evolution. I am filth. I am hate. I am war.

He was definitely not all right by then, and I'm not sure what happened to upset him in the intervening days.

He began insulting counselors, refused to follow the rules, wouldn't go to group, and then, perhaps spurred by things said in groups, according to Julie, he decided he hated us, and announced that he was never coming home. Apparently, someone had talked to him quite a bit about what a burden it must be for him to have a famous mother, they had suggested to him that perhaps I never spent time with him, or maybe he had been shunted off so I could be free to pursue my own life. Nick ran with the ball they tossed him and went wild with it. He was trying to score a touchdown, but had no idea for what team, and after a week or two there, he had no idea which end was up. He hated them, he hated me, he hated John, and he hated Julie. He hated everyone, and when they asked him if he felt 'abused' by us, he said yes. And they told him he could have himself made a ward of the court if he chose to.

When Julie returned to the hospital, she saw the state he was in. He was completely confused and very manic, frightened and hell-bent on becoming a ward of the court although he was no longer sure why he had come to that conclusion. She told us we had to bring him home and fast, before he got even more confused, and the hospital agreed with her. He had somehow felt too much pressure on him, and he couldn't cope with it. Something in him had snapped, and Julie said he hardly knew who or where he was. But he had complicated the situation dramatically, by asking to become a ward of the court. In the end, I called my lawyer, who knew someone in a city near the hospital. My lawyer's friend called the hospital for us, and Nick was so confused, and difficult by then, the hospital also thought he needed to come home to us. He had somehow become unstrung, panicked, confused, and couldn't pull himself back together. Their specialty was not handling psychotics, it was handling kids who were suffering from addictions. Nicky's problems seemed far greater to them, and to us.

They wanted Nick out of there as badly as we wanted him home. He had been there for exactly two weeks, and although he had been depressed when he left, he had been functional. Now he sounded completely bonkers, and out of control.

Julie asked us to have a bodyguard meet her, to

help bring him home. Nick was in such a state that she was nervous that he might bolt, or panic on the flight. And we sent someone very nice out to fly home with her and Nicky. But as soon as they got to the airport, after leaving the hospital, she called. He had already calmed down a lot. But what worried all of us was realizing that he had come as badly unhinged as he had in the hospital. He didn't sound like he was in any kind of shape to come home, and we were once again faced with what to do with him when he got off the plane. He needed a kind of interim base where he could slowly pull himself back together. I called his psychiatrist, who couldn't think of anyplace appropriate to put him. Nick wasn't dangerous to himself or anyone else, didn't belong in a hospital, and according to the doctor, he still didn't feel Nick needed medication. As usual by now, I felt utterly helpless. And it was obvious to me that Nick was too sick to come directly home. I couldn't manage him myself, and had to think of the other kids at home as well.

I met Nick as he came off the plane, with a fair degree of trepidation. He had been telling me on the phone how much he hated me for the past week, how I had let him down, how little I cared, and all I was interested in was my career and my fame. He was no longer rational and seemed to blame me for all his problems.

It would have been useless to try to reason with him on the phone during his hospital stay, to remind him of how much time I spent with him and the other children. Nick had become a full-time job by then. I was constantly dealing with his school, his psychiatrist, talking to Julie about him. There weren't enough hours in the day to devote to him, spend quality time with the other kids, work late into the night on TV shows and books. I was hardly sleeping. And I was always behind the eight ball. Always apologizing for being late, or spending hours on the phone, trying to dig up new resources for Nicky. It was a challenging existence, but perhaps in some ways something Nick wasn't entirely aware of. He didn't know how many hours it took out of a day to try and help him. All he knew was what he didn't like about his life, like most teenagers. Like many kids his age, he was extremely self-centered, and very demanding of everyone's attention and time, particularly mine.

But as I stood waiting for him at the airport on the fifth of July, 1993, all my problems seemed to disappear when I saw Nick, just as they did the day he was born. All I saw was that smile, those eyes, and that face I loved so much. And as he saw me, he beamed at me, and ran over to give me an enormous hug. The first thing he said to me was 'I love you, Mom,' and then he looked down at me with the sheepish look I knew so well, and added, 'I don't know why I got so mad at you. I think I got confused. But I'm not mad anymore. Everything's fine now.' I knew it was the moment I saw him, but I also knew that he had hit the nail on the head. He got confused there. Either their treatment plan simply hadn't worked for him, or something in their groups put too much strain on him, through no fault of theirs. It was hard to figure out what had happened, but it had surely done him no good. Our goals for him had not been met. If anything, he was sicker than when he had left, more confused, more depressed, though at least relieved to see me. Maybe it was just a natural progression of his disease, and might have happened anywhere. The timer on the time bomb of his disease was constantly ticking for Nicky.

But he still needed help, and in extremis Julie had come up with a temporary solution. At this point, one has to realize that we still had no idea what was wrong with Nick. Whatever ailed him, and it was obviously considerable, was still a mystery to us. As yet, no one had given us a firm diagnosis of his problem, or a solution that would work.

Our game plan that day was to put him into a program where Julie knew several people who ran it. She had called, and asked for their help, and they were willing to take him, straight from the airport, which was a godsend. It was another drug program, which wasn't entirely appropriate for him, as his problems were more psychiatric than drug related, but he didn't appear to qualify for a mental hospital at this point, and we had no one to check him into one. We needed a place to put him until he recovered some of his balance. And although we knew drug programs didn't fully address the problem for Nick, the only option we had were the resources Julie had to draw on. He wasn't functional enough to be at home just then. So far no doctor had felt a mental hospital was suitable for him, and we believed that all Julie could do was help to get him into drug programs where they knew her, however limited the benefits to Nicky. We were still groping in the dark for solutions. And we had not yet realized that the drug programs, where he didn't fit in, and couldn't function adequately, only unwound him further. But we had nowhere else to turn.

When I saw the program we took him to that day, I wasn't sure it was the right place for him. I was almost sure it wasn't. It was a small building with no greenery, no garden, no place for him to exercise. But we felt we had no choice. Although he was calmer than he'd been a few days before, he was still too confused and too wound up to take him home to the other children. We hoped to keep him there for a few weeks, and this time he agreed without negotiation. He knew he wasn't well enough to come home. But he didn't like the place when he saw it. All I could do was promise to bring him home as soon as I could. And I knew he trusted me to do that. I had given him my word, and he knew that when I did, I lived by it.

What we didn't bargain for, although we should have by then, was how the people at the program would react to me. I was suddenly faced with a now familiar dichotomy. While on the one hand, they apparently were impressed by my celebrity, and everyone wanted autographs as soon as we arrived, they also seemed resentful of me. Julie knew several people there, and had chosen the program, and they had agreed, in an unofficial capacity, that she could be part of Nick's treatment. She had the advantage of both her skill and experience, and knowing him better than they did. One of the problems for Nick in drug programs was that as other kids began to normalize and find balance again, without drugs, Nick would only seem to get worse and function less well than the others within the confines of their rules and structure. He was in effect far less functional than they were, and far less so than he appeared. It was easy to expect too much of him, and to be fooled by the effect he presented. He was brilliant and sweet and funny, and everyone who met him fell prey to his charm. And at first, he usually appeared more 'normal' than he really was.

Within a short time, they attempted to apply some of their normal rules to him, regarding responsibilities, attending groups and dress code. And Nick refused, or was unable, to comply with them. And at the same time, the program decided not to let Julie collaborate with them on Nick's treatment. When I called him there, he was unreachable, and they were uncooperative with us in small, unimportant ways that were hard to pinpoint. But I felt I had to bend over backwards to prove that we were ordinary folks and not expecting special treatment. But one thing was clear to us, and to them eventually. The more they tightened the rules on Nick, the less he was able to function, until he could no longer function at all.

The problem of their attitude was a small one compared to the mental state that Nick was in. He didn't cause any trouble this time. He didn't ask to become a ward of the court. But it was obvious within days that he was unable at that point to conform to their rules and do what they wanted. He had fallen apart so badly in the past month that, in the face of all their requests of him, all he could do was shut down emotionally and stay in bed, sleeping. They seemed to be challenging him beyond his capabilities, and he was slowly turning into a vegetable, losing touch, losing his grip, losing his will to live, through no fault of theirs. His reaction must have been part of his illness at the time.

After endless hours on the phone, discussing the situation we were in, Julie and I made an executive decision to take him out of the program and bring him home. Our attempts at treatment for him that summer had utterly failed, and if anything, had set him back further. He seemed more dysfunctional than ever.

I took him up to Napa with me, babied him, coddled him, and cajoled him as best I could. But for a long time, I got nowhere. He was in a deep depression from which Julie and I couldn't seem to rouse him. She came to see him every day, and sometimes she just came and sat with me in my kitchen and cried after she saw him. It hurt us both to see him in so much pain. We could hardly get him to come out of his room, or out of bed, and I realized then that it was time for desperate measures. At Julie's suggestion, I called the psychiatrist Nick had seen all year, and told him that we felt Nick needed medication, and quickly. He said he couldn't give it to him until an evaluation had been done, and he wanted to recommend someone else to do that. He gave me the name of a psychologist who could do the evaluation for us, and I was upset. I wanted him to give Nick the medication we thought he so desperately needed, without waiting any longer. But I took the name of the doctor he gave me, and without waiting another minute, called him.

The doctor whose name I had been given to do

the evaluation took a day or two to return my call, as Julie and I grew ever more frantic. And Nick grew more depressed by the hour. He was fifteen years old, and he was so depressed, he could barely function. But when I explained the situation to the psychologist, he promised to help us. He said he would do the evaluation as quickly as he could, and if he agreed that it was necessary, he would ask the psychiatrist to prescribe medication. But first, he had to do the evaluation. He didn't want to be hasty or careless. But I was worried about the delay, and what it might mean for Nicky.

Nick was so depressed he wouldn't get out of bed. I felt as though Nick's life was on the line, and reading his journal entries from that time confirms it. I truly believed then that Nicky was losing hope, and Julie and I were both afraid of what he would do about it.

It was a miserable time. I was told that the evaluation would take several sessions, and with great, great effort, I talked Nick into getting out of bed and going to the Peninsula to see the doctor. He was willing to talk to the new doctor, which was a miracle, but by then, maybe even he knew how sick he was. There was nothing manic about him at that point, it was all depression. But I was relieved when he liked the doctor, and cooperated with the tests. After he went for a session, the doctor broke the news to me that he couldn't finish the evaluation, as he was going to be traveling. He was deeply apologetic, but there was nothing he could do about it.

He said that he suspected from the psychological tests he had already administered that Nick was perhaps atypically manic-depressive, but he didn't want to be premature in his diagnosis. He had to complete the tests first. Furthermore, he said patiently, it was very unusual for a boy of fifteen to be manic-depressive in his opinion, and he wasn't sure he should be given medication. He didn't want to be hasty or presumptuous in his assessment. But I wanted him to hurry.

But when I called the psychiatrist who referred him, to ask him to speed things along, I found that he was out of town as well. There was nothing we could do except wait. I made a plea for medication in the interim, to tide Nick over till the doctor got back. Prozac. Valium. Aspirin. Rolaids. Anything. Just give this kid a break. But the psychiatrist had told us that we would have to be patient, and Nick had to wait for the evaluation to be completed.

It was a time of terrifying frustration. I am a capable, reasonable, rational, intelligent, fairly strong-willed, competent person, with ample funds at my disposal, terrific resources, and an ability to get things on track quickly. If I couldn't make things happen for Nick, and get help for him, I shudder to think of what happens to people who are too shy or too frightened to speak up, people who don't know their way around, or have someone like Julie to help them. She validated everything I had thought for years about how sick Nick was, and gave me the courage to keep on fighting. But what happens to people who don't have a Julie in their lives, who get no validation? All I can say is, given what I know now, if you believe that someone in your care is suffering from manic depression, or a similar illness, and you feel you're not getting the help you need for them, don't wait, don't screw around, don't be patient, try someone else. Try every route you can lay your hands on to help them. There are a lot of doctors out there, some good, some bad, some lazy, some brilliant, some stupid, some who care, others who don't, and some who will help you and really make a difference. You have a right to what you need, someone who cares about your loved one and will help you. Do everything you can to find people who will help you. Keep trying, keep asking, keep begging. It makes all the difference in the world to find a good doctor and you have a right to do that. *Always* listen to your instincts. You know the patient better than they do.

Don't ask me how, but we somehow managed to tread water for a month, and went back to see the same psychologist again. He completed the evaluation, finally. He told us he would sum up the results, and then have his conclusions typed. I assumed that this would take a few days at most. I didn't think Nick could wait much longer.

Nick had gotten back on his feet somewhat by then, but he wasn't in great shape. The only thing that had saved him was Julie, with her loving, firm, devoted, constant help. She just refused to give up, and tried everything she could to keep him going, and give him the hope that we would eventually be able to help him. Even Nick realized by then that he needed medication. And he was willing to try it, if we could get someone to give it to him.

He was able to go back to school, and much to my surprise and our collective delight, he actually felt well enough to start a band. Encouraging him to do that was one of Julie's tools to keep him going. He wasn't in terrific shape at that point, but things were looking up. He called the band, rather unattractively, 'Shanker,' but it provided the little fun he had in his life. And it revived his old passion for music. But when he wasn't in school, or practicing with his band, he was either sitting on his couch watching TV in the dark, or in bed, sleeping. Classic signs of depression. And I was developing a strong sense that a kind of lethal hopelessness was setting in. Fearing that it might lead to a disaster, I called the doctor doing the evaluation several times. He still hadn't finished up the report, but promised he would 'soon.' At Julie's urgent recommendation, I asked for medication for Nick again, and was denied. And when I tried to get Nick to go back to the psychiatrist he'd seen all during the previous school year, Nick refused to go back. But he liked the doctor who had done the evaluation, so I turned to him for help. And he agreed to see Nick several times a week. But he still wouldn't give him medication until the evaluation was completed. I'm not sure what he was waiting for, but I felt as though I were waiting for three wise men on camels to appear beneath a star from the East, bearing Prozac.

What I remember most about the fall of 1993, when Nick was fifteen, was that I was afraid to walk into his room. I had such a powerful sense of Nick's despair (and who could blame him, no one seemed to be helping him, we were just putting Band-Aids on fatal wounds) that each time I walked to the door of his room, I was terrified of what I

195

would find when I entered. I was afraid he'd kill himself before we could help him. And I finally bluntly told the doctor that one of these days, we would find Nick hanging from the belt of his bathrobe, and what would he say then? How sorry would he tell me he was? What was it going to take for someone to help him and give him the medication I felt he so blatantly needed?

I'm not sure if it was that comment that spurred him, but within another week or two, he finally gave us his report. And when the doctor met with me and John, he looked somber. He talked about Nick having some learning disabilities and that 'his behaviors were suggestive of a hypomanic quality that may point to a variant of a bipolar affective disorder.' For the first time, the possibility of Nick's being bipolar, even atypically, had been touched on. And although he didn't write it in the report, I believe that he said he thought Nick had ADD, (attention deficit disorder) and was possibly suicidal. He talked about a significant depressive component to Nick's current experience, although he did not seem to believe that Nick was suffering from major depression. But he was willing to recommend medication. Hallelujah! The only miracle, as far as I was concerned, was that Nick was still alive to take it.

They put him on a medication in the Prozac family, and it helped a little, but in my opinion, not enough. He was still depressed a lot of the time, though not quite as extremely. But there was still a lot of room for improvement.

A song Nick wrote for his band, Shanker, tells how he felt at the time.

I'm all alone
I'm all alone.
Sky is white
The pain is bright
And I wanna get stoned.
I'm all alone.
Destiny, my destiny
dance with me, dance with me, destiny
Destiny, my destiny
No escaping, that's for me.
My mother moans, get off the phone,
she don't like my fucking tone.
Mama may have
and Papa may have
But God bless the child that's got his own
God bless the child that's got his own
I have been shown my heart of stone
Feel it in my broken bones
Love I can't have
The Dad I won't have
The child was left here all alone
I was left here all alone
Destiny, my destiny
Dance with me, dance with me, destiny
Destiny, my destiny
No escaping that's for me . . .

It is a beautiful melody, with a mournful sound.
It nearly broke my heart the first time I heard it.

It was a tough winter for Nick, and the medication didn't help him enough, but at least it was
something.

It was a tough time for all of us. We had
learned earlier that summer that there were two

unauthorized biographies planned about me which upset me greatly. We had also just recently been told that one of the biographers had somehow obtained knowledge of the record of Nick's adoption. All children in the state of California have a right to have their adoptions sealed. In fact, it's automatic. We had never asked for it, but as they do for all children, they had sealed Nick's adoption records, when John adopted him when he was seven.

But the biographer was threatening to mention it in the book, and Nick was frantic about it. Particularly in his very depressed state, he didn't want anyone to know he was adopted, especially his younger siblings. At his request, we had continued to keep that information from them, so they wouldn't feel he was 'different' from them. He was emphatic about it. And John went to court to try and protect the seal on Nick's adoption. That was all we wanted, to protect Nick, and the rights he had by virtue of being a minor, and having been adopted in the state of California. What mattered most to us was that it meant everything to Nicky, and he was already so fragile, we didn't want the biographies to upset him further.

The papers reported that we were trying to stop the book, and suing the biographer, but we weren't. John went to court, and lost. The judge ruled that because of my celebrity, Nick's right to privacy, and to keep the seal on his adoption, had been preempted. Our lawyer was outraged, and Nick was crushed. We had a right to appeal, but Nick was in no shape to deal with it, or to appear in court, as he probably would have had to. We dropped the case, and Nick was bitterly disappointed. But the biographies, at that point, were the least of our worries.

Nick was behaving strangely in school all through September, October, and November. He was quiet, and seemed mellow, but he was not doing his work, and his lack of impulse control was getting seriously out of hand, and getting harder and harder to explain to his teachers. One day, when he said he was bored, he walked quietly up to the teacher in front of the class, and without malice, or explanation, but just a lazy hand, quietly poured a soda out onto the teacher's foot, and then walked back to his seat with the empty can when he had finished. The teacher was horrified, and I began getting frantic calls from the school. It pained me to say it, but it was obvious that Nick had to be treated as a 'special needs' child. He could not function in a normal school on an ordinary basis any longer. They were going to have to accept him as emotionally handicapped, if they were going to keep him. And they were not prepared or equipped to do that.

The week before Thanksgiving, they called and told me I had to withdraw him. He had lasted there exactly a year. But it was time for a new school now. Nick and I had visited a school months before, and it was somewhat unusual, but now it was perfect for him.

I went to speak to the headmaster of the new school, told him the situation, and didn't hide anything from him. He was willing to take Nick on, and deal with his problems. I broke the news to Nick and he was thrilled. He had loved the school when we saw it. It was tiny, informal, and the headmaster was bright and creative, and sur-prisingly undaunted by Nicky's problems.

Nick started there in December, and things went as smoothly for him as possible, at least for a month or two. But there was no denying anymore that Nick was getting sicker and sicker. And Julie decided that she had better go on an exploring ex-pedition for us. She was still coming to the house every day, to work with Nick, and he was seeing the psychiatrist who had done the evaluation, although Nick seemed to be progressing slowly.

What Julie wanted to explore for us were mental hospitals where we could put Nick if we had to, for a brief time, if he fell apart entirely, became suicidal again, or where they could at least do a thorough evaluation for us and explore the bipolar issue further. I was disappointed by the evaluation Nick's psychiatrist had done that summer, and felt that he seemed to have done surprisingly little about it.

At the same time, John suggested a famous mental hospital in Kansas. We talked about long-term, or even permanent, hospitalization for him. John thought it might help him, and it was un-deniably difficult keeping Nick at home. But I wouldn't even consider sending him away long-term, unless I felt we had to. I had promised Nick I would never do that to him, and as long as he was able to function while he was living at home, I intended to keep my promise. Besides, I felt strongly that one of the best things Nick had going for him was his family. If we 'put him away' somewhere like that, there was no way that we could visit him with any regularity. I had small children at home and it just wasn't realistic for us to start commuting to

Kansas to see him. It was a great place, and John thought they could help Nick. But I didn't want him to leave us. We never mentioned it to Nick, or he would have panicked. He didn't want to be away from me, John, Julie, or his siblings for a minute.

Nick got a little respite then, he was taking the medication, settling in to his new school, and he got an unexpected break that I thought might do a lot to boost his self-esteem and his spirits. There were times when I was still hoping for external forces to make a difference for him. But as with all manic-depressives, the powers that drive them, or drown them, are internal. But at least this one experience provided a positive moment for him. A TV show was being developed at that point, which was a news program for kids, written, produced, and reported by kids with adult supervision. And after an initial interview, Nick was hired as one of their principal 'reporters.' It was a terrific opportunity, and a fun thing to do, and for a while he loved it.

He interviewed teens with AIDS, tattoo artists, and someone at a piercing parlor. He did a piece in the Haight on runaways, interviewing kids, and commenting on the interview afterwards. There were serious moments in the show, and zany, wild ones. And with Nick's personality and good looks, he was perfect for it. And for a while, he handled it well and was in everyone's good graces. We all particularly enjoyed the show he did on Halloween. He interviewed costume shops about the hottest costumes that year, and did the entire interview straight-faced, while wearing a huge pink tutu. He actually loved doing the show and we loved seeing him on it.

But the problem that did him in eventually, and ended his brief TV career, was his usual nemesis: impulse control. He began getting argumentative and difficult about the assignments he was given, and quarreled with the producer and director more than once about the subject matter. He finally walked off the set one day, and told them the interview he was supposed to do was 'just too stupid.' But I think, in retrospect, that what was happening to him was that he could no longer take the pressure. No matter how much fun it was for him at times, or how well he did at it, he couldn't keep up the performance. He walked off the set that day, and afterwards declared that he just didn't want to do it any longer. But like all the things he 'wouldn't do,' it was always more a matter of what he 'couldn't' than 'wouldn't.' But it was disappointing when he left the show, because it had seemed like such a good thing for him. Nick had had the same problem earlier with modeling, when he refused to wear the clothes they gave him and walked off on modeling assignments.

And as Nick was ending his fledgling media career, Julie had been spending three months traveling around the country, off and on, looking at hospitals for him, to see if we could find some place extraordinary, where they could help him on an as-needed basis. And finally, she found one. It was in a place I could get to fairly easily, my mother and stepmother could also travel to see him, and if he was there for a brief stay, Julie could arrange to leave her own family, and stay with him.

They were willing to do an evaluation in February, in a week, during Nick's ski break, and they would give us whatever suggestions they could as to how to help Nicky after they did it. It was something to hang on to, and we managed to talk Nick into going. He wasn't enthused, but we promised him it would only be for a week, and the one thing he knew was that he could trust us.

He went, willingly, but he must have been nervous about it, because we later discovered that he took an inordinate amount of Valium, without telling anyone of course, the hour before he got there. But in spite of that, they managed to do the evaluation. It reached our hands more quickly than the first one had and listed an incredible amount of mental and psychological problems, but confusing the situation even further, it found no evidence of either manic depression or ADD.

He came home in exactly a week, just as we had promised him. And it hadn't been as bad as he had feared. But it hadn't really advanced us much either. All we had after his week there were more questions about the nature of his disturbances, but no answers.

11

Up and down, and up and down
better and worse, and better.
Just like a seesaw.
And finally, a diagnosis.

When Nick got back from his week at the hospital, he settled back into the new school he'd been in for the past two months, and Julie came up with another miracle. She came up with a new psychiatrist for Nick. I would have been lost without her. Life with Nick, without Julie to deal with him, interpret for us, comfort us, comfort him, and come up with a constant cascade of new ideas, and help us implement them, would have been nothing short of a nightmare. She reminded me at times of Anne Sullivan, who brought light and life and language and joy into the life of Helen Keller. Julie truly was a miracle worker, and for that, and her vast heart, I will be eternally grateful, more than I can ever say here. I don't know what fates crossed her path with mine that breezy October day when Nick was fourteen, but for once they knew what they were doing.

Before Julie found the psychiatrist she recommended to us, I called everyone I could think of to find one. People were getting used to me calling them, asking about doctors and psychiatrists and schools and hospitals. I was a one-man band, and played a single tune for more years than I care to think of. But I managed to come up with half a dozen names this time, all over the Bay area, and listened to a variety of excuses as to why they couldn't see us. Most of them were kind, but they weren't taking on new patients. But I knew I had to find someone soon. I felt that the doctor Nick had been seeing for the past six months wasn't making much headway, and Nick was disenchanted with him, as was I. I had recently gotten discouraged when relating something inappropriate Nick had done, and he asked if I ever said 'no' to Nicky. Of course I did, but the question made me feel that he had a less than perfect grasp of an extremely difficult situation. No, no, Nicky, don't get depressed and sit in your room in the dark for three days at a stretch . . . no, no, don't wander around the house all night and fall asleep on the floor somewhere, wrapped in your bedspread . . . no, no, Nick, don't come down to dinner half naked. And for Heaven's sake, no, no, don't look like you're contemplating suicide, or be so depressed and racked with misery that every time I see you, my heart bleeds.

The point that was hard to get across at times was that Nick wasn't just a disciplinary problem. There were clearly times, many of them, when he was barely able to function. The simplest tasks were too much for him. He could not do chores, or have responsibilities. He could not feed a pet, remember to empty his waste basket, close the refrigerator door at four A.M. so everything in it didn't turn to mush, and making his bed was totally beyond him. He just *couldn't* do it. He wasn't just lazy, he was dysfunctional. And his lack of impulse control made him increasingly difficult to manage. And the older he got, the more we saw of it.

When he was fifteen, as he was then, his six-year-old sister was far more capable than he was, and in fact often offered to help him. The range of tasks he was reliable at was so small that getting him to flush the toilet was a major accomplishment. I was grateful each time he did it. And the scary thing of course was that along with the total irresponsibility was an equally alarming lack of awareness. He would leave something highly flammable touching a lightbulb, or let a wobbly candle burn too low, or a child hang out a window. He was dangerous to himself because of it, and inadvertently to others. But to answer the doctor's question, YES, I had said no to Nicky, and it got me nowhere.

I made appointments with four new psychiatrists to see what I thought of them, before I burdened Nick with the same task. I wanted to filter them for him, because new people and new things, new places and new challenges made him visibly nervous. In fact, Nick didn't do well with stress or overstimulation of any kind. He couldn't travel with us anymore. Our household, with all its kids, pets, staff, visitors, and the normal comings and goings of a flock of children, seemed to make him extremely anxious. Whereas the rest of us were used to it, the older he got, the less able he was to cope with the stimulation and confusion.

So as to spare him stress, I wanted to do the groundwork for him by interviewing new psychiatrists. And all I could think of as I went from one appointment to the next was a scene in the movie *Baby Boom*, where Diane Keaton is interviewing nannies. One is weirder than the next, ranging from women fresh out of cults to others who looked like they should have been carrying a whip and wearing leather. The psychiatrists I saw were not quite as exotic, but some of them were just as funny.

I particularly liked the one who said he felt our entire family should be in therapy, and extended family as well, aunts, uncles, grandparents. I looked at him in amusement, as I explained that our immediate family consisted of eleven people, the youngest of whom were six, seven and eight years old, and the others only slightly older, and hardly responsible for Nick's problems. And if we were going to pull in 'extended family,' it would entail flying in nine additional people from as far away as London, New York, and Tokyo. The prospect of that didn't seem to faze him. All in all, he would have been interrogating twenty-two people before having enough insight to address Nicky's problems. And he looked at me straight-faced as he said it.

Another one looked so depressed that it depressed me to talk to him, and I didn't think Nick would like him.

The good ones (I assumed) weren't taking new patients, the more offbeat ones seemed to have plenty of time for Nick, and I could see why, but I just didn't feel comfortable with them.

But the man Julie found for us sounded terrific.

Dr Seifried was intelligent, sensitive, practical, and reasonable. In a physician–patient relationship with a boy as troubled as Nick, at least one of them had to be sane, and for the moment it didn't look like it would be Nicky. We spoke on the phone at length for the first time, and he told me very sensibly that it sounded like a chemical issue with Nick, and more than likely the family had little or nothing to do with it, given what he knew about us. He had no interest in examining the rest of the kids, John, me, the birds, the dogs, or Maxx's rabbit. He focused entirely on Nick, and said that problems like his are usually not caused by the family, or the environment they live in. 'In fact,' he said, much to my delight and surprise, 'if it's chemical, even I may not make much difference to him. What he probably needs first of all is the right medication.' Hallelujah! I wanted to cry as I listened, or kiss him. I had known for a year that the right medication for him was the real issue.

Nick started seeing him as soon as he got back from the hospital, and he saw Nick frequently, before coming to see me at the house. And I liked him the minute I saw him. He had a happy, intelligent face, warm eyes, an easy smile, and a great sense of humor. He was incredibly bright, immensely practical, and it was obvious that he knew what he was doing. And what's more, in the sessions that he had with Nick, Nick really liked him – a real bonus.

He didn't mince words when he discussed Nick's problems with me. He had read all the material we had, the first evaluation, the second one done at the latest hospital, reports from his school, and had asked me a lot of pertinent questions. But his diagnosis was pretty straightforward. He believed Nick had Attention Deficit Disorder and depressive illness, and there was a possibility that he had some slight neurological damage. There was also a chance that his experimentation with drugs for the past three years might have caused additional damage. There was also the possibility, as we'd been told before, that Nick was atypically bipolar, which had made it hard to diagnose. Apparently manic-depressive teenagers are harder to diagnose than adults, which could have been why his previous psychiatrist had been hesitant about his diagnosis. Another thing that had troubled me for years were the comments of well-meaning friends, who said that Nick was just a 'normal teenager' or a boy with 'a lot of spirit.' My efforts to convey how deeply troubled I felt he was were dismissed, which left me feeling lost and lonely.

I had a sense of overwhelming relief for about twenty seconds as I listened to Dr Seifried. The suspicions I had had for most of his life were correct. There was indeed something wrong with Nicky. Something pretty major. But it hadn't been my imagination. He was a mess, in fact. But it was such a relief to hear another human being say it out loud and validate my fears. But the relief and excitement I felt were instantly swept away by a sense of panic, and a feeling of 'Oh, shit . . . now what do we do for him?' That was an important question, and it didn't have an easy answer.

As he had suspected from the first, the doctor said it was primarily a question of chemical readjustment. It was all about medication with Nick, how good it was, how well it worked for him, and finding the right ones. It had nothing to do with my toilet training, or John's, or the children's, 'telling him no,' or writing contracts. For the most part, it had to do with chemicals and medications to balance Nick's system. He would get psychiatric treatment too, of course, to try and reason with him, keep him balanced, and try to deal with his poor impulse control, although that was chemically generated too. All we wanted was to help him lead as normal and happy a life as he could. But most important of all for him, essential in fact, were the medications.

'How do we find the right ones?' I asked, somewhat innocently hoping that there was one magic pill that would do it. For Nick, as yet they hadn't been an adequate solution. The medications he'd taken hadn't made enough difference for him.

'That's a good question,' the doctor said. 'To put it scientifically,' he said with a smile, 'from now on, we throw a lot of darts against a wall and hope some of them stick. This is a very crude art form, and it's the best we can do. Nick is going to have to be patient.' Patience wasn't Nick's long suit, nor mine, but it sounded as though we didn't have much choice here. What helped was that the doctor was so honest and straightforward. I liked him more than I had ever expected. He had given me relief, comfort, validation, reality, hope for Nick, and a whole new set of problems to contend with. I tried to talk about the long-range implications of Nick's disease, but the doctor felt it was too soon to do that. There were a lot of things to ascertain first, and Nick was still very young. He said that it was very unusual to be clearly diagnosed manic-depressive at fifteen, which was why all the doctors we had seen had been loath to do that. Incorrect diagnoses can be made that way, and determining him as bipolar would be a major pronouncement. It was even more impressive when you thought that he had probably been that way fairly overtly since he was roughly twelve or thirteen. As it turned out, it was a very early onset of the illness, and as it usually manifested itself in an individual's early twenties, I couldn't help wondering what it would be like for Nick when he reached that age. With a ten year head start on most people who manifest mental illness, would he be that much worse, or were we likely to have brought the disease to heel by then, or at least taught him to live with it with the proper medications? The doctor I was already so fond of told me that there was no way of knowing, but I had a vaguely uncomfortable feeling that he was not overly optimistic. But I was not ready to hear it. I had heard a lot for one day, and despite my familiarity with Nick's problems by then, and the relief I'd felt to hear them given a name, I was reeling from the severity of the verdict for Nicky.

As I would come to frequently over the next four years, I mentally compared Nick's problem to juvenile diabetes, which is more severe usually than adult-onset diabetes. But it is a disease that requires constant and conscientious administering of medications to keep the patient alive and functioning. It's not something you can do casually, it is a life-threatening disease, as Nicky's was, and it is also far more serious when manifested at an early age in children.

Thinking that made me ask the doctor even more seriously about the kinds of medication Nick would be taking, but he wasn't sure yet. He didn't want to put Nick on anything as major as lithium for the moment. He wasn't absolutely convinced it was appropriate yet, and taking lithium at Nick's age presented a lot of risk for him, particularly a potential challenge to his kidneys. Nick was going to have to live with his illness for a lifetime. And he was going to be dependent on medication for the rest of his life. There was no cure for Nick's illness, particularly if in time he developed into a typical manic-depressive. The only thing I didn't understand at that point was how readily manic depression could be fatal. I had no idea then of the high suicide rate among people suffering from bipolar disease. I have now been told informally that 60 percent of all manic-depressives attempt suicide, and 30 percent are successful. Had I known that then, I would have been panicked, though I'm not sure I would have done anything different. We were already doing everything we could for him. But I thought we were fighting for the quality of his life. I did not understand then that we were fighting for his survival, nor did I ever understand how high the odds were that we would not win that battle.

The one thing I felt certain of, as I listened to what Dr Seifried said, was that I didn't feel any stigma attached to Nick's problems. I felt sadness for Nick, and what he had been burdened with, and relief to have at least a slightly better idea of what to do about it. But I wasn't ashamed for him, or for us. If

213

anything, I felt more protective of him than ever, and grateful that we had come this far and finally found a doctor who, I believed, would help him.

The medication the doctor wanted to try on Nick was Prozac, and if he did well with it, we were going to try adding another medication to it later, or even several, but the doctor had not yet determined which ones. We were hoping that the Prozac would help him with the depression. As the doctor had said, it was now a crapshoot we had to learn to play, of trial and error. And the one thing we agreed on was that we were not going to discuss this with Nicky, he was not ready to hear it, and still far too fragile. All he needed to know for now was that we were switching him from his current medication to Prozac.

And at first, he seemed to do well on his new medication. He liked his new psychiatrist a lot, thought he was 'cool.' He liked his new school, and his spirits seemed to lift, probably due to a variety of factors. Julie was still seeing him at the house five days a week, and on weekends if there was a crisis. A crisis could mean an argument about a concert he wanted to attend, or the fact that he hadn't brushed or combed his hair in months. He had decided to grow 'dreadlocks,' which with his silky fine hair was a cultural challenge. All he looked was home-less, but he was happy about it. I was somewhat less so, but it was the least of his problems. I was more concerned with what was under his hair, rather than how he combed it. Or maybe I just say that now, there were times when he drove me nuts with his unkempt appearance. I still had fairly mundane standards, although Nick had taught me many things about 'norms' and 'standards.' And sometimes he looked cute, even to me, in his crazy outfits.

As spring came, he seemed to be doing better, though he was still depressed at times, still difficult much of the time, still couldn't sleep at night. He roamed the house like a hamster in a Habitrail, which I know now was classically manic-depressive. It is typical of the disease to turn day into night and vice versa, which meant he was often awake till four and five A.M. and near-comatose when we tried to wake him up in the morning. The medications challenged him in that area too. The Prozac often kept him up at night and had to be administered in the morning. We hadn't added any other medication to it. His doctor wanted to proceed slowly, but he was ready to add to it if necessary. I felt that working with Dr Seifried was entirely different from the other psychiatrists we'd worked with. He was readily available, acutely interested in Nick, and well aware of, and sympathetic to, the challenges we were facing. I had a list of phone numbers for him, which even now cover an entire page in my address book, including his sister and parents in Ohio. And when I called him, he would return my calls within hours, or sometimes minutes.

The correct dose of the medication Nick was on was a constant issue, and one we fiddled with for quite a while until we felt we had the right balance between too much, which made him jumpy and anxious, and too little, which didn't help him and left him depressed and lethargic. But he was clearly less aggressive, and less acutely unhappy than he had been. It may not have been the perfect solution, but it was helping.

And rather optimistically, Julie and I decided Nick needed something to do in the summer. It wasn't good for him to just languish in Napa. He wasn't mature enough, reliable enough, or well enough to handle a summer job, he was too mercurial and about as responsible as a ten- or eleven-year-old, at best. So although he would turn sixteen in May, a summer job was out of the question. But lying around in Napa, isolated from his friends, with nothing to do, was likely to depress him. So we began a search for a summer program that would suit him and keep him busy.

As usual, Julie threw herself into the project with her usual zeal, and came up with a million suggestions. The trouble was, Nick was tough to place. And even on medication, not easy to manage. His impulse control was still negligible, and he would do almost anything that popped into his head, if it appealed to him. Only weeks before when visiting Julie's house, he had decided to slip out and take a walk, and had done so on the freeway, totally unconcerned with the potential danger. He had no real sense of risk to himself, and Dr Seifried had explained that Nick's perception of pain was also likely to be somewhat imperfect, not due to the medications he was on, but as a result of the ADD and possible manic depression. He had already proven that to us, in fact, when he decided one night, alone in his room, that he didn't like his hair, and had taken first scissors, and then a razor to it, chopping it all off and giving himself, he thought, a home-made buzz cut. But the buzz cut didn't come out right, according to him, no surprise. So he decided to shave it all off, and in doing so, slashed his head in about a hundred places. He appeared in my room, with blood dripping down his face, and looked as though he had been stabbed. He was in tears, not because of the injuries he'd caused, but because he didn't like his hair. And I cried with him, because it broke my heart to see such plain evidence of how sick he was. He wore a hat for weeks to hide the scabs. But it had brought home to me once more that he was potentially a danger to himself, if not to others. And with an imperfect perception of pain, he was just as likely to slice a finger off, or part of one, while slicing bread to make a sandwich. People with Attention Deficit Disorder apparently do not always notice it when they've been injured, and just keep on going. He had to be constantly watched, which again made it a real challenge to find the right summer program for him.

The problem was finding a camp for normal kids, that was willing to take responsibility for administering his medication. He could not afford to miss a single dose, just like a diabetic. But when we talked to the camps, one by one they told us that they were not equipped, or prepared, to take on a high-risk, high-maintenance situation like Nicky's. Which ruled out any kind of summer program for normal kids. We thought of Outward Bound as well, at John's suggestion, but they explained that a boy like Nick would not only potentially endanger himself, but the other boys who might rely on him. He was a great kid, but there was no hiding from the fact that he could not be relied on.

Which left us only programs for disturbed children, and there were plenty of those. But we discovered rapidly that they were attended by children or teens with far more manifest disturbances than Nicky's. Outwardly at least, Nicky was more functional than they were. Which left us, once again, nowhere.

Until we found what Julie, John, and I thought was the perfect program. We were nothing if not creative. Looking back on it now, I really wonder how we did it. It wasn't until I started writing this, looking through records and files, and pulling out memories from my head, that I realized how many things we tried. How many crazy, and not so crazy, schemes we concocted to help him.

But this time Julie had managed to find an outdoor camp which catered to 'special needs' children. It seemed to focus mostly on kids who had used drugs, but they said there were some other kids like Nick there as well. So it seemed an appropriate choice for Nick. It was all boys, and would be a healthy, rugged experience, and together, Julie and I convinced him he'd enjoy it, although as Nicky loved to say, he hated nature. It was only a four-week stay, and I was going to try and take the younger children on vacation during the time Nick was away. And sadly, there was no way he could join us. He just wasn't up to traveling with us, and hadn't been for years, and even he knew it.

I don't mean to portray to you in all this that Nick was sitting in his room, empty-eyed and weeping for all these years. On the contrary, outwardly, to most people, he seemed like an ordinary teenager, obstinate, wearing crazy fads, unruly. He had opinions about everything, which he voiced willingly, no matter how unpopular they were, he had friends, and he was more knowledgeable than ever about his music. But the fact was that behind that carefully painted scenery, there lurked a host of demons. Nick knew it, and so did we, as did Julie and his doctors, but no one else did. He covered it well for short periods most of the time, and most people just thought he was difficult. He was just a teenager after all, wasn't he? And his brilliant mind, good looks, and charm seduced them. But to those close to him, there was no denying his illness. And on the rare instances when I would confide my concerns to close friends, they would usually pooh-pooh it by saying all teenagers were difficult, and Nick was no different. But Nick was very different, and we knew it. No other teenager I knew required a team of people to keep him dressed, clean, and safe from slicing a finger off when he made a sandwich. No other teenager found it as great a challenge to turn a light on or off, close the freezer door, or flush a toilet. No other teenager was awake all night, tortured by his private demons. But Nick covered it as best he could, and we did the rest for him, and helped him to look 'normal,' whatever that was.

In fact, that spring, we came to an important decision for us, to maintain our sanity. It was my idea this time, and we had to sell it to Nick, but it proved to be one of the things that made Nick's illness liveable for us, and gave me some modicum of peace of mind. And in the long run, Nick not only adjusted to it, he liked it. We decided to hire attendants for him.

When the children were small, and actually to this day, one of the gifts I gave myself at our summer home, where we had a big, open pool, was to hire lifeguards in the summer. With six young children and three teenagers, I was constantly worried about accidents in the pool, and someone drowning. Having young college boys for the summer to watch the kids diligently at the pool gave me peace of mind that was worth everything else I had. Besides which, nine kids is not nine kids. Nine kids is nine kids plus ten friends. On any given day in Napa, there were fifteen to twenty kids in the pool, and the lifeguards were essential.

The attendants for Nick were the same concept for me, someone to keep their eyes on him at all times, see that he was safe, and drive him places. Like all kids his age, he needed a lot of chauffeuring, but he also needed more supervision and more monitoring than even my six-year-old. There was no hiding from the fact that we needed to keep a constant eye on Nick. And doing that, while attending to the other children's needs, was a constant challenge. I thought the attendants would make a huge difference for us. He needed to be prodded into the shower, have someone help him wash his hair (once he gave up on his 'dreads'), administer his medicines, and do the usual things one had to do with a child, like tell him to clean up his room (just empty words to Nick), and do his homework. An attendant would be a godsend. Though it took a little while to sell it to Nicky, and to find one.

Julie began interviewing. We tried to get people who had some experience with problem kids, and for lack of a better place to look for them, Julie began tapping into her old resources, and talking to people who had worked for her in drug programs with adolescents. The problems were different here, but some of them were willing to try their hand at a new routine and a different set of problems. And most of them were overly optimistic when they started out, thinking they were going to change things for Nick, and he was just a slightly out-of-whack teenager. Again, because he often appeared so functional, he often fooled people into believing he was. And then he would turn on them in a rage, become fiercely oppositional, or outrageously insulting, or behave like a five-year-old. To a man (and one woman eventually), I believe they were unprepared for what they were facing, but most of them were incredibly good-hearted, willing to learn, and devoted to Nicky.

Some people adapted quickly to the job, and grew rapidly fond of Nick, others never did and left after a brief stay, and it took a while for us to understand what we, and Nick, really needed. But in the four years we had attendants for Nick, there were some exceptionally wonderful people with him, whom he loved, and who truly came to love him.

But for me, having an attendant with Nick made life easier, less stressful, and kept Nicky safer. I didn't have to worry as much about him. I knew Nick was in good hands when there was someone reliable with him, and once Nick adjusted to the idea, he actually liked them. They did exactly what I had promised him they would, took him where he wanted to go, paid constant attention to him, he was the central focus of their attention, and he loved that when he was younger. He told his friends they were bodyguards, which made him feel important.

Later on, as we became more adept at meeting Nick's needs, and more aware of them, we hired psychiatric attendants to work with Nick. There were always two people who worked with Nick, alternating days and shifts, and fill-ins when needed. They worked with him seven days a week, endless hours, and were inseparable from Nick. The last two men who worked with him became particularly dear to us, and to him, and it is clear even now how much they loved him. Paul worked with him for more than three years, and Cody for well over a year. It is rare to have found two men like Paul and Cody, and Nicky came to view them almost as older brothers.

His attendants spent more time with him than anyone else, and were with him from fourteen to twenty-four hours a day, depending on his schedule and his needs of the moment. It was surely more time than they spent with their partners, spouses, friends, or their own children. And as lovable as Nick was, it wasn't always easy to be with him. He had an intensity about him. A sense of urgency that meant everything had to happen 'now' with him, faster than fast, as soon as he thought of it. He had fuzzy concepts of time, so that something that had happened hours, or even days ago, seemed like years before to him. And something in the distant future had to happen right this minute.

Julie's house was well over an hour away from mine, an hour and a half at heavy traffic hours, and when he traveled between her home and mine, he and his attendant would have to take that into account. Paul says now that in the three years he drove him back and forth, Nick would always claim it took just under twenty minutes. As a result, he would drag his feet, cause them to leave late, and then just laugh and say, 'Tell my mom there was an accident on the bridge, Paul. It's okay.' I realize now, looking back in light of that, that if as many accidents had happened on that bridge as he said, there would have been more casualties on it than in the Korean War, but their tardiness never seemed to faze Nicky. He would always explode into the house with a big grin, a kiss and a hug for me, and an apology for arriving halfway through dinner.

There was a childlike cuddliness about Nick, more than ever in later years. He loved being close to the people he loved, physically as well as emotionally. He would follow me around, just happy to be with me, he did the same with Julie, and he was happy just 'hanging out' with his attendants. Paul says now that when he went off to do something, and would leave Nick with Julie or me, he would instantly get a page on his beeper, invariably followed by the code '911,' to indicate that it was an emergency. Given the possibilities with Nick, he would immediately call in to see what had happened, only to hear Nick's cheerful voice say to him, 'Hi, Pauly. What's happening? I just wanted to see how you were doing.' It was hard to get mad at Nick over things like that. There was something about the way he did them that touched your heart. It was his way of saying, 'Hi . . . I need you . . . I love you . . .' He found it easy to say those things too, but he had a way of reaching out and just

223

touching you that made you realize again that you were important to him. And the men who cared for Nick, and went everywhere with him, were very important to him. Especially in the case of Cody and Paul, he looked up to them, admired them, respected them, and genuinely loved them. And it was as obvious then, as it is now, that they truly loved him. And he knew it.

In some ways, these men knew him better than anyone else did. They saw his foibles, his weaknesses, his fears, his strengths, his unguarded moments. Cody tells another story, of Nick's generosity. Apparently, whenever they would pass a homeless person on the street, Nick would stop, and rather than give them money, he would give them a brand-new full pack of cigarettes. And if he didn't have one on him, he'd stop to buy one. Nick was generous to a fault, in other ways, too, giving his friends his favorite possessions without hesitating, or buying thoughtful gifts for them, his siblings, or for me. He loved giving people presents (as I do).

The attendants' job became particularly challenging during Nick's years while he was on tour with his band. These men who had come to him to care for him, and administer medication, suddenly found themselves in deafening concert halls, with flashing lights, in a crowd of hot, sweaty, tattooed bodies, watching Nicky sing, and helping him and his roadies and band members haul equipment on- and offstage, or sit in a van for fifteen hours with nine teenage boys going from one town to another to play yet another concert. In order to do that, they gave up time with their families, weekends, holidays, and probably suffered hearing loss from Nick's music, but he loved them for it. With Nick, life was always full of surprises.

One of the other things his attendants did was go to twelve-step meetings with him. Drugs were not the main issue with Nick. His greatest challenge in life was learning to live and cope with manic depression. But when feeling down or out of control, or not adequately covered by the medication he was on, drugs were always a lure to him. Going to twelve-step meetings shored him up against a temptation that could only complicate his problems and interfere with the medications he was taking. Nick knew with certainty that he had to stay away from alcohol and drugs. And to be sure he did, we tested him daily for drugs with urinalyses, and raised hell with him when he dallied, which wasn't often. But when we said he wasn't on drugs, we knew for certain that he wasn't because of the testing.

What dismayed me in those early years were the tales he told about his hospitalizations. Although he was usually remarkably honest with us, he thought nothing of telling outrageous stories to the outside world when they served a purpose, or enhanced his image. When he went to a mental hospital, he told his friends he had been to rehab, or worse, jail. Because he thought it made him sound more interesting. And when I scolded him for it, he would laugh at me and say, 'Just be cool, Mom.' I learned to be very cool over the years. Very. A lot 'cooler' than I'd ever planned. Nick taught me a lot of new lessons.

But whatever his early views about drugs, and how 'cool' they were, in his late teens he became rabid about them, taking a strong stance against them. Not only for himself, but his younger siblings. He became what the kids call 'straight edge,' which is violently opposed to drugs, alcohol, or sex. He managed two out of three anyway. And we teased him about the rest. And the only times he used drugs in the last years of his life were when he attempted suicide. Any other time, whether it was for a beer, or a puff on a joint, we came down on him like bricks and put him in the hospital to adjust his meds, and warn him of the risk he was taking with his health and his own delicate balance. But in his last years, we never had to do that. He monitored himself, and had clear and very reasonable views on the subject. And as Julie pointed out to me not long ago, it wasn't an easy fight for Nick, because of his illness and the challenges it presented him, the fight to stay clean, to not allow himself an escape through readily available illicit drugs was harder than anyone could imagine. It was a real victory for him, and one he was deservedly proud of.

So that was what Nick was up to the spring he turned sixteen. He was living with Prozac, going to school, had two attendants alternating shifts to monitor him, and in June he went off to his summer camp for 'special boys.' He was a little leery of it, but only because he was not in love with the great outdoors, and he would have rather stayed home and gone to concerts. And he had just joined a band called 'Link 80,' and was excited about playing with them. He was anxious to get back to the city to have an opportunity to play more, and rehearse with them. But we convinced him that his outdoor experience would do him good, although he teased me about it. I hate the outdoors as much as he did.

Julie took him to camp with a four-week supply of meds, all our phone numbers, including mine in Europe while I traveled with John and the kids, and a long list of instructions from Nick's doctor. All was well when John and I flew to Paris with the kids. It was a special trip for me, as I spent much of my childhood and adolescence there, had gone to French schools, and still had school friends and family there. I hadn't been back in years, and I was dying to show my children the landmarks of my childhood. I was only sorry Nick couldn't be there. But maybe someday . . .

I got the first call from him a few days after we got to Paris. It was the middle of the night for him and he sounded panicked. It had been too much to hope that everything would go smoothly, and now I was six thousand miles away, eating crêpes, and taking the kids on the metro.

'What's up?' I asked, trying to sound casual. But I could hear the nervousness in his voice. I suspected part of it was psychological, because I had never left home before, and Nick liked to know I was close at hand for him. He had unusual separation anxiety for a boy his age, but the psychiatrist said that was not only due to his illness, but also because I had never left him. 'How are you doing, sweetheart?' I said, hoping to reassure him by the sound of my voice. He didn't like being left anywhere, and for the first time in years he didn't have me, John, Julie, or even his attendants. But at sixteen, we hoped he was ready for it, and listening to him, I suspected easily that he wasn't.

'They're not giving me my medication, Mom, and I'm getting crazier by the day.' He sounded anxious, and it was rare for him to call himself 'crazy,' or to acknowledge how severely he needed his medication. I worried for a minute that he was making it up so that we'd bring him home, like his old stories at camp about torture and torment, when he was a child of ten and thought I needed some excitement.

'Are you sure?' I was worried, but didn't want him to know it.

'Of course I'm sure.' He sounded insulted by the question.

'I'll call Julie,' I promised.

'I want to come home, Mom.' He sounded five years old and he tugged at my heart with his tone.

'I know, sweetheart. Just hang in,' I encouraged him. 'We'll all be home soon.'

'Get me outta here . . . they're not going to give me my meds.' I could tell he was near tears as he said it.

'Yes, they will,' I promised. 'I'll call Julie.' Julie, the fixer of all crises and problems. Julie, who had long since had to give up her other private clients because Nick was such a full-time project. What on earth would I ever have done without her?

I urged Nick to hang in, and called Julie immediately, although it was the middle of the night for her, but she never complained about midnight phone calls in a crisis. Like me, she found it unlikely that they were withholding Nick's medication, but when she called them, they said that he had to be responsible for taking his own meds, and had to report to the med room by seven A.M. or he didn't get them. And so far, he hadn't been able to do that.

We were both panicked when we heard that. We had counted on the camp giving Nick his medication. Not expecting him to be responsible for them, which he couldn't handle.

And Nick must have been feeling even more panicked than we were, and desperate, because he apparently broke into their store of medicines in the infirmary that night and helped himself to something, God knows what, to ease his anxiety, and they were furious about it. But getting himself to the med room at seven A.M. every day had been more than he could cope with.

The next day, the phone rang as we were leaving our hotel room in Paris to catch a plane to London. It was two A.M. for Nick, and he sounded frantic.

'I'm leaving here, Mom. I can't stay here. They still haven't given me my meds.' Shit. It was Father's Day in the U.S. I was six thousand miles away, and we were about to miss the plane to London. But I couldn't just abandon him, either, and I knew from his tone that he was desperate and frightened. And without his medication, his impulse control had to be at its lowest ebb. God only knew what he would do to relieve the situation. And all I could do was try to speak to him calmly.

'Nick, you can't leave. Just a day. Give me one day. I'll get Julie to you tomorrow.' Lucky Julie. Back on a plane to rescue Nick. It was such a damn shame the camp hadn't worked out. It would have been so nice to give him a normal experience for a change. It was both worrisome and disappointing.

'I can't wait,' Nick said flatly.

'Yes, you can. Just till tomorrow. I can't ask Julie to come up on Father's Day. She'll come and get you tomorrow, and I'll be home soon. You can stay with her till I get there.' He had already spent a couple of weekends with her when the attendants needed a break, and I knew he liked it there. 'Look, I'll call you in . . .' I calculated rapidly, 'about three hours, from London. Just sit there.'

'Mom, I'm walking out of here.'

'No, you're not, Nick.' I tried to sound firm rather than panicked. 'You're going to sit there until someone comes to get you. Twenty-four hours. I swear.' And with that, someone interrupted our conversation. I could hear in the background that someone at the camp had discovered him on the phone and scolded him for calling his mother in California.

'I'm not,' Nick said honestly. And I knew what he meant. I wasn't in California. I was in Paris. He was calling from the director's office. Nicky was never shy about doing what he felt he had to, to get what he wanted. And this time was no different.

'Nick, I'll call you in three hours. I promise.' I hung up then, and we just barely made the plane to London. And the instant I walked into our hotel room there, the phone rang. It was Nick. He had kept careful track of our itinerary, and I was glad that he used it, given the situation he was in at his end.

'Are you okay?' I asked him. His voice had sounded happier when I answered the phone. He had obviously calmed down, which was a comfort to me.

'Yeah, I'm fine.' And then suddenly, I wondered.

He sounded too ebullient. Maybe even a little manic. But without his medications, that didn't surprise me.

'Where are you, Nick?' I said calmly.

'In a phone booth on the highway.' He had done it. Walked right out of the camp in the middle of the night, two weeks off meds, and in the middle of nowhere, on a highway. My worst fear was that he would hitch a ride with a truck driver, and disappear forever. Although I tried not to sound it, I was frantic.

I asked him if he'd go back to camp, just to please me, but he was adamant and I knew that would get me nowhere. He was beyond that kind of reason at this point and his lack of impulse control had already taken him too far to turn back. I had to think of other options. 'What's nearby, Nick? Can you see anything? A town?' I was groping, as John walked past with a worried expression. There was no denying that with Nick there was always a drama. There was no such thing as an easy day, or a carefree vacation. And now, as usual, my whole being was focused on Nicky.

'There's a motel,' he said blithely.

'Where?'

'Across the street.' He had already walked a long way down the highway, which made my heart race.

'What's it called?' He told me and I jotted down the name. 'Okay, now I want you to listen to me, Nick, and I mean it. Go to the motel, get a room. Call me if you have to, and I'll give them a credit card number to guarantee it. Get in the room, and stay there. I'll have someone there with you as soon as I can, but I want you to promise me you won't go *anywhere*, or you're in BIG trouble.' I tried to sound as though I meant it, and somewhat ominous rather than frightened as I was. I couldn't imagine who I was going to send there to get him.

'Can I order pizza?' He sounded happy with the plan. Happier than I was, but at least there was a motel for him to go to.

'Sure. Order as much as you want. I'll call you when I know who's coming. And remember, *Stay there!*'

'Okay, Mom. I love you.' He sounded happier again. Crazy kid, but how I loved him.

'I love you, too, Nick.'

All my afternoon plans with the kids went out the window, as I reached for the phone again. But we were used to it. John took them on a sight-seeing tour without me. 'Mommy has to take care of Nicky.' How often had they heard that? Too many times, I knew. But that was the reality of my life, and his, and theirs, and John's. There were no easy options. I was always disappointing someone to take care of him. But they had grown up with it and understood it, or at least I hoped so.

I called Julie and relayed the situation to her. She was as panicked as I, but it was Father's Day and she couldn't leave her husband and children.

Next I called Camilla, our beloved longtime nanny, who had stayed home, mercifully, and not come on the trip. Now I knew why. There was a God after all. I called her, found her at home, and told her what had happened. She called me back five minutes after I'd explained it. If she drove to the airport like a maniac, and didn't bother to pack, she could catch two connecting planes and be with him in five hours. If we could just keep him in the motel room for that long, he'd be in her competent, loving hands. And I'd know he was safe five hours later. She could assess the situation from there, and bring him calmly home to Julie.

'Go!' I said, and she dashed off, without even taking a change of clothes with her, or a toothbrush, as she pointed out later.

I called Nick back then, and told him Camilla was on her way, and threatened his life again if he moved from the motel room, and he swore he wouldn't. But he sounded perfectly content, said he was watching TV, and had ordered pizza for breakfast. Terrific. Me, I had been too nervous to eat lunch, and now I had to survive five hours of anxiety until Camilla got there. I called Julie and told her what was happening, and she was relieved too. And then, hoping that everything was as much in control as it was going to be, I called the camp Nick had just walked out on. I wanted to see what they were going to say to me. I had already called home to check, and they had left no message for me. They also had my itinerary, but had not called me in London, either.

When they answered, I asked to speak to Nick, and they told me he was busy.

'Really? What's he doing?' I asked sweetly.

'Horseback riding,' they lied.

'How wonderful.' Nick hated horses. 'When will he be back?'

'Soon,' they said vaguely, sounding nervous. They were lying to me, and they still hadn't called me to tell me he was missing.

I called again that afternoon for me, morning for

them, and they continued to report on his activities. And on the third call, I forced a showdown. They claimed they'd been trying to reach me all day at home, and at my hotel, which was a bold-faced lie, and I said so. I asked them if they knew where he was, and they finally admitted that they didn't. And when I asked if they'd called the sheriff to tell them that an emotionally disturbed teenager was missing, they said they hadn't, but were 'going to.' I was livid. From what I knew, I felt they had endangered my son, first of all, and foremost, by not giving him the medication he relied on to remain balanced, and which we felt he needed them to give him. There was no excuse they could possibly offer to placate me. What would they have done if they had truly lost my son, particularly in the state he was in, and some harm had come to him? I told them I would call them when we found him, but I wanted to wait until Camilla was there, because I didn't want them taking him back to the camp now. I didn't trust them with him.

And a short time later, Camilla called. She had him safely in hand, and was at the motel with him. He seemed happy enough, and had ordered four hundred and eighty dollars' worth of pizza, which confirmed what I thought, when I thought he'd sounded manic. He had also bought a cigar, and was smoking it when Camilla entered the room.

And the rest of what Camilla told me was typical of Julie. Camilla had run for the plane, as she'd promised to do, and then switched planes for the second flight to get Nicky. It was a small plane and she hadn't bothered to look around when she took her seat. She had been distracted and thinking about Nick. And when she got off the second plane, she saw a familiar face getting off the plane behind her. It was Julie. Father's Day or no, Julie had been worried sick about Nick, and in the end had left her family, to be with him. She had taken a different flight to make the same connection as Camilla, but neither of them had seen each other as they were boarding.

They went to the motel together, and as they entered the room and saw Nick smoking his cigar, he grinned when he saw them.

But the rest of what they both told me on the phone was considerably less amusing. Nick had told them both almost immediately that he felt completely unbalanced, and for the first time, told Julie he wanted and needed to go to a hospital until he got 'normal.' He had been too long off his medications, and he knew it. It was the first time he had ever asked to be hospitalized, and it both concerned and impressed me. He told Julie he felt completely out of kilter, and was frightened by it. But at least he was safe and she and Camilla were with him.

I let the camp know that he was safe, and then Nick's doctor, who agreed that hospitalizing him was a good idea under the circumstances. And when I spoke to Julie, she suggested the hospital that had evaluated him four months before, as she'd been impressed by them. And Dr Seifried promised to fly out to see him. My next call was to the director of the hospital, who promised to find a bed for him as soon as we got him there.

By then I had spent the entire day on the phone. The children and John were back from their tour, and I was still too distracted to talk to them. I had to get Nick on another plane with Julie and Camilla, who had agreed to fly him to the hospital together. And I was immensely relieved that they were with him, although I felt guilty not to be there.

Meanwhile, neither Camilla nor Julie had clothes with them, nor Nick, who had left everything at the camp, and they had promised to send his things to us.

They were back on a plane two hours later. As usual, we had snatched victory from the jaws of defeat, but I was a nervous wreck after I hung up the phone. I had already decided that the rest of us would go to pick Nick up on our way home from Europe. And at least he'd be safe now. And Julie was going to stay at a hotel near the hospital in the meantime. But we knew that within a week or two, we'd have him on track again with the Prozac.

I hung up the phone finally, and went to catch up with my other children. Sometimes it was hard to be lighthearted for them. The burden I was carrying was by no means a small one, and they knew it. Even when I didn't tell them what was happening, they almost always sensed it. Particularly Sammie, who was twelve then. The war between Nick and Sammie had long since ended. She adored him. She was completely devoted to him, and very protective of him.

Seeing my face, she interrogated me immediately. 'It's Nick, isn't it?' I admitted that it was, but reassured her that he was on his way to a hospital for a few days, and would be home soon. But I could see in her eyes how worried she was about him, as we all were.

She was angry at me for putting him in the hospital, and viewed it as some kind of punishment I was meting out to him. She knew from him how much he hated being in programs and hospitals. And whenever he was, she viewed it as the ultimate betrayal on my part, rather than a safeguard. I explained to her that he wanted to be there this time, which she found incredible. But as she happened by, Victoria, who was only eleven, was far more pragmatic about it. As Sam berated me for 'locking him up,' Victoria looked at her and shrugged her shoulders.

'Come on, Sam, he's sick, you know that. He needs it.' Out of the mouth of babes. They all knew it. They had grown up with it. They accepted him for who he was, and even though he made their lives difficult sometimes, particularly when he ate up so much of my time, they loved him. And fortunately, he knew that.

12

A long, hard summer

The rest of the trip to Europe went well. The kids
had a good time, and so did John and I. But the
reports I was getting from the hospital where Nick
was were not terrific. What we had anticipated as a
short stay was now being stretched out longer. They
felt that he needed residential treatment and would
benefit from staying for an indeterminate amount
of time, perhaps the entire summer, or longer. And
Nick was miserable about it.

I wasn't sure which way to turn. He sounded
upset, but they kept assuring me they could help
him. The director of the hospital was someone I had
spoken to and liked, and at first the counselors and
therapists he had there seemed interested in him.
But within days, the director left for a month's vacation, and the counselors were beginning to sound
frustrated and hostile. The longer he was there, the
less Nick was cooperating with them. He was
sounding angry and aggressive, and they were
playing our old, familiar theme song, to which I
knew the lyrics only too well. Neglected celebrity
child, and spoiled, indifferent mother. Great. But

there was no denying that Nick wasn't well. Even with medication, he seemed to be getting worse instead of better. I wasn't sure if it was because he was upset about being in the hospital, or if he was actually getting worse, from a psychiatric stand-point. Dr Seifried flew out to see him, as promised, and agreed that Nick wasn't ready to come home yet. And once again, once hospitalized, Nick was becoming less functional, and cooperating less than ever.

John and I went to see him on the way home, and I didn't like what I saw. He looked pale and tired and sounded irrational and desperate. He wanted to come home with me, but he seemed too wound up for us to handle. He needed to calm down again before I could bring him home, no matter how badly I wanted to free him. And I tried futilely to explain that to him. He thought I was abandoning him there, and he was afraid I would leave him there forever.

The problem the hospital had with Nick was that he didn't fit in anywhere. He was too bright and too sophisticated to fit in with the kids his own age, who were there for a variety of reasons. But when they put him in with the adults, although he inter-acted well socially with them, and in therapy groups, he actually had nothing in common with them. Their life experiences were just too different. He wasn't dealing with children and wives and jobs he couldn't cope with. But he ran rings around the adolescents, and some of the counselors. And as usual, he was creating mayhem all around him. He was once again unable to follow their rules, ignored their smoking taboos, and had set fire to the carpet in his room, and scorched an entire wall by putting a paper clip into an outlet and doing something exotic and extremely dangerous with it to light a cigarette. Fortunately, he wasn't hurt. But they were already pretty tired of him by the time I saw him. And Dr Seifried wanted some new medications tried, but they had not yet done that, and Nick said he didn't want to.

All I could do was urge him to cooperate with them, calm him down as best I could, and promise him that I'd bring him home as soon as he could travel. And I meant it. I had no intention of sticking him away in a hospital somewhere indefinitely, unless they could prove to me that they could help him. They promised they could, of course, but there was no evidence of it yet. In fact, he seemed a lot worse, and more irrational and agitated than he had when I'd last seen him. But he had also been off his medications for two weeks, and I knew that that had wrought havoc with him. All we could do was wait now and see what happened.

I left Nick with a heavy heart, and flew home with John and the children. But I was still worried. I wasn't sure if Nick was just having a 'bad spell' for a while, an irritation of sorts caused by being off Prozac for two weeks, or if his illness had taken a turn for the worse. And no one seemed to know which it was. We'd just have to see how things progressed, but I was depressed about it.

Once I got home, Nick called me several times a day, always with a tirade about how I had abandoned him, how much he hated me for it, and how I had betrayed him. He was certain that we were lying to him and leaving him there. Even Julie couldn't calm him. The only thing that seemed to help were visits from my mother, who would travel considerable distances to see him, and despite the length and rigors of the journey, would arrive wearing a silk dress and pearls. Immaculate as usual, as Nick would sit with uncombed hair, playing Scrabble with her. But the longer he stayed, the looser his grip on sanity became, and the less feasible it was to bring him home. It was a vicious circle from which there was no escape for the moment.

And as I read his journal entries written during his hospital stay, I am once again aware of how troubled he was, and how desperate he must have felt. It breaks my heart to read them. They were written in July 1994, when he was sixteen years old. He was pretty sick then, immensely tormented, but still lucid enough to write in his journal.

'The Quiet Room'

Caged in, locked down, a spitting screeching animal, no saner than a rabies infested rodent, foam dripping from its lock-jawed mouth. I bang my head into the walls, round and round in circles, white ceiling, mattress in the middle of the room, bare and singular. Makes it seem even more empty. On my knees I squeal at the dense, thick walls to rescue me. I pray to the empty sky I cannot see and the empty God who doesn't inhabit it to relieve my pain, fix me, heal me, save me. No answer. I sit in the corner, hands covering my eyes from this taste-less plain reality, this awful reality I can find no escape from. I'm alone, head down, trapped in my wooden and plastic cage. The only light streams in through the glass square in the middle of the door filled with chicken wire to keep me from any hope of escape. They think I might hurt myself. I look in the plastic mirror and see a haggard boy in it. It is so they can watch me, make sure I'm broken down to nothing, crying out for rescue, begging for the salvation they offer, but I won't break. This will never end, no matter what.

Mental stability has reached its bitter end, all my senses are infected. I will never get out of this hell. Everything questions my mental health. It makes me lose control. I just can't trust myself. If anyone can hear me, slap some sense into me, but they turn around and I end up talking to myself. Anxiety has got me strung out and frustrated so I lose my head or bang it up against a wall. Isolated and angry, it hampers my recovery, and keeps me from being healed.

Confusion has me strung out and desperate. My whole world is made of disillusion and pity, nothing more than a mirage, transparent, nonexistent. I reached my hand out to try and touch my soul, but it was gone. I lost it somewhere. I am a scared little boy, and I don't know where to run. My little boy legs won't carry me much farther. I am weak when I always thought I had strength. My feet are in the air, my head is on the ground. Reality has set me spinning. I thought I could get up but there was more to it than that and I asked myself . . . where is my mind? . . . I thought I'd know what it was to be a man, but now I know I didn't understand. Secrets collecting dust, rotted to ashes long ago in the back of my head, and now the skeletons are coming to life in my closet.

In this same journal he talks about his friends, and a girl he is in love with. He also talks about being sick and insane, and for the first time many of his entries are completely incoherent and irrational, very different from the others. Yet some are brilliant.

'On a Scooter'

Confusion, pulling me every which way. Anger throws tulips in my face and the sky refuses to part for my ego to be comfortable. How will I stand this? How will my body hold up through the drive? Chewing on my lips, clawing the bedspread. Run, run, run, spitting product of our father's loins, poison the mother's milk, and make the children cry with infection. Bleeding out of my eyes, striking out at thin air, scratching at my chest, trying to find out whether the heart inside me is still beating, or if there is even a heart still inside me. Do you think I'm crazy? I'm pushed and pinched, shoved into a narrow box and labelled. I'm fucking NUTS and this place made me that way. I was normal before I got here, and then they took my reality, tossed it in the blender and liquefied all my mental assets. They make others like me every day, pumping us out like they were a factory. And I guess, in a way, they are.

'Need'

I need it. I want it. I want to feel at peace, my soul at rest. I don't want this pus-filled anger to gnaw at me night and day, my rage just a hollow tomb that I enclose myself in day and night . . . It's so lonely when you don't even know yourself. I'm empty. I'm weak. I just want to be filled with good feelings and happiness. None of this hatred, this contempt that has been rotting away at my belly for years. How can I cure myself? How can I find a way to get that cancer out of me? I want gentle rain to wash the fear and loathing out of me. I want the rage and resentment to be lifted. How can I be at peace? I want it. I need it. Need. Need . . .

'Fucking Rotters'

Why is he saying those things? Why does such blasphemy cross an educated man's lips? I have a heart, I have a soul, I can love, I do love. I am loved. He makes me feel worthless, like an unfeeling, unwanted soulless fuck, and none of it is true. Within five minutes of shaking my hand, he's assessed that I'm nothing, that I will only amount to nothing, and that I am a weak shell of a human being. Does he believe those words? Does he truly think that's me? Well, I don't. Fuck him. He doesn't know me from Adam. Who is he to pass down such judgments, to inflict such stinging words on one who he does not know? He's superior to me and I cannot tell him he's wrong, tell him to go fuck himself, and I just sit, dumbly nodding and confirm all his cruel assumptions. Fucking bastard. He doesn't know me, and he doesn't care to either. I can love. I love many. And I can make people feel loved. I am worth something. I am a good person. I don't think anybody has made me feel that shitty in a really long time. It's cruel, unfair, and untrue, all his accusations, all his false truths, none of it is real. I have a soul and a heart, and I know how to use them. He made me feel so low, so useless and *pitiful. Is that why I'm here? To be broken down, to be told I'm nothing, that I never will be anything? Yeah, that sounds good, let's go and get berated by some true professionals, and what can I do? Nothing, that's what, because his word might as well be God's word. Who'll believe me? If he says I'm fucked for life, shit, I'm fucked for life. He's a PROFESSIONAL. Fucking rotter. He doesn't know. He sits in his office and reads the reports and makes people feel worthless, makes us feel like shit. Maybe it makes HIM feel good. Maybe he's the one with no heart and no soul and he doesn't give a fuck who he hurts. Well, I have feelings and it sucks to get shit upon.*

'Indecisions'

What's happening? Where am I going? I sit in the silence of my cell. It's so quiet, it hurts me. My eardrums throb and ache, begging for sound, for the sweet comfort to be found in another human voice. Anger bubbles up and recedes as fast as it appeared. Confusion is the only thing present to constantly keep me company, confusion and agitation rotting my mind. Slowly driving me mad. Where will this road end, where will it take me to? What is happening? I just don't know. Maybe I don't want to know, maybe the answer is just as hellish as the indecision, the dark uninformed abyss that I am floating in right this minute. I watched the sun rise this morning. I watched it cast its healing light on the birds as they chirped and the trees as they shivered in the morning breeze. A deer appeared from within the woods, and it slowly chewed the dew-moistened grass before me. This sight, this vision, if you will, moved me indescribably. I was filled with a peace, a peace that I wanted to soothe my very soul. But it didn't. I still ache.

'Tired'

I'm so tired of being held down, of being held back. I feel like a hamster running in my little mill, expending all my energy, but going nowhere. I'm sick and tired of the fight, of the battle, of kicking and screaming at every last turn. But they won't stop provoking me. They won't stop easing me with freedom and love because they like to see me fight. They like my rage to explode because they know I can't win, and I will never be able to defeat them because they are too strong. They humiliate me and break me down at every turn, making me angry and hurt. But they don't care and I'm getting there too. Nothing can stop me now 'cause I don't care anymore. I'm going crazy in this place, it's driving me to my end. I can't stand it anymore. They dehumanize me because they want to see me squirm, they want to see me cry. Fucking bastards. I'd kill them all if I could. Fuck them. I'll never give in. Never.

'Finally'

Truth has exploded within me to own my shit, to do it, to be the very best I can be. No more lies, no more shit. No more fucking up. I'm finally going to Walk the Walk! I feel so light, the burden of my secrets lifted from my chest, my truth and desire echoing in my head. I'm going to really do it, truly honestly do my very, very best. I know I can do it, and I'm scared shitless but the joy overpowers the rest of me, it has finally taken control and I know I can truly, honestly do it. All I need is to be true, to be real, to actually do all I've been saying I want to do. I've always fucked up, no matter what the consequences. Now I want to be honest and good, despite the consequences. I feel it in my heart, I'm coming back. No matter who pisses on me, who's angry. I don't give a fuck. I'm doing this for me, so I can get better and feel good about myself. NOTHING WILL STAND IN MY WAY. Nothing but my ego and my sneakiness that is. I truly honestly do not care anymore what people say or think, but I am going to do it. My dreams will finally come to light, and I can see what they really are, who I really am. This might be tough, but fuck it. I finally am ready to walk the line that my words have painted, the line of truth and happiness and goodness and self-respect and love. I want it, I want it, with every inch of my being, with my every pore. Every breath I take feels different. I was more honest in the last twenty minutes than I have been in the last six months! I am there, I have reached the first step and I am ready to bite my lip and close my eyes and run the rest of the way up. I can do it!!!

'Forget That Shit'

This is so stupid and fucked up. I try to do it. I fucking try to get honest and be all I can be and I get attacked. Verbal assault coming from all sides. Just as I try to let down my soul and build up my courage, I get shot at from all sides. Put back in my cage, ranted and screamed at, telling me I'm a liar, that I don't know what's right, and who's wrong. All I tried to do is get honest and see what

Nick at sixteen with, left to right,
Maxx, Vanessa, Sam, Zara, and Victoria

Sam and Nick

*it got me? Fuck that shit. I get nothing but pain.
Being berated is not my idea of a first reward for a
first step. I feel so alone, so homesick. Why is this?
I'm just alienated, and no one gives a shit. They
want to keep me in the dark. I'm less trouble that
way. Fair and square, right? It's not worth it, all my
efforts are in vain. I've been left broken and insane,
cut off from the world. I miss my family, miss my
girl. They all think that I'm sick. They're full of
crap. Fuck that shit!*

They promised me at the hospital that they would
do everything to help Nick get better, treatment,
therapy, medication. But he sounded more
depressed every time I talked to him, and eventually
he just folded up the show and stopped talking to
anyone. He couldn't follow their rules, they weren't
doing anything for him, and all he wanted was to
come home. He stopped cooperating with them
entirely, and their solution to that was to fill him
with Thorazine, put him in the 'quiet room,' and let
him sleep most of the time.

I figured it out when every time I called him, they
said he was 'having a nap.' How many 'naps' can
you take in a day's time? I would call back four or
five times a day, and he was always sleeping. Once
again, I felt I had betrayed him. We had tried something that not only hadn't helped him, but had
made him worse. And they still hadn't tried the new
medications.

The counselors urged us to leave him there. Julie,
Nick's doctor, and I talked it over, and came to a
decision rapidly. Once again, the experience had
been disappointing, and Dr Seifried agreed that

there was no point having him there any longer. It wasn't helping. It was aggravating the situation. It was time to bring him home, no matter what condition he was in, or how bad it got. And from my perspective, he didn't belong in a hospital, knocked out on Thorazine, far from his family and his home. He belonged with us. We would take care of him. I called him again that afternoon and demanded they wake him up. He sounded groggy when he came to the phone, but he had no problem understanding what I told him.

'You're coming home, sweetheart.' There were tears in my eyes as I said it.

'I am?' I could almost see him smile as I said the words. 'When?'

'Tomorrow.'

Nicky let out a scream of glee. And he sounded saner than he had in weeks. He had been there for thirty-nine days. Wasted days, most of them spent in the 'quiet room,' because they didn't know what else to do with him. Like caging a beautiful, injured bird. I just hoped that his broken wings had healed enough for him to be able to fly again. He'd had a very tough seven weeks. Poor Nicky.

They got one more shot at him before he left. He apparently lit a cigarette again the morning he was supposed to leave. He managed not to set the wall or the carpet on fire this time. He did no damage at all, but he had broken the rules. They called Julie at the hotel, and told her he wouldn't be able to come home for another day. He would have to spend time in the quiet room for a day to atone for breaking the rules, which was understandable, but annoyed us. We were anxious to get him home.

She called me, furious, and I added my voice to hers. I called the hospital and told them to have his bag packed in an hour. They spluttered at first, but I think they knew I meant what I said. They weren't going to stop us now. They had done nothing for him except lock him up, like a car in a garage. We'd had enough of it. And now, my son was coming home, and nothing was going to stop him.

They put him in the quiet room while he waited for Julie to arrive. They made their point right up till the very last hour, but he didn't care anymore. He knew help was on the way. The nightmare was over.

'I fucked up again'

Oh well, last minute mistakes. At least I still get to go home. I shake with excitement, with anticipation for what will come. I can't wait to get on that plane. It's just a pain to sit here in the quiet room until I leave. I hate this place and I can't wait to leave. I'm not in the mood to miss it right now. I want out. They're all so concerned with telling me that I'm going to fail, that I can't do it, that my relapse has already begun. Well fuck them. I know me better than anyone else does and I know I can do it. I wish people had faith in me and didn't read into things so hard. I smoked in the bathroom because I needed a cigarette, not because I secretly want to stay here, or because I'm a fucking pyro. I need to go home. I need normalcy. I need balance. I need my life back.

It was all we wanted for him too. And all we could hope for.

13

A new home for Nicky

Nick came up to be with us in Napa when he got home on the twenty-ninth of July, and for once, he was actually happy to be there. After five and a half weeks in the hospital, even Napa looked good to him. He seemed edgy to us, and anxious, and not as well as he had been when he left, but he sounded better than he had on the phone. I think he was shaken by the experience. He still seemed far from well to me.

He played with his band a few times, and got tired of Napa eventually, so we let him go to Julie for a few days. But she called me in a panic shortly after he'd arrived. He had tricked her, and run away. It was a first for him, not counting the time he sat on the park bench laughing at us, eating doughnuts when he didn't want to change his sneakers. But this was for real, he was older, and he was sicker. He was sufficiently unbalanced these days that his disappearance was a real concern to us. Not to mention the fact that he hadn't taken his medication with him, naturally, and we knew he would be in bad shape soon.

Trying to fight back panic, I called a police lieutenant I knew, and Julie called all his friends, trying to figure out where he'd gone. This was literally the only time he'd run away, and it was difficult to imagine where he'd gone to.

He had been out of the hospital for exactly two and a half weeks, and he was obviously still confused, and behaving strangely. But within hours, Julie had figured out where he was. He was with a girl he knew. We sent two policemen over, and her parents tried to pretend he wasn't there. I called them then and explained the situation to them. There was no way to handle it except to tell them that he was sick. And two minutes later, they let the policemen in. And there was Nick.

I called Nick's psychiatrist, and we talked about what to do. It was obvious that Nick was still in bad shape, and he suggested we put him in a small hospital where he put patients sometimes, in the East Bay. It wasn't a fancy research facility, but he'd be comfortable and safe, and the doctor would see him every day. It broke my heart to lock him up again, but if he was going to start running away, we had a much bigger problem on our hands than we'd ever had before. It was dangerous for him to just disappear, and even more so to have him miss his medication.

John and I drove into San Francisco and picked him up, and quietly drove him to the East Bay. He didn't ask where we were taking him. I think he was too scared. He called friends from the phone in the car, and tried to be nonchalant about it. Julie met us at the hospital, and Nick's doctor was there. It was a small, clean, well-kept place that looked like a nice hotel. Nick didn't even argue with us this time, or ask how long he would stay. I cried when I filled out the forms for him, and went upstairs to kiss him goodbye. He wouldn't look me in the eye, and he looked defeated when he turned away. It broke my heart to see what was happening to him. Clearly, what we were doing wasn't helping him, and the medication wasn't strong enough, but what other options did we have than to put him in the hospital again? Particularly if he was going to run away.

The only thing I felt good about was the hospital itself. It was immaculate, and the staff was nice. He had a decent, comfortable room and there was a swimming pool he could use. I felt in my heart that he would be safe and well cared for there. I particularly liked the nurses and the doctors, they all seemed like exceptionally nice, caring people.

But as we drove back to Napa, I had a heavy heart. It was hard to imagine him ever being all right again. And as the summer came to an end, Nick only got worse. I was driving down from Napa to see him two or three times a week. It took me two and a half or three hours each way in heavy traffic and deadly heat. I would bring him pizza or ribs, and we'd sit together in a locked room. But he was angry at me. Very angry. He shouted at me, threw a chair at the wall, he never touched me, or aimed anything at me, but every time I saw him now he was in a rage. He was like a caged animal with nowhere to go. He was not only losing his grip on his sanity, he had lost both control and hope. It was painful to imagine his future at that point.

And after listening to how much he hated me for

two hours, I would drive back to Napa for another three hours. The round trip and visit took all day. And as always with Nick, it took me away from the other kids, and that summer I began to see it was taking a toll on the rest of the family. And worrying about Nick, I was beginning to drag badly. I was exhausted and disheartened. It was hard to be optimistic about him. In retrospect, with a whole spectrum of years to choose from, I think the end of that particular summer, when he was sixteen, was the most depressing of all. Psychiatrically, he was the most disturbed he'd ever been, or ever was later. And as he raged, and cursed, and threatened and accused when I saw him, it seemed inconceivable that he would ever lead a normal life again. I was beginning to fear he would be hospitalized forever, and for a long time there was no glimmer of hope whatsoever.

The trips to visit him seemed endless, the outlook bleak, and my marriage to John was at low ebb as well. I think we were both discouraged by how little hope we saw for Nick, and perhaps as people do when they feel helpless, right or wrong, we either blamed ourselves or each other. I was constantly involved in talking to the hospital, Julie, or the doctors, visiting him several times a week, upset about not being able to spend more time with the other kids, and getting no results from Nick. And perhaps John felt that I was too often absent or distracted. I'm not sure what he felt, we didn't talk much about it. All we knew was that we weren't happy. The past few years had been anything but easy, with tabloids, unauthorized biographies, dealing with and worrying about Nick, as well as the ordinary strains of any marriage. And just as a bonus, a local radio talk show had begun making disparaging remarks about me. It was just one more thing to make me sad, and to add to my sorrows.

Labor Day came and went. The kids went back to school, and I continued visiting Nicky. At least by late September Nick's spirits had lifted a little, and he was less aggressive than before.

He had been doing his homework in the hospital, and was caught up. But in spite of being solidly on the Prozac again, and somewhat happier, he still seemed shaky to me. After six weeks in the hospital this time, he came home on October first, and with the exception of two weeks in August between hospitals, he had essentially been hospitalized for three and a half months, one hell of a long time. It was obvious that his condition had deteriorated over the past several months, and taking care of him was now a full-time job. He was easily upset, explosive, anxious, withdrawn, and frequently angry at me. It made life at our house a living hell. Not only for me and John, but also for the kids, and even for Nicky himself. He had worsened considerably and I realized that if this was the way our life was going to be, the other children were going to be sacrificed to him. There was no way to have a peaceful night anymore, a quiet hour, a relaxed dinner, or even an easy five minutes with Nick in the house now. His volume had been turned up way too high, and seemed to be getting louder.

The doctor and I talked about it, Julie was constantly at the house, and within a month she made a suggestion that was anathema to me, and would surely change all our lives, ours, hers, her family's, and Nick's. At first, I rejected it out of hand. I wouldn't even consider what she had said. Her suggestion was that Nick come and live with her family, which I knew would be a huge sacrifice for her, and seemed like a terrible loss to me.

Julie had two children. Serena, who was eight at the time and a son, Chris, who was four. She had discussed it with her husband, Bill, who was willing to give it a try. I wondered if he realized what they had offered us. If Nick went to live with them, I knew only too well, they would never have another moment of peace, or privacy or tranquillity. And their house was far smaller than mine. There would be no way for them to escape him for a quiet moment. Even in my house, Nick seemed to take up and fill every inch of space, and I knew he would utterly change their lives. My own children came to dinner now with a look of anguish on their faces, knowing that every dinner hour would be a forum for Nick to create a crisis and act out.

But, however willing Bill and Julie were to take him on, I was adamant about not giving up my child. This was his home, we were his family, I was his mother, and as such I was bound to do whatever I could for him, close at hand, until my dying day. Moving him out felt like total defeat to me. But what made me consider it at all were the kids. I knew that if Nick got any worse, or even stayed the way he was at the time, there would be too little of me left for them. I never had enough time for them anymore. I was too busy chasing after Nick, arguing with him, and trying to be in fourteen places at once to make sure that he was safe. He was virtually unliveable for us, and now when he was up all night, he would pace our bedroom and argue with me for hours. About concerts, plans, his hair, his friends, his dog, his food, his room . . . anything that came to mind. And when he wasn't manically attacking me verbally, he was holed up in a black mood in his room, and I was terrified of what he'd do. The situation was grim. And I realized that if I could not help him, I owed the children more than this nightmare. I couldn't sacrifice them to him. Until that point, I had been convinced that I could juggle him and them. But through no fault of his own, he was making that more and more impossible for me, and I knew they were getting the short end of the stick, and as long as he was there, they always would. As much as it broke my heart, the time had come to make a choice, them or him. I had no intention of abandoning him, or 'giving him up,' but living under one roof with him full-time had become a nightmare from which none of us could wake up. The children above all were paying a high price for living with him. And my marriage to John had certainly been impacted by him, though I couldn't blame its demise on him.

It was a decision I came to agonizingly. And in my mind, it was perhaps the worst thing I ever did. I cried myself to sleep each night (when Nick finally left my room in the wee hours). I didn't want to let him go. I wanted to be there every moment of the day for him. I had promised that to him the first time I laid eyes on him, and relinquishing him now to someone else, particularly in view of the condition he was in, seemed like the ultimate failure to me.

I discussed it with my therapist and his, and

everyone felt it would be best for him, if not for me. Our house was too big to keep good track of him, even with two attendants chasing after him, and the normal turbulence of a busy family seemed to make him anxious rather than give him peace. At least we could give it a try, they urged. But I cried every time I thought of it. In my eyes, if I let him move out, I was failing him. I felt as though he were two and not sixteen, and in some ways he was. He was still my baby.

Sending Nick somewhere else to live is one of the few things I regret in my life. And although it worked out wonderfully for him, and he was happy there, I felt guilty about it for years. For some reason, I talked to him about it five months before he died. With tears running down my face, I apologized to him, and told him how much I regretted hurting him. He took me in his arms, and told me it had been the best thing for him, and how much he loved me. And I think he meant it. I was so glad I said it to him, knowing that I had said it, and that he didn't resent me for it, somehow freed me. He called it 'tag-team mothering,' and it was clear to me for all the years he lived with them, how much he loved the Campbells.

It was an arrangement that worked well for him. The Campbells were utterly selfless in their sacrifices for him. In the end, they were what kept him from having to exist in an institution. They made it possible for Nick to grow up happily, to have a life that worked for him, and to allow my other children to flourish without the pressure of living with their brother's illness every day.

It only worked because of Julie's enormous

capacity for loving him, her generosity of spirit, and her constant fairness about respecting me as Nick's mother. She never tried to take my place, usurp my role, play games with me or him. She upheld me as his mother from first day to last, and we developed a profound love and respect for each other, which now transcends him. It really was tag-team mothering, just as Nick said. He said we ought to write a book about it one day, and perhaps this one will serve the purpose. But we used to laugh sometimes about the fact that it took two women to mother him. And when he was with me, I would call her in a high squeaky voice complaining about some crazy thing he'd done, and she would calm me. When he was with her, she would call me five times a day, sounding hysterical and telling me he was driving her insane. But somehow we found the perfect balance that suited him remarkably, and worked for us. It was a juggling act of Herculean proportions. But all of our decisions were made jointly. We maintained a united front for him, every inch of the way, and when we disagreed about something, which was rare, we worked it out and compromised. We taught each other a lot about the fine art of mothering. I learned new skills from her, and she learned old ones from me. I made her more conservative at times, and she taught me to give him independence, self-respect, and freedom.

We shared him at first, and he spent several nights at home, like a form of joint custody. But in the end, he was happy to stay at her home all the time. The truth was that our house and its constant activity made him too nervous. There were too many people, too many kids, too many dogs, too much confusion for him. He was happier at Julie's, although he came home frequently during the day, and at night for dinner, and just to hang out with his brothers and sisters. And he spent the night on holidays and Christmas.

But if I had known how well it would work out, I would have cried far less on the day he left. He was a lucky boy to have had two women to care for and mother him and love him so deeply. The tag-team mothering we invented for him, and managed for three years, was a brilliant solution for Nicky. We all benefited from it one way or another, especially Nick. And I know from everything he said how much he loved it, and Julie, till the very end. We were a great combo for him. His tag-team mothers.

And Julie's words about me echo everything I feel about her:

I wanted to share some of my thoughts and feelings about Nick and Danielle. First and most importantly, I want to make it clear that I could not have done or dealt with Nick without complete and constant support from Danielle. Danielle is truly an amazing person. She taught me so much about being a good mother and doing the right thing. Instead of taking the easy way out. Before Nick came to live with me, a lot of people had recommended that she commit him to a mental institution. He had failed every program we put him in. He had been kicked out of every school we had found. The home contracts we had tried had failed, and Nick was completely out of control. It would have been very easy to commit him, and truly believe she had done everything possible to help. But instead, she allowed him to move in with me. Danielle never gave up. And even though he lived at my house, she was literally involved in all decisions that had to do with Nick. I can't remember a time that I couldn't get a hold of her. If Nick wanted to do something, and I wouldn't let him, he would follow me around the house arguing for hours. About every couple of hours I would call, ranting and raving that he was going to make me crazy. So she would proceed to argue with him for the next few hours. By then I would have gotten my second wind. Then I would take the next shift. When I think of some of the things we went through with Nick, I'm amazed at how we coped. But I believe it was because we truly supported each other. We had an agreement that if one of us felt strongly enough about something, the other one would support it, regardless of how we felt, and then present it to Nick as our own belief. Because of this, Nick could not divide and conquer us.

Nick had an incredible mind and he could convince himself and most people of anything. When I think of the stories he would tell about us to justify his actions, it would blow my mind, and more than that the fact that he could get people to believe them. When people came over, I always wondered what wild tale they had been told about me. One time when he had been put in a hospital for a time out, he had convinced the staff the only reason he was there was because I had broken my jaw and was grumpy. The fact that he had been kicked out of school had absolutely nothing to do with it. Another time he had convinced his group and counselor that his mom had a headache so she made him get his long hair cut off. The fact that he had been brought to their hotel room by night security for stealing and driving and wrecking a golf cart, was insignificant. Needless to say, the early years with Nick were a challenge.

I don't know what force brought Danielle and Nick to my office that day. But I do believe it was fate and that we were supposed to find and help each other become better and healthier people. And in the end, I believe we all got as much as we gave. I loved Nicholas so much and I admired the way he fought every day to be happy. And how hard he worked to break down his defenses and let us in. We did it one brick at a time, and at times he would let three down, and then be startled by his vulnerability and put six back up. We learned to see Nick as a person and not a behavior problem, and I believe that's when he started to believe he had worth.

One time, he had done something wrong so he was not supposed to go out. But he was really looking forward to going to this concert. We had been locked in this pattern for about a year, any time Nick really wanted to do something, he would get in trouble right before and not be allowed to go. So he would go on feeling persecuted and hating the world, and we would feel sad and frustrated for him. So this one day, we decided we would honor his feelings of really wanting to go to this show more than his acting out. I told him we were going to let him go. He asked why and we just said because we could see how important it was to him, and that he had value. After that, things began to change slowly. Nick started to explain how hard it was to control his impulses, rather than saying he just, 'didn't give a fuck.' I started giving him little exercises to try. I remember one was whenever Nick did get in trouble, rather than call his mom and apologize and telling her how bad he felt for letting her down, he would end up cussing her out. So we would call her and put on speaker phone so I could hear the conversation and I would write down what he was to say. And the amazing part was he would say exactly what I wrote. That was when I realized that Nick really did want to do and say the right things, but that he didn't know how. Inside he felt so inadequate in dealing with this world. He had such poor impulse control that he often did and said mean things. Then he felt so bad and he had such a limited ability to feel and own his pain that he would convince himself that it was everybody else's fault but his own. And his justifications were good. Luckily for me, God had given me a brain not only as good as his, but also as fast.

We would debate for hours over the simplest things and somewhere along the way, he started to listen and learn. And I listened and learned. And Danielle listened and learned. And we started to become the people we wanted to be, and we helped each other. Nick used to teach me how to spell and use proper grammar. Danielle taught Nick how to love and be able to tell the difference between a friend and an enemy. I taught Nick to think more with his heart instead of his head. Nick taught his mom that sometimes there are no answers to the questions. If I had to do it all over again, I would do it all again and probably in just the same way. Danielle and Nick have given me way more than they took. Even though the day Nick died, and for a few months afterwards, I truly could not figure out how to go on. I was so paralyzed by the loss. Slowly I realized that to love and trust so completely, and be loved and trusted so completely, is a gift that only comes around once in a few lifetimes. While the pain is temporary, the love is permanent. I love you, Danielle, and thank you for sharing your son, your unconditional love, and most of all for teaching me the true meaning of integrity.

14

A miracle at last

While I found psychiatrists and new solutions for Nick, and drove endless miles to visit him in hospitals, and Julie learned how to live with him, hire his nurses, and fold his laundry, John provided, at times, something even more important. As a mother, I deal in the practical and the concrete. I buy shoes for the kids, take them to the dentist and the doctor, watch them at ballet, make peanut butter sandwiches, and buy them new toys when their old ones get broken. I am always there for them. And what I offer them is pretty straightforward.

John's real strength is sometimes more esoteric. He chases down ideas until they become real, pores over articles and discovers new drugs and treatments for what ails us. He hunts down pharmacologists, hears about new medicines, and comes up with some pretty wild ideas. Like all people who live together, I often ignored him. It's difficult to focus at times on some new cure for malaria, which no one has at the moment anyway, when I have to buy the dog a new collar, and can't find Zara's other sneaker.

But John is an absolute bloodhound about things that intrigue him. Only a few months before Nick died, John went to see a psychopharmacologist at Stanford, and not only discovered an adverse reaction between two of the drugs he was taking, if a third one was added, but researched some entirely new drugs for Nicky. Unfortunately, we never got the chance to try them.

But shortly after Nick moved in with Julie, we heard of a doctor at UCLA, who specialized in manic depression and Attention Deficit Disorder. We discussed it with Dr Seifried, who encouraged us to see him. And I believe the doctor in L.A. suffered from ADD himself, and was apparently brilliant on both subjects. In truth, he would change the quality of Nick's life forever. Without his visit to the doctor at UCLA, I suspect Nick's life would have come to a tragic end far more quickly than it did.

They sent a hundred-page questionnaire for us to fill out about Nick. And I did it because I was the only one who had most of the information. There were a vast number of questions about my pregnancy, the delivery, and the first years of Nicky's life, some of which I had even forgotten. They needed other information as well, and I referred to the thick medical files we had on him. By then, Nick's medical records looked like the New York phone book. With the questionnaire in hand, all filled out, John and Julie went to L.A. with Nick and the meeting went very well. The doctor didn't waste any time, having reviewed our answers to his questions, and after talking to Nick, he wrote out a prescription for lithium. He said he believed Nick was manic-depressive. It was the first clear diagnosis we'd had. He said that if lithium was inappropriate for Nick, it would do nothing for him. If on the other hand it was the right solution for him, we would see a miracle within three to four weeks. His blood levels would have to be monitored at first to establish the right dose for him. It sounded vaguely complicated when they told me about it, but well worth it, despite a potential risk to his kidneys. But by then we felt we had no choice. It was his kidneys or his life.

The lithium was worth a try at least, and by that point, in order to improve the quality of his life, I was willing to risk his kidneys. His kidneys wouldn't be much good to him if he committed suicide, or eventually wound up in an institution. It still seemed like a possibility, and one I was willing to do anything to avoid.

Nick began taking the medication in November, a year after he had started taking his first medication. And he could still take the Prozac he took with the lithium. In fact, the doctor in L.A. thought it an ideal combination, and Dr Seifried agreed with him. He was totally in favor of trying the lithium on Nick and agreed with the L.A. doctor's diagnosis. Nick was beginning to seem truly manic-depressive by then.

Lithium allowed Nick to feel and believe that he was normal. But the prospect of taking it, and facing the fact that he had a disease, must have been endlessly traumatic for him. The night he came back from UCLA with the prescription in hand, he went quietly to his room and then announced he was going to jump off the roof. Fortunately, we were able to calm him down quickly. But after a fairly pleasant day in L.A., that was his immediate reaction. It reminded us yet again how badly he needed help. But from that day on, there was no further talk of suicide in his daily life, or in his journals.

Nick was nervous about taking the lithium, but nonetheless submitted himself to constant blood tests. Once or twice he said it was a dumb idea, and insisted he didn't need it. He had denial about being manic-depressive and the lithium would be the final test, we realized. If it worked for him, it would prove the acute chemical imbalance we had long since suspected. It was the final lap of an endless witch hunt. And trying to pretend it wasn't as important to us as it was, we all went about our business. It was difficult not to watch Nick like a laboratory experiment and he must have felt under constant scrutiny, which he was. But he was back at school, visiting us at home frequently, and enjoying playing with the band he was still in, Link 80.

But there was no denying the results three weeks later. Nick was a changed person. Happy, good-humored, sane, well-balanced, calm, and getting A's in school. The miracle had worked. The idea had been brilliant. Since I am violently allergic to penicillin and it risks my life, I have never thought of it as the miracle drug everyone else claims it is. But there was no question in my mind about lithium. For Nick, it was a miracle drug. Our long search for help had paid off for him. It worked! It helped him! And with the wonder drug it became for us, and for him, a whole new life began for Nicky. After what I saw it do for Nick, I will forever sing its praises. It made him feel a little queasy at first, but he got over it. And we had to keep trimming the sails a bit, adjusting the doses, but it gave him the opportunity for a life he would never have had otherwise. It gave him normalcy, and a chance for a productive life, which he took full advantage of from then on. And in no way did it impact his kidneys.

The key to making the drug work for him was in the delicate balancing act it became to keep it at the right levels for him. It was a juggling act we were constantly aware of. We never dropped the ball. Without the medication, or too little of it, one slip, and one only, could prove fatal if he were to become fatally depressed and attempt suicide. But for three years, it made Nick's dreams come true, and ours for him. It gave him life as surely as blood or oxygen or his heartbeat. Without it, we could never have helped him. With it, he had a real life.

He went back to the hospital three times in the next year, for five days or a week each time, to adjust his medications. Considering how often he'd been in for the year and a half before, it really was a miracle. And the hospital he went back to was the small, friendly one in the East Bay. He was comfortable there, never objected to it, and I liked it because I knew he was safe and well cared for there.

Sometime during this period as well, Nick managed to spend a few hours one afternoon with his biological father. Bill came by his school, and I don't know if it was an accident or prearranged.

They spent an hour or two together, and I think Nick was startled by how ravaged Bill seemed by his drug life. And after that afternoon, they did not meet again. Ever. Nick had satisfied his curiosity and seemed ready to move on.

Being on lithium allowed Nick to pursue a normal life. He went to school, and concentrated on his music. During that entire year, he devoted himself to his band. I knew it was important to him, but I had no idea just how talented he was. I began to hear ripples of how good they were, and how well the band was doing.

But the best and worst of the lithium was how normal it made him feel. The danger there is what happens to most manic-depressives who take lithium. At some point, they decide they're fine, cured obviously, and no longer need it. When that happens, disaster strikes, as surely as the sun comes up each morning. But Nick took it for nearly two years before challenging it, which gave him plenty of time to enjoy life, and his music. And I was thrilled for him. We all were.

15

Music, MUSIC, MUSIC!

When I saw Nick play with Link 80 for the first time, he absolutely bowled me over. He had a talent and a stage presence, an energy and a charisma that took my breath away when I saw him. And as I told a friend when I watched him onstage, I felt like Mick Jagger's mother. It was incredibly exciting!

He had talked about the band a lot, but he was fairly modest about his talents. I'm not sure he even realized how gifted he was. He was just as busy writing lyrics, and rehearsing and performing, as he was organizing and selling the band. He handled all their bookings for a long time, until they got a booking agent, ordered artwork, made flyers, ordered merchandise to sell at their shows, booked their tours, and called all over the country to promote them. He really had enormous talent, and was willing to work as hard as he had to, to sell it. And I realize even better now that he was enormously respected by people in the business.

'Nick's and my friendship first sprouted at a Link 80 Subincision show at the Club Cocodrie in San

Francisco. We both had heard a lot about each other, and seen each other in passing, but had never met till that afternoon. After seeing Link 80 perform, I suggested setting up a show with my band, the White Trash Debutantes, so we exchanged telephone numbers. We did not speak for another three weeks. I remember it well, it was 1 A.M. and I was ready to turn out the lights when the phone rang. It was Nick calling about a show. My first reaction was to ask him if he knew what time it was, and have him call back in the morning. Before I knew it, we were engaged in a lively conversation that lasted nearly an hour. Nick was a charmer and a go-getter. He had big plans for the band, and what was better, he had the ability to get them done. Well over seventy-five percent of the people you meet in the music industry are 'slackers,' and it was refreshing to meet a young guy with such energy and drive. Our show never transpired, due to a riot that had erupted at the club the week prior, and our gig was canceled. However, our friendship grew. His childlike innocence was very endearing. Although Nick was barely seventeen, I found him wise beyond his years. He tried to understand people from all walks of life, and would often support the 'underdog' even when it was not 'cool' to do so. Maybe because he had suffered some of the same pain in his own life, he could relate. Nick brought his own struggles into his music for all to share. It was a form of therapy, I am sure. When he took the stage, he brought with him all his frustrations to help make the show more exciting and wild. However, what I found most memorable about his performance was the humble way he thanked the audience. He so much wanted to get his life together, make his mom proud of him, and find success in his real love – MUSIC.

I am going to miss Nicky not only for his gift of music, but for the times we spoke about the ups and downs that life brought us. He would always have an open ear for me, and I also would listen to him. Nick had so many plans for his new band, Knowledge. Nick Traina was a very special person who touched everyone he met. I will miss him very much.'

Ginger Coyote
White Trash Debutantes

Nick's booking agent wrote of him:

Nick was much more than some disenfranchised punker. He embraced beauty, art, poetry, and goodwill as readily as anger, pain, and malice. The intensity of his range was inspiring, and I had hoped to become lifelong friends and partners in his personal and musical discovery of self and life. I miss him and think of him often. I'm mad at him for fucking up, and cheating me and everyone who loves him of time with him. I have dreamt of him – met with him if you will – as I have with other people I love who have left this world before me. He seemed good – really good, as though the demons had gone to rest. I pray his soul is at peace.

Steve Ozark
Booking Agent, Ozark Talent

Myk Malin of Burnt Ramen Studio engineered a demo recording Nick sang on, in late 1995, when

Nick was seventeen, and talked in a letter to me about how difficult Nick still was at the time. He said Nick felt self-conscious doing the 'scratch vocals,' although he did them.

He goes on then, 'The next time I saw Nick was May '97. He had heard some stuff from the studio that was good and wanted to come in to record two more songs. My impression of Nick was totally different, that time he was self-assured and extremely nice.' They recorded two cover tunes, and Nick gave him a copy of his most recent Link 80 CD, *Seventeen Reasons*, and a Link 80 sweatshirt. Myk asked Nick if he could use two of his songs for a compilation called 'Ramen Core', and Nick agreed, and then promised to come back soon to do some more recording. Myk talks about the enormous impact Nick left, and says he wishes he could have helped him.

'In the grand scheme of things, it's difficult to say what really makes a person unique. But it is the savage poetry of his short life that made a great impression on me.' I was deeply touched by his letter.

A memory I will always love of Nick is when I went to see him at a small club filled with smoke and lights and wild-looking kids, many of them in punk rock outfits. There was lots of rainbow-colored hair, and I felt a hundred years old as I waited for him to come on, and watched everyone milling around. There was an aura of expectant tension. I was excited to see him play finally, and thought it would be fun, but I had no particular expectations, and I was in no way prepared for what I saw when his band came on, or the frenzy of the audience that loved him so much.

Nick's band came on, adjusted their instruments, checked their mikes, and within instants exploded to life before me. And although I'm hardly impartial in my assessment of him, Nick was terrific. I was totally unprepared for his professionalism, how powerful the music was, his voice, his stage presence, or the quality of his performance. Nick leapt and jumped, reeled and careened, like a boomerang exploding in midair. I loved it!

And between sets, he told the audience that I was there, and that if it weren't for me and everything I'd done for him, he wouldn't be there. Tears filled my eyes as he said it. And it delighted me to watch the audience go crazy over him. They reached, they screamed, they sang with him, they begged for more. And after the performance, he was besieged by groupies. It was an incredible experience watching him, and I was vastly impressed by his power and magnetism as a performer. There was absolutely no doubt in my mind, as I realized something I never had before, Nick was going to go a long, long way as a rock star.

Afterwards, he came to find me, and I told him how impressed I was. Our friend Jo Schuman was with me, and even with her vast expertise in the music scene, she was as impressed as I. I was so proud of him, and as he dripped sweat, he put an arm around me, as girls clamored to get near him. It was an unforgettable moment in my life. One of many that I will always cherish. And I've been told by his friends that whether I was in the audience or not, he always dedicated at least one song to me at each performance.

I saw him at a bigger nightclub after that. It drew a tougher, older audience and had room for a far bigger crowd. The audience looked blasé when he arrived onstage and he looked nervous, at least to the practiced eye of his mother. He started off somewhat cautiously, and within minutes it had happened again. He had taken a huge hall of strangers, and turned it into a sea of writhing, screaming, dancing, singing, shouting people. Nick onstage was magic.

I loved going to see him. I loved what he did, how he looked when he performed, and when I went back to see him at the small club again, I squinted at him from the distance, trying to pretend I was a stranger. What I saw was an incredibly handsome young man, and I was startled to realize that he was very sexy. He was muscular and well formed, and I could see why the girls screamed when they saw him. He had so much charm, a dazzling smile, his arms seemed to reach out to the crowd and pull them to him. He had incredible charisma. And aside from that, he had real talent. He had a great voice, and the lyrics that he sang, when you could understand the words, were very well written. He made me so proud, and I had so much fun going to his concerts. The best part was that we were proud of each other.

My son and I were both very lucky. At an early age, we had both found our passions. I was about his age, nineteen, when I wrote my first book. And now, he was willing to work his tail off to get what he wanted, and enjoyed it while he did it. There was absolutely nothing else in the world he loved more than his music and his band.

*Nick onstage, at shows, in
concerts, at sixteen*

One of Nick's closest friends was another young performer on the music scene, perhaps his best friend, Sam Ewing. Nick and everyone else called him Sammy the Mick, and he and Nick used to love to horse around before, during, and after Nick's concerts. He talks of the unstoppable passion Nick had for his music, and how much he loved singing. They were like two kids just playing and having fun, but no matter how much Nick played around, nothing in the world could stop Nick when he was singing.

'I always tried to sabotage Nick when he was onstage. I would trip him and throw things at him, and push him offstage. And once, he hit the ground hard. I jumped up and actually lifted him off his feet. He wanted to scream, but Nick continued to sing. I turned away from him and he just went on singing. I whipped around and kicked his feet out from beneath him. He fell to his knees, still singing. I reached down to push him over, and he pulled my shirt off. I jumped on top of him, and we wrestled. And all the while, Nick sang his little heart out. I grabbed a water bottle and dumped it on his head. He did the same. The entire crowd was doused. And through it all, Nick just kept on singing!'

Not all his performances or their antics were as rough as that, but the two had a great time together. Sammy went on some of their short tours, and supported Nick, particularly if he was down, or bone tired after a string of shows and concerts. Sammy the Mick was always there to cheer him on and boost his spirits. The two got identical tattoos with the word *brothers* on them. He loved them. Another manic passion.

And Nick gave Sammy a birthday cake after a performance at the Club Cocodrie, and presented it to him onstage. Inevitably, it turned into a food fight. There were a thousand Nick and Sammy stories. They flirted with girls together, sang together, and generally fooled around, egging each other on to behave like wild, happy children. Sammy the Mick came to Hawaii at Easter with all of us that year, and he and Nick looked like choir boys, in gray suits, on Thanksgiving. They were the best of friends, and full of fun, and it always warmed my heart to see them together.

Nick was not only singing but managing the band when he was eighteen, booking them on tours around the state. He arranged publicity, organized a video. He seemed to be juggling a dozen people who were peripherally involved in his career, and he did it all between constant performances and rehearsals. We had always respected each other, but now we had more than just admiration for each other, we had something in common. We both worked in creative fields that we loved.

I loved talking about his work with him, he took it so seriously, and I knew he would go far with it, because he was willing to put his heart and soul into it. He couldn't have done otherwise. It was his passion. It was what he lived for. From those early lip-sync contests at school, he was suddenly the real thing. He was on his way to becoming a rock star.

I think one of his finest moments, and my favorite

memory, was his last spring with us; before he went on tour, his little brother Maxx entered the lip-sync contest at school, the same school where Nick had gone, and the band he was portraying was Link 80. Samantha dressed him up to look like Nick, dyed his hair black like Nick's, gelled it, and Victoria carefully painted tattoos identical to Nick's. It was a thrill even for me to see one son onstage, so competently imitating the other. And Nick just loved it. Nick watched him, fascinated, grinning from ear to ear, and cheered him on from his seat. He had brought the rest of the band with him, and Maxx was thrilled to have him there. It was one of those absolutely perfect moments that I will forever cherish. I will never forget Nick's smile as he watched Maxx, or Maxx's look of adoration for his older brother. Nick was his hero, and he adored Maxx.

Nick's relationship with all his siblings was extremely good. From whatever skirmishes he'd had with his younger siblings in his early years, once he matured and was on lithium, he had grown into a loving, protective, very conscientious older brother. He felt a particular kinship with Maxx, perhaps because they were boys, and autographed a poster to him on Maxx's eleventh birthday that said 'To the coolest Traina since me, love from your big bro, Nick.' Maxx idolized him, his 'coolness,' his music, his sense of fun. Nick never lost his child-like playfulness, but over the years he added to it the wisdom and insight, sensitivity and compassion he'd added to his own soul, through years of crawling bravely through his pain and struggles. He had a lot to give us all, and didn't hesitate to do so, but over the many layers of his soul and spirit was a thick overlay of just pure sheer fun. He loved to tease his sisters, and play with them, admired them enormously, and the last year he would look at them in awe, and then talk to me privately, feeling, as I did at times, both stunned and old. 'How did they get so grown up and so beautiful?' he would say to me in a whisper after they left the room. He was crazy about them, adored his baby sister Zara, and was fiercely protective of them all, particularly of Sammie.

Nick and Sam always shared a magical relationship. A spoken and unspoken bond that, when they were together, shut all others out. She would have done anything for him, and done anything to protect him. I knew, from watching them over the years, how deep their bond went. They were like Siamese twins of the soul. And although she always fought us bitterly over the idea that there might be something 'wrong' with Nick, I think she knew it herself, and wanted to do anything she could to protect him from getting hurt. More than anyone else, he confided in her, and she in him. All of which was why what came later was perhaps hardest of all for her. Although I know full well how much the entire family suffered when we lost him, sometimes I feared that Sam took it the hardest of all. But one cannot measure grief or pain, who am I to say how deeply the others felt? I know that each of his siblings felt his loss as an irreparable blow, as I did. Beatie, surely, felt the same agony we did. He was, for his entire life, her baby brother, the baby that had been born to be hers. Like Sam, she protected him fiercely, and used her own professional psychiatric expertise to help him when she could be useful.

In the last two years, when I took an occasional vacation with friends, Beatrix always stood in for me, making responsible decisions, and reaching out to him as best she could. She hospitalized him once, when he would listen to no one else and had stopped taking his lithium for a while. She had a gentle, persuasive way with him, and he respected and loved her. And he was particularly proud to be a part of her wedding. Nick's relationships in the family were usually powerful, and for the most part very good.

After Nick was gone, wrestling with her own agony, Beatie wrote this about what she was feeling.

Tears

I am drowning in my own tears.
I stumble wearily through the blur of days
    while dreading nights
I am a captive of my nightmares and the
    darkness.
Dusk is the daily reminder that the
    nightmare is alive and well.
There is no escape for me.
My heart screams in agony.
There is no reprieve, no help for me.
There is no balm for my wounds because
    they are so deep.
I am writing and my search for safety is
    fruitless.
Everywhere I look I see others grieving you.
    They are thrashing.

You were my sunshine, my carefree
     abandon.
Your smile was my hope.
I do not know how to live without you.
I am 30 but feel the burden of someone a
     hundred.
My soul is old.
I scurry about frantically because the
     alternative is so tempting.
I fear the indulgence of staying in my bed,
     my cocoon.
In the dream I pleaded with you to stay.
Your eyes danced, your smile embraced me.
I begged for the mercy of getting you back.
Your words 'you know' echoed each time I
     asked.
'You know' meant 'I can't stay.'
I struggled to keep the grip on your hand,
     your smell, your touch.
The notion of waking up without you on
     Christmas is devastating.
There is no Santa Claus.
I rise early each day to walk off the demons.
Instead of peace, I have cried through many
     miles in many cities.
I am so tired and this journey seems endless.
I am trying to no avail.
Struggling is not familiar to me.
You have left an abyss and I am hanging by
     a thread.
I am curious, so I peer over the edge.
I take nothing for granted.
Even breathing is a challenge. Asthma is a
     frequent dictator.

Often I hear my jagged breaths before I feel
them.
The harsh sound pierces through the music
of my Walkman.
My anguish breaks out.
I have a rock in my throat.
I wheeze. Being still offers no comfort.
I feel awkward and uncomfortable in my
own skin.
I am a snail without a shell.
I try to retreat into the safety of hiding.

Nick also had a strong tie to Trevor and Todd,
his older brothers. They are John's two sons, but
our plan to bring the children up as one family had
been successful and taken hold from the first. Nick
never felt less than a full brother to Trevor and
Todd, nor did they. Other than Beatie, Trevor is
probably the most 'respectable' member of the
family, a serious citizen, young businessman,
conservative by nature, though well able to enjoy a
good laugh and full of fun. Nick always said he was
'perfect,' so 'cool' (the ultimate compliment from
Nick), and so 'totally decent and nice.' He loved
and respected Trevor, enjoyed spending time with
him, and they went to movies and shows together.
But seeing them together always made me smile.
One couldn't have found two men on earth who
looked less alike. The one in all his rad, mod, funky,
punky, earring, nose ring gear, the other looking
like a Ralph Lauren ad. They are both handsome
boys, but with ten years between them and different
interests and passions, they existed in different
worlds. Trevor designed a Web site for Nick and his

band, which, sadly, never had time to see the light of day before Nick left us.

Nick had more in common with Todd, though he loved them equally. But Todd was outwardly 'cooler,' lived in L.A., and as a struggling young movie producer was more familiar with the vagaries of Nick's music world. For years, they had shared similar taste in bands, laughed at the same things, and Todd was outrageous enough, although nine years older than Nick, to play the same pranks with him. They both had the same fondness for whoopee cushions I did, laughed at the same jokes, and whenever Nick could get away with it under Todd's nose, and he tried hard, liked the same girls. They were soul mates of sorts. And like the rest of us, when Todd lost Nick, he felt as though he had lost a piece of his heart and himself.

Todd and Nick admired each other, understood each other, and were close to each other. Nick's favorite thing in the world, and the ultimate treat for him, was visiting Todd in L.A. Todd even let the entire band stay with him on some of their brief tours to L.A. He was proud of Nick, as we all were, and his eulogy to Nick said it all when he said, 'I am proud to say that Nick became the person he wanted to be. He did tell us all how much he loved us. Nick was a strong person. Nick was a loving, caring, talented, truthful, fully functioning, fully realized person who turned his life around on his own accord. He became the person he wanted to be. He was a success. I'd have to say that Nick Traina was one of the greatest successes I have ever known.'

And on his monument, he put something that

touched my heart and soul, and surely Nick's, and said it all:

'Dear Nick, You were my shadow. You were my buddy. You became an inspiration. I am so happy for the times we shared. You will always be my bro. I will miss you so much. Love, Todd.'

When Todd was nineteen, he got a tiny purple fox tattooed on his hip, which no one knew about. It was in a spot none of us was likely to see. But Nick saw it, thought it was the 'coolest' thing he'd ever seen, and vowed to do the same one day. But in usual Nick fashion, of course, he took the ball (or the tattoo in this case) and ran with it – all the way. Nick didn't do things in half measures, or subtly. When he did things, you knew about them. They were painted in bold, neon colors, and way beyond life-sized. Nick went 'all the way' with his tattoos. No tiny little barely visible fox for him! (Todd's now-famous tattoo is still legend in the family. I've heard a lot about it, but have never seen it, and doubt that I ever will!)

Nick got his first tattoo when he was seventeen, and it was a trauma for both of us. I hated it, and so did Nick after he got it. He agreed to have it removed, and he did, though the process must have been painful. He got a second one, and had it removed as well, to humor me. But on his third one, I gave up. Eventually his arms were covered with them. That last summer, he had 'Traina' in large Gothic letters blazoned across his shoulder blades. And at the very least, he added another one to his chest which said prophetically 'Only God Can Judge Me.' I hate tattoos generally, but somehow on Nick they looked all right. He was so good-looking and they somehow fit with his persona onstage. The last performances I saw of him, he sang with his shirt off, as his tattoos danced, his muscles rippled and his body glistened. What he did was exhausting, but he never seemed tired when he did it. He looked as though he could have gone on forever.

At seventeen, Nick put out two single records, and he was eighteen when his first CD was released. And I was so proud of him. He made several, and was also asked to sing at other people's recordings. He was good, very good, and the other musicians and performers he worked with knew it. And the lyrics he wrote always had a message that his audiences liked. There were songs about Brotherhood, Unity, against violence and racism, about young people rising up to outshine the old, and even some about me, and his father. Kids loved his songs, and although I couldn't always decipher them, they seemed to know all the words when he sang them:

Time
I spend all my time hoping
That you're going to find another way
And yer not gonna shut me up
Cuz I've got too much to say.
If you live to be happy all the time
Then you overlook what's there.
And I wish I had more time
Cuz life's too short not to care.
Wasting away on detachment
You think it doesn't apply.

But only when you apply yourself
Will you be able to see the lies.
Everybody will tell you something
And who knows who makes sense
But to actually admit
You don't know shit
Takes an awful lot of strength
Keep your life focused
And always do what's right . . .
And cherish every minute God gives you
Don't go without a fight.

Used To

There's no point in fighting me
Cuz I've already lost
This life is but a battle
That I've already fought.
Every day I bow my head
Surrender to myself.
I used to be so strong
I used to not need help
I used to be a boy
I grew into a man
But I'm not even living
I don't know what I am.
A life that's just spent dying
Is not a life at all.
Walking through this life
And through this living hell
It really can't last much longer
I've lost all I once had.
I know it could be worse.
But still it's pretty bad.

from 'Spacey'

. . . I'd like to stay a secret,
Like walking in the dark,
If no one knows you, no one cares
So no one breaks your heart.
In half-closed dreams I see myself
And I'm standing on my feet
But all my time's spent sitting down
I'm always half asleep.
This world has nothing left in it
It died when I was born.
I used to have a purpose
But there is none to have one for . . .

from 'Ha Ha Ha'

. . . this world is in such disarray
It's pathetic and it's sad
So while I'm doing good
And I should be happy now
I can't seem to figure what happiness is about.
And so everything will end
The same way it begins
I will die with nothing.
I will never win.

Julie said once that his songs were his suicide note, and many of them poured out his sorrows. But there were a lot of more upbeat ones, and angry ones, and rebellious ones. He wrote a lot of songs, and later on, he did happier, more positive ones with his new band, Knowledge.

He loved touring, too. It was an adventure to him. He loved the people he met, the clubs where he played. He loved everything about the music scene. It was as though he had grown up to be exactly who he wanted. And I loved seeing that in him, that raucous pleasure and sheer glee that came from doing something he loved. He could play, jump, dance, scream, shout, and sing for hours. I feel just like that as I pound away on my typewriter through the night. No day or night is too long, or too tiring, as long as I can keep writing. And Nick felt exactly the same way as long as he could keep singing.

I was impressed by the fact that he managed not to let it interfere with school. And he did fairly well at the school he had gone to since he was a sophomore. But I also think that he was relieved when the school put him on 'independent study' when he was a senior. It gave him more time to practice and rehearse, book tours for the weekends, and from time to time, do his homework.

Nick viewed his transition to independent study as a blessing, but it actually came about for a variety of reasons. For one thing, he stayed up late at night and was tired in the morning when he came in. They had a couch in the front of the school, and he was never embarrassed about just crashing there, and snoring loudly. It didn't exactly impress his teachers with his enthusiasm about their subjects. But when forced to, he could also sleep in their classrooms. The headmaster called me from time to time to discuss it. Nick was outspoken, but well liked, and he did reasonably well, but he was still Nick. A lot of the time he did what he wanted, and as much as they could, they let him.

The final incident that led them to release him

Nick did fantastic jumps and hops onstage.
These at about seventeen

from classes was a little more delicate, but I think convinced them that he was just too independent and eccentric to have in the classroom. He disagreed with something someone said, and in a spirit of fun, dropped his pants in front of everyone. They called me immediately, and later that day, I discussed it with Nicky. And I looked serious when I did it. He on the other hand looked vastly amused and told me to 'chill out, Mom.' No. This time I wasn't 'chilling,' I told him. I was unhappy about it, and told him it was inappropriate behavior.

'Everyone does that at school, Mom!' he insisted with that big, goofy grin of his, which was different from the seductive grin, or the dazzling smile of the performer. But I argued with him, 'everyone' did not do that, which was why the school had called me.

They felt that he was a little beyond what they wanted to deal with in class. But they were willing to keep him as part of the student body, as long as he came in for tests, and sent in his assignments. Nick was enchanted with the arrangement. He never dropped his pants anywhere else that I knew of, except once, at a freshman high school dance he played at Samantha's school when he was eighteen. And I was mad as hell about it, and he must have mortified Samantha. But she loved him so much, and was such a fan of his, that she brushed it off and said everyone thought it was funny. It was Nick's old battle with impulse control again. Now and then, he'd lose it. And other than that, he never dropped his pants onstage. But I'm sure his fans, particularly the groupies who followed him every-where, would have loved it!

Nick's career was something I was very proud of him for. He did a great job in a short time, and Link 80 did extraordinarily well considering how young they all were, and how little experience they had when they got together. And I was particularly proud when I went to Europe when Nick was on his big tour, walked into a music store in London and saw Nick's CD's . . . that's my boy, I wanted to tell everyone in the store . . . look, he's a star! That's my baby! What a good job he did. He was a shooting star. A bright, brief flash across the Heavens of the music world. A comet. Would that he could have stayed there, high in the sky, singing his heart out forever.

16

Two warning shots rang out in the silence

John and I shocked the rest of the family to its core when we separated in the summer of 1995. Nick was seventeen. And we actually separated in August, but didn't tell the children till September. We were trying to find the right time to break the news to them. But as with any bad news, there is none.

The children were particularly shaken by it, because we had been fairly discreet about our disagreements. Things had been strained and often chilly between us for three years, and maybe it was just that the children were so used to it, they thought we'd live that way forever. At times, even I did.

And I thought the day we broke the news to them was the worst day of my life. But much to my chagrin, we've had worse since then.

We told the kids over Labor Day weekend that we were getting separated, which was all we were doing, for the moment. We were all devastated. It was the end of a dream for me, and John, the end of a safe, magical time for the children. And it took a lot for us to get there. John and I had not made the decision lightly.

And when we told Nick, he hardly seemed to notice. He was perfectly cool, and seemed totally unaffected, unlike all the others. But he began acting out two days later and continued to do so for weeks until we put him in the hospital for two weeks in October. He didn't have the stability to cope with it. But the rest of us weren't coping with it that well either. It was a tough winter, a hard year. But eventually, to the best of our abilities, we all adjusted. John and I still made an effort to keep up communication, and even spend time together with the children, particularly over the holidays. But it was a hard time for everyone, Nick no more than the others. Once he settled down with it, he handled it as well as everyone else did.

The only landmark I remember that year was in December when I actually said out loud to a group of friends at a dinnertable that Nick was manic-depressive. They weren't close friends, and it was the first time I had admitted it in public. It felt like an important moment, and said to me, and to them, that I loved him the way he was, was proud of him anyway, and accepted the hand fate had dealt us. The people I said it to were quiet at first, and then asked some questions about it. I remember that my voice was shaking when I answered. But it was a first step for me. It was the beginning of being open about Nick's problems, and not hiding them. And it gave me an opportunity to say how proud I was of him. He was working hard on his music then, and doing wonderfully on the lithium. I still considered

*Thanksgiving,
1995*

*Nick on Mother's
Day, 1996*

Summer 1996, left to right, Victoria, Nick, Zara,
Maxx, Beatie, Todd, Sam, Trevor, Vanessa

it the miracle drug that had saved him. And even today, wouldn't say anything different.

He turned eighteen in May of '96, and it was an important event to him. Perhaps too much so. It symbolized freedom to him, and adulthood. It was as though he expected cannons to go off on the first of May, and everyone to see him differently all of a sudden. But of course, they didn't. He still had to have attendants with him, and Julie to monitor him, still had to see his psychiatrist constantly, and take medication. I think somewhere in a secret place he had hoped that the problems would all disappear like magic on his birthday along with his illness. But even once he'd turned eighteen, he was still stuck with the same limitations, and he was unhappy about it.

He started threatening to move out of Julie's house, where he'd been for nearly two years, and suddenly refused to do things he was expected to do, or knew he had to. 'I'm eighteen now, you can't make me!' He sounded five when he said it. And there were a lot of arguments from the moment he turned eighteen. He wanted everything to be different for him, and it wasn't. It couldn't be. He was still emotionally young for his age, and had the same lousy impulse control, which was only slightly held in check by his medications. But he was still just as liable to do something wonky. And even for a kid without the problems he had, eighteen is not usually synonymous with total autonomy. But Nick was tired of other people making rules for him, and having to live by them.

And in the mental hospitals where he stayed occasionally, there were mental health workers who explained their rights to people like Nick, and told them they had the right to make choices. The choice Nick made in September was to stop taking his lithium, and the reality was that we couldn't force him to take it. Officially at least, he was an adult now.

We had tried to give him independence in other ways. He had graduated from high school in June, and was taking courses at a local junior college, and we were proud of that. And Julie and her family had just moved in the fall, into a house that suited her and our needs perfectly. It was a large, comfortable house for her family, with a room for Nick if he needed it, and a little mother-in-law cottage where Nick could live independently from her, while still being close enough to be safe. Nick could sleep there if he was in good shape, and behaving, and he loved it.

But in spite of that, he felt he needed to make a bigger statement about his coming of age. He absolutely refused to take his medication, and we all knew it was only a matter of time before disaster struck him. We just didn't know what form it would take then. But no amount of cajoling, wheedling, or even threatening would make him take it. He said he felt fine, the lithium had cured him, and he no longer needed to take it. It was typical behavior for a manic-depressive. Many of them stop taking their medication from time to time, usually because they feel so normal on the lithium that it's deceptive, and they convince themselves that the problem that led them to it has vanished. Nick was no different, but as the days and weeks rolled by, he became more and more difficult and unmanageable. He was like an express train careening seriously offtrack, and I was desperately worried about what would happen. But I had an unavoidable trip to England for a few days where I got a series of frantic phone calls from Julie. Nick needed to be hospitalized but he wouldn't agree to go. Now that he was eighteen, he didn't have to do that either.

We no longer had the right to hospitalize him when we felt he needed it, or if the medication needed adjusting. He had to agree to go, and of course he wouldn't. The more he needed it, the more he refused. It was an insane system. This time my daughter Beatrix went to Julie's and spent hours with Nick, cajoling him into going to the hospital. They must have had a hell of a time with him, and called me several times late that night. But he finally went and bounced right back out two days later. But I came home that night and saw him as soon as I got back. It was obvious that he needed help. Without his medication, he was getting wildly manic, and we all knew that crushing depression would follow.

I spoke to his psychiatrist the next day, but our hands were tied. We couldn't prove he was a danger to himself. He never really had been, and he was certainly not a danger to anyone else. He wasn't aggressive in any way, he was just acting crazy. And living with him must have been driving Julie up the walls. Living with someone in a manic phase is like spending your vacation in a Waring blender. Definitely not easy.

I was particularly aware of it when he called me nearly two weeks later from Julie's house, at four o'clock in the morning. I happened to be working, which was unusual even for me, but I was finishing a project. Nick wanted to know if he could bring someone home to dinner the following week. I assured him he could. And then he called me back every half hour after that to confirm it. He was friendly and adorable on the phone, but wound up like a top. And I called him back the next day with an idea that might or might not work. But I was ready to try anything to convince him to take his medication.

I asked him very inelegantly if there was anything he wanted. If bribery would do it, then that was okay. We had to get him back on lithium and Prozac. Nick thought for a long minute, and then said yes, there was something he wanted.

'Will you go back on lithium if I get it for you?'

'Okay,' he said easily. And I held my breath wondering what it would be. One forgot at times how childish Nick was, particularly off his medication.

'What is it?'

'T-shirts for the band.' That was it? That was all? He was willing to go back on lithium for T-shirts for the band? I almost cried, I was so relieved. And I called the doctor after I hung up, but for some reason the doctor decided to wait till Monday. It was something functional and practical, maybe it had to do with tests or blood levels, or waiting for results, but he'd been off it about six weeks then, and the doctor felt comfortable letting it wait a few more days until after the weekend, and I agreed with him. Nick didn't seem to be in any particular danger. He was just irritable, high strung, and wound up. And if Julie could live with it for three more days, I could.

I went to L.A. that weekend, with Tom, the man I'd been seeing for just over a year by then, the only one I'd dated since the separation. Nicky was extremely fond of him, and the two had formed an instant bond, in typical Nick fashion. Nick either liked you, or he didn't, and he had an uncanny sense about people. He had fallen in love with Tom as soon as they met. Tom is straightforward, kind, intelligent, honorable, and Nick sensed all of it. He was always telling me how much he liked him, and urging me to do something about it.

And we had a great time in L.A. that weekend, although I was in constant contact with Nick and Julie. Nick seemed to be hanging in, and we were all anxious to get him back on his medication on Monday. But in the meantime, Tom and I had a good time in L.A. with friends, and for the first time began talking seriously about the future. We talked a lot about Nick too. Tom was as worried about Nick's unmedicated state as I was. We always talked about Nick, and Tom had taken a backseat position of concern about his illness since he knew him. He cared a lot about Nick, and always inquired about him.

I was still happy about the weekend when I got home. And on Monday morning, my world seemed instantly blown apart when Julie called me, screaming into the phone that Nick was dead. Paramedics were there and trying to revive him. I was hysterical, breathless, horrified, and with shaking hands, dialed John. And I called Tom to tell him seconds after. He was as devastated as I was. What seemed like a thousand phone calls followed.

The paramedics had been able to start his heart again, but had to do so twice more on the way to the hospital. He had obviously overdosed on something, but no one seemed to know what, or why, or how it had happened. Julie had been vacuuming when she got a sudden strange feeling, and went to check on Nick in his cottage. The paramedics said afterwards that although he'd been unconscious for several hours, his heart must have just stopped when she got there. It was a moment of utter panic for all of us. John and I took off for the hospital minutes later. Tom offered to come as well, but it seemed too awkward, and I promised to call him. And all the way across the bay, I prayed that Nick would be alive when I got there. I was barely coherent.

And when I ran into the hospital when we got there, Nick was in terrifying shape. Julie was there waiting for me, and a few minutes later, Nick's psychiatrist arrived, and Camilla joined us shortly after. I was in hell, terrified of losing Nicky.

As best we could figure it, the lack of lithium had apparently gotten to him finally, and he appeared to have attempted suicide. He had used heroin, and an unknown assortment of drugs and poisons, to do it.

Beatrix joined us at the hospital right after I arrived, and Nick was incoherent and wild-eyed in the emergency room of a trauma hospital, where they had brought him. They warned me immediately that he was in an extremely critical condition, and even if he survived, was likely to be brain-damaged. He recognized no one and nothing, his eyes were open but he appeared not to see, could not speak, and was flailing his arms, and making terrifying bovine noises. It is a sound I will never forget, sort of terrible monsterlike moans, and I couldn't help wondering if this would be it for Nick forever, *if* he survived it. But one thing came clear to me very quickly. All those things one says when one isn't faced with a situation like this one, about not wanting your child to survive if he'd be brain-damaged. I didn't care if he'd be a vegetable for the rest of his life, I didn't want to lose him. I didn't care what it took to keep him alive, but I wanted to do it. I didn't want to lose him. I was absolutely certain of it.

But he was in dire shape for hours. And they said that if he were to survive even moderately functional, he would have to come out of it fairly quickly. And four or five hours later, there was no sign of improvement. I went outside once or twice, to cry and call Tom. But there wasn't much to say. The situation looked hopeless.

The entire trauma team was still working on him, but they were getting nowhere.

Finally, as Nick continued to moan and had no consciousness of his whereabouts, I sat down next to him. We had been there by then for eight hours. I took his hand in mine and started talking to him, no matter that he couldn't hear me. Julie tried to talk to him from time to time too, shouting at him to come out of it, to look at us, to hear us. The whole event had been traumatic for her, as she had kept him going with CPR until the paramedics arrived. She had saved him. And if she had vacuumed for five minutes longer, he would have been gone now. I was acutely aware of what I owed her. My son's life, if he survived it, which at that point, was still uncertain.

I talked to Nick endlessly for an hour, sitting close to his ear and telling him over and over again how much I loved him, that I was there, and that I was waiting for him. And John and Beatie stood by, feeling helpless, and watching.

'Come on, Nick . . . I'm here . . . open your eyes . . . look at me . . . it's Mommy . . . I love you, Nicky . . .' It was an endless rote of words, and for a long time it seemed hopeless, but I had convinced myself that somewhere, in the dark hole where he had fallen, he would hear me. I had almost given up, when he turned to me with wild eyes, moaned horribly again for a minute, and then pursed his lips together, trying to make a sound. I wasn't sure if he could see me.

'Mmmmmoooommmm,' he said, and I stood there and cried. He sounded terrible, but he had said 'Mom.' It was like snatching him from the jaws of death as I continued to talk to him, and they worked on him. I felt as though I had pulled him back from the abyss where he had fallen.

Hours later they moved him to the ICU, and he was slightly more coherent, but nothing was assured yet. And they only had a vague idea of what poisons and drugs he had taken. And a slightly better picture of the damage he had caused himself. He had injured his liver, kidneys, spleen, and deafened himself, perhaps temporarily, perhaps not, and his legs were paralyzed. The motor skills in his arms were affected, his vision, and perhaps his heart. And they were not clear yet about the full damage to his brain.

But when I finally left that night, they thought he would survive, though he was not completely out of the woods yet, and wouldn't be for several days. I went home for a few hours to the other children, and explained what had happened. Everyone was worried sick about him.

We had worked out shifts at the hospital. John stayed until I got back, and Julie, Camilla, and I agreed to take eight-hour shifts with him for as long as we had to. And Beatrix was going to be there as much as she could, when she wasn't working.

By the next day, things had improved, but only slightly. They were doing a thousand tests on him, and Paul, his attendant, sat at his bedside and cried like a baby. We all did. My beautiful boy was hovering on the edge of death, and I could only imagine what had brought him to it.

The next week was something of a nightmare, but he got better day by day. He went from neuro-ICU to coronary-ICU to renal-ICU and at one point, as they wheeled him from one ICU unit to another, for tests and closer observation, Nick looked at me with that grin I loved so much and said, 'Why don't they just leave me in the parking lot so I can smoke?' Very funny. I wanted to shake him for what he'd done, and make him swear he'd never leave me. The thought of what had very nearly happened made me shudder.

He admitted to having been depressed and fed up and not thinking clearly and the neurologist had started him on lithium and Prozac again within hours of his arrival.

Three days after he came in was Halloween, and I arrived with an armload of decorations for his room, a silly T-shirt, and orange-and-chocolate cupcakes. He loved Halloween and I didn't want him to miss it. Little did I know it would be his last one. I wore a purple wig and a witch costume to amuse him.

But he was lucky this time. By the end of the week, he still couldn't feel his legs, but he could walk, somewhat awkwardly, they had figured out that his heart was all right and he hadn't damaged the lining, his hearing had returned, the rest of him was still a mess, but he was no longer in danger.

I was commuting to the hospital, an hour away, twice a day, and running between Nick and the other children. It was a shocking experience for all of us, which left us rocked to the core, half angry and half hysterical over what Nick had done and very nearly accomplished. I think we were all reverberating from the emotions. The younger children, in particular, were badly shaken.

Nick stayed at the trauma hospital for eight days, but at the end of a week, they very responsibly asked us to move him. They said they weren't equipped to help him psychiatrically, and their hospital wasn't set up to protect him. They were afraid that he would try it again, which sounded absurd to me. I was sure he had learned his lesson. He was being wonderfully affectionate, and seemed happy to be alive, and maybe by then the lithium was helping a little, or at least the Prozac. His friends were visiting him and he seemed in remarkably good spirits. The rest of us, particularly Julie and I, looked exhausted and frazzled. I had never in my entire life been through anything so stressful. But miraculously, they were beginning to think that he might recover completely. His brain functions had been assured by then, and he had sustained no permanent damage, which really was a miracle. The only lingering problems he had were some liver disfunction, and the fact that his legs were still partially numb. But they said they could stay that way for six months or more. He was going to have to get therapy to help them.

The trauma hospital had been extraordinary with him, and I was immensely grateful to them. There were so many people to be grateful to. Julie, the paramedics who had continued CPR, the emergency room staff, the people in the ICU, a wonderful neurologist who really cared about Nick, and an extraordinary psychiatrist who got Nick's number the first time she met him. She was the one who suggested we move him, and quickly. And if only to humor them, I did. Eight days after he arrived, Nick went by ambulance to a hospital in the city with a psychiatric unit. He was put in a room with a suicide watch on him, and I could finally visit him easily, without negotiating the bridge or rush hour traffic twice a day. It made my life a little easier, and gave me more time at home with the other children. I finally began to relax, knowing that he was in good hands, and I no longer had to worry about him. All we had to do was get him on his feet, literally, keep an eye on his liver, and get enough lithium back into him to settle him down again. Compared to what we'd just been through, that seemed easy, and every minute of every day, I was grateful that he was still with us.

In fact, by the time we'd settled him in, he was not only in good spirits, but somewhat feisty. His friends were visiting him, and somehow I managed to close my eyes to the danger signs, although I am not usually prone to denial. But I considered what had happened an aberration, because he had been off lithium at the time. I knew that once back on, it was unlikely to happen again. But what I underestimated entirely, or had never been told, was how lethal his disease was. In my view, it was something that could make him unhappy all his life, but not something that could kill him. I missed that message completely.

Supposedly, sixty percent of all manic-depressives attempt suicide, and thirty percent of all manic-depressives are successful at it. I'm not totally sure of that statistic but if it is even close to accurate, it's very impressive. I never realized that Nick had a thirty percent chance of dying as a result of his disease, or I would have been even more panicked.

As it was, I wrote him a poem, which told him how I felt about what he had done. It said it all, and Nick carried it in his wallet forever after and said he loved it.

TO NICKY

because I love you
You didn't come into my
    life
    easily or smoothly,
    without decision

or confusion,
you came as a surprise,
    a person and event
    I had to decide
    how much

314

I wanted.
I struggled,
    wanting you,
        not knowing you,
            not sure of you
or myself,
    or how to have you.
But nonetheless,
        I chose you,
    with no idea how
        I would house
            or clothe
                you.
No one to help me,
        No one to share,
            No one to care,
    only me and Beatie.
You were ours then.
And even then,
    you did not come home
        easily
            or smoothly.
Instead of one watermelon
    hidden in my dress,
            you looked like
                seven,
    you made people smile
            and chuckle
        as Beatie and I waited
            for you,
    and then you came,
        not easily or smoothly,
        with as much noise
            as you could muster,

crashing into my world
        as you and I held
hands,
and I promised you an
eternity
    of love and protection.
    you ate for twelve,
        and I loved you
            for two hundred,
my perfect gift,
    most cherished child,
            funniest,
    most beautiful,
        you were so anxious
to be part of things,
        you talked to me,
        and told me every-
thing
    long before you were
        supposed to.
    it all came
        much too easily and
smoothly
and you began wearing
my hats
    and beads,
        disco dancing
    and loving clowns
        and wearing my heart
on your sleeve,
    as you ran the world
while still wearing sleepers.
    you owned my bed, my
heart,

my life,
   you wore black turtle-
necks
in school, instead of white,
   and learned to say and
spell
   everything perfectly,
      but backward,
   you made me laugh,
      you made me cry,
   you played airplanes
      with my heart,
and you and I always
knew
   that you were
      a special person.
      too special,
         too wise,
too omniscient
   and too blind,
   you saw the world
      too clearly
   and not at all,
      and you and I
have known each
other's souls
and hearts and minds,
   while inside you burned
      with a fire
         that nearly ate you.
and through your eyes,
i saw your darkest hours,
      and brightest lights
      and brilliant sunsets,

   we lived through
storms,
and stood hand in hand
   in the rain,
      and I promised you
         I would always
            be there.
but yesterday,
   beloved boy,
      you hid from me
in a place
   where,
      but for a moment,
         you told yourself
i could not find you,
   hiding as you once did
as a child,
      beneath my bed,
         inside my head,
behind curtains,
      and inside boxes,
      so sure,
         so very sure
   that this time
      no one would find you.
they called
   to tell me
      you were dead,
that you had been
   ripped
      from my heart,
         my head,
   that you had gone away
      to a place where

316

no one could find
you.
you thought to hide there
    for an hour,
        a day,
    you sought white
lights,
        you went to play,
        you tried to free
            yourself
            from the agonies
                that bound you,
    but i,
        knowing the places
            where you hide,
that you will always be
            my child,
    knew
        that, if they let me,
i could find you.
i ran through the darkness
    filled with rain,
        knowing just
how great your pain,
    and found you
        hiding there,
a small black tiny ball
        of terror
            and silence,
there was nothing
    in your eyes,
        no win,
no prize,
    and even then,

my love,
you could not go
    easily and smoothly
        i will not let you.
i will not let you
    run and hide,
        i will not let you
            flee, or die.
I reached down deep
    into that dark, dark well
where you had fallen
yesterday and grabbed
you.
    no life to live
        when you are gone,
no laughter,
    no smiles,
        no sorrow greater
than this one,
but it was your choice
    this time,
        not mine,
i held out my hand to
you
    once more
        and would not
            leave you.
you sat there
    poised
        for so long,
deciding which way to
turn,
    i knew your anguish,
        felt your pain,

know infinitely
   the terrors that burn
you.
      and then slowly,
   barely,
      nearly not at all
        you turned,
      you looked at me
      and saw me,
and said Mom . . .
   and slowly, slowly,
      ever so slowly,
        crawled back
        up
          the mountain
and now you are here,
      poised on the ledge,
   still balanced
      on the edge,
   still here,
      still mine,
        still hurting,

the last sunrise
   that never came,
      the final hour
      not to be
        this time,
your hand in mine again,
   i will never let you
        go
   easily or smoothly,
i will bring you back
      again,
i will always know your
pain,
   i will never let you
run swiftly into darkness.
   you will not go as you
came
you must never do this
again.
   you must stay now,
   if only because I love
you.

Once Nick was settled into his new hospital, I tried to calm down myself, and was looking forward to a weekend with my children. Tom and I went to visit Nick on Thursday night, and Tom made Nick promise, for whatever it was worth, that he would never do anything like that again. Nick promised he wouldn't, and looked as though he meant it. We ran into Todd at the hospital too, and the four of us sat and chatted for a while. And I know Beatrix and Trevor had also been to see him. And I let Samantha go for a few minutes, and bring him food. He hated the food there, but otherwise, he seemed comfortable and happy. And Sam, particularly, was thrilled to see him. He had scared all of us, and it was as though we each needed to touch him and see him, to reassure ourselves that he was still with us.

Tom and I had a nice evening with the kids on Friday night, and were relaxing with his arm around me when the phone rang.

It was the hospital, and they quickly told me that Nick had tried it again, but they had saved him. They had found him almost immediately, had to start his heart three times this time, but they already felt that he was out of danger by the time they called me. It had all happened very quickly. And they believed he had overdosed on some drugs that friends had brought him. 'Friends.' Not my definition of friendship, to bring a mentally ill boy drugs in a psychiatric ward, on suicide watch. I was too stunned to react at first, but Tom looked distressed. I told him what had happened, and a little while later he left. He was tired too, and wanted to go home and get some rest. We had all been through the wringer.

He thought I should go to the hospital that night, but after he left, I didn't. I was too angry at Nick to go. I knew he was out of danger, and I didn't want to see him. I just couldn't. And there was nothing I could do to help him. He was safe. He was alive, and I needed some time to absorb what had happened. Julie and I talked on the phone, and I called John and Dr Seifried. But it was obvious that the demons that were driving Nick now were stronger than he was. And I was heartsick when I went to bed that night, but grateful again that he had survived. But I was beginning to wonder how often I was going to have to be grateful after Nick dared the fates to take him.

I fell asleep, too exhausted to undress, and went to see Nick in the morning. He looked awful. His system had received another huge shock. His legs were worse again, and having his heart started three times once it stopped hadn't done much for his complexion. He looked almost transparent, and was still fairly groggy.

I was upset when I went home, deeply troubled by the turn Nick's life seemed to be taking. And as I had tried to point out to him that afternoon, to no avail, he was taking all of us with him. If he went down, like passengers on a ship, we were all going to go down with him. The bonds that we shared, the unit that we were as a family, were irrevocably tied to him and to each other. We talked about it, and I know he felt some remorse, but I'm not sure he truly understood it. I reminded him that if nothing else, he would break Samantha's heart, not to mention mine and everyone else's, if he succeeded. None of us would ever be the same again without him.

And when Tom came by that night, it was obvious that he had done some serious thinking. He needed a break from the relationship he said, and time to clear his head. It was suddenly clear to him what he'd be taking on, if we stayed together. And I was devastated over his conclusion, but even in my disappointment, I couldn't really blame him. Nick had gone down in flames twice in ten days. It had to make Tom wonder what his life would be like if we ever got married. I'm sure it was a frightening prospect. It was, even for me, knowing how fragile Nick was, and how easily tragedy could strike us. I understood it, but for the first time in his life, I was angry at Nicky. For the first time, his illness and the manifestations of it, had actually cost me someone I loved dearly. And for the next several days, I was torn between grief and resentment.

Nick sensed it when I next visited him, although I didn't say anything, but I was sad, and we were so close that he knew it. He asked what was wrong, and I was vague, and then he asked for Tom, and met my eyes, and knew before I even told him. I didn't have to. He understood it. He guessed Tom's reaction to his latest drama. I tried to make light of it, and said things would be okay, but it was actually Nick who reassured me, and told me Tom was a great guy, and that he'd be back. I wasn't as sure he would, but it gave us a chance to talk about Nick again, and what he was doing to all of us. I suppose at that point I didn't fully understand that he had no choice. I felt as though it was a decision he was making coherently, which of course it wasn't. We had a good talk, and a good cry, and a big hug, and I tried to explain to him again how devastated I would be without him. I wish he had understood that, and could have done something about it, but he couldn't.

Nick was right about Tom of course. His 'breather' lasted for nearly three weeks, a long three weeks to me, and he came back with apologies and greater insight, the night before Thanksgiving. We agreed to take things one day at a time, and not make plans for the future. I had a lot to be thankful for that year, not only for Tom's return, but Nick's survival. He came out of the hospital the day before Thanksgiving, and was back at Julie's, under impeccably close supervision.

All of the children were with me for Thanksgiving, as was John, as we still shared the holidays with the children. And Nick and his friend 'Sammy the Mick' arrived in time for dinner, all dressed up and beautiful in shirts and ties and suits. It was a Thanksgiving I will never forget, full of joy, and grace and gratitude for all the things in life that matter.

And when we sat down for turkey, I looked silently at Nick and counted my blessings, praying it would never happen again, and that he would never leave us. I wanted to believe with all my heart that he wouldn't. It was his last Thanksgiving.

17

Third Warning

Nick had inadvertently given us an ace in the hole
with his second suicide attempt. It was an experience I would have much preferred not to live
through, but in endangering himself twice, he had
given us the legal right to hospitalize him whenever
we felt he needed to be, or if he stopped taking his
medication. Because in doing so, he would jeopardize his life, as he had so amply proven. We would
never have to wait again for six weeks after he
stopped taking his lithium. We could put him in the
hospital the first day he missed it. No arguments,
no explanations.

We could 'slap' him with what was called a 5150,
a public health statute that would allow us to
suspend his rights and keep him in the hospital for
three days, and then follow it up with a 5250,
which would give us up to two weeks longer, and
so on. We had even discussed the possibility of a
conservatorship, but there were disadvantages to
that, too, and we had decided against it.

And with his lithium levels high again, Nick
seemed normal. He was working hard with the

band, back on his feet, and in relatively good spirits. He had no memory of the hideous experience we'd all shared at the trauma hospital. He had scared the hell out of everyone but himself. And he went back to business as usual with Link 80.

By Christmas he was leaping around again, and playing rock star. My romance was back on track. The children had settled down again, after the shock Nick had provided them, and all seemed to be going well. Although I had a constant underlying feeling of nervousness about Nicky now. He had shown us what he was capable of, without his medication. But now we had the legal right to force him to take it if we needed to. But he no longer objected to it, and he took it as he was supposed to.

In January he went on a short tour to L.A. with the band and was busy playing back-to-back concerts. I had finally begun to relax again. The last nightmare was two and a half months behind us. And then I got a phone call early one morning from Julie. He had done it again, this time at her house, right under her nose, with her children nearby. He had quietly overdosed himself during the night, but late enough, and close enough to her, right in the main house, that he had been almost certain she would find him. It was a plea for help. She revived him again, and he was awake and moving this time when the paramedics arrived. Nick went back to the same hospital again, with the psychiatric ward, but this time Julie and I agreed to tell no one but John about it. It was time to eliminate the drama, and to deal with the real issues.

It turned out that his lithium levels had been down, as had been his spirits, but only slightly. But still enough to make him try to kill himself. But despite our vow of silence this time, we knew how serious this was. I spoke to the doctors about not only a conservatorship, but institutionalizing him. It broke my heart to do it, but he clearly needed more supervision than we could give him. I spoke to several attorneys, and a judge friend about the conservatorship. Unfortunately, the court would appoint a conservator, other than myself, or the court itself could perform that function. And my greatest fear was that if they decided Nick was dangerous, to himself and no one else, or just too much trouble, or even insane, then I would no longer be able to decide what to do to help him. I would lose complete autonomy if I got a conservatorship on Nick, and he could even wind up in a state institution, and I would be unable to release him. It was something to think about, and I kept my own counsel. I needed to make the decision myself, and discussed it only with John and Julie.

Nick bounced back all too quickly, meanwhile, and appeared deceptively normal.

We discussed long-term hospitalization with his doctors at length, and we pointed out to them that Nick didn't look like the other people in institutions. He was functional, he had a successful career with his band. It seemed criminal to lock him up, but the hospital psychiatrist said that he was less functional than he looked. It was hard to believe that. After discussing it at length with both psychiatrists and legal counsel, we decided against the conservatorship, and two weeks later released him to Julie's.

The hospital psychiatrist said that if we could

keep him alive until he was thirty, we'd have a good chance of keeping him alive for his normal life span. Suicides, 'accidental' or otherwise, were more common in people in their late teens or early twenties. That was 'only' twelve years away for Nick, and seemed like several lifetimes. But Nick appeared to 'get it' this time. We all had a long talk with him, and tried to appeal to everything from his reason to his conscience. And he looked sad when he asked the doctor how long he would have to be on medication. I think he knew the answer to the question before he asked it.

'Forever,' he said simply, and Nick nodded. He was finally facing the fact that he would be manic-depressive forever. It was a bitter pill for him to swallow. And we compared it to diabetes. We also told him that if he missed a single pill, or refused to take one, this time we would put him in the hospital and keep him there for a very long time. Three attempts in three months were terrifying. And I was terrified.

Before he left the hospital, I wrote Nick this letter. He had written me a letter apologizing and objecting to being in the hospital at all, and as always, I tried to appeal to his heart and his reason, with mine.

Thursday night
30 January 1997

My Darling Nick,
Your letter today touched me so very, very much, and I love you so much more than I can even tell you. It is wonderful of you to reach out to me, to share your feelings with me, and

to apologize to me for the worry I have on your behalf. But I want you to know, now and always, how incredibly proud of you I am, just of you, as you are, as a human being. I will be very, very proud of you if you are successful with your music and I think you are hugely talented – but that's just kind of an 'add-on,' an extra – I am proud of you right this minute, without your accomplishing anything spectacular in the world, because I think you are a wonderful, very special person, you always have been, and always will be, and are right now, at this very minute.

The sadness and worry you see in my eyes sometimes, as you said, is that I do indeed worry about you, and I am sad when you are sad, and I know that this is very hard for you right now. I am sad when I think you have almost slipped through our fingers. I am sad when you aren't happy with the way your life is, as you are sad for me when I am less than happy with mine. But the 'disappointment' you see is not disappointment over you, it never has been, and isn't now. You don't disappoint me. You reach out and touch my very soul, and into me. You have a wonderful knack for that, you always see me as I am. Of everyone around me, through the hard times I've had in the past year or two, you are the one who has most touched me and comforted me, and soothed my heart. I want you to know that!!!

The disappointment you see at times, is not over you, and never has been (I brag about you constantly!!!), but more over the state of my life at the moment. I spent a lot of years building something, many things, our family, my career, my life with Dad. And at the moment, I seem to have slid downhill and am ass over teakettle somewhere at the bottom (like Chutes and Ladders, I thought I'd made it all the way to 99, hit a chute, and wound up again at 2 – just the way you feel at times). But I hope to learn from it, and hit the ladders again and make it back up. The disappointment you see is at what has happened in my life, vis-à-vis my marriage, and over the hurt I feel when the press beats me up, and over the sense of helplessness I feel to help you more than I can and have. But I am not disappointed over you.

But this is the way life is at times, we all fall on our asses, we all slide down the hill in one way or another, and we all climb back up. I'm actually feeling better about life than I have in a while. I see some sunshine out there on the mountaintops again, not just for me, but for you. And hand in hand, with the people we love, and who love us, and our friends, and just a teeny bit of luck, we make it back up, when life knocks us down. You have given me a hand more often than you know. And my hand is always right here for you. I will always be there for you, sweetheart, and when life is sad for you, no matter how big or old or grumpy or pissed off or disappointed you are, you can always crawl into my lap and sit for a while.

There are some things we have to do alone,
that first leap of faith over the abyss that looks
like it's going to swallow us up – we have to
do that on our own, we have to believe enough
to try – just as you have to believe in yourself,
and a (positive) power stronger than you are,
even now. But beyond that eeny teeny tiny
(and often seemingly huge) first crawl out of
the pit – there are people to catch you and to
love you and to be there for you, just as I am,
and Julie is, and your friends are, and your
family is. We're all here rooting for you, sweet-
heart . . . and me, most of all.

Thank you for caring about how I feel, and
for all the wonderful things you are, and do.
You may not feel too wonderful right now, but
you are.

I wish all sorts of terrific things for you. I
hope your music brings you all the joy and
excitement and satisfaction you deserve, but
whether or not you become a 'star' publicly,
you will always be a star to me, and already
are. You are a star as a human being, sweet
Nick. And you shine more brightly than you
know.

So dust yourself off, smile, and know that
you are the joy of my life not a disappoint-
ment. I just want you to be safe and well and
happy – and if we stick you in a 'closet' from
time to time to keep you safe, it's a bit like
locking a jewel up in a safe to keep it from
harm. It may not 'help' the jewel, or improve
its quality, but it keeps it from disappearing,
and keeps it safe. It's kind of a dumb thing to

do with a person, I guess, but you are a jewel to me. I could not bear losing you – and if you think I look sad sometimes now, you can't even imagine how sad I'd look if something terrible happened to you. It doesn't bear thinking about. So keep safe, try to be brave, crawl out of the pit, even in tiny baby steps, take whatever leap of faith you can, and here I am, with my arms out to you, my heart always yours . . . and more love for you than I can tell you.

Even in the worst circumstances, there's a little shred of something to be happy about. Grab it, hold it, keep it. You have often been that shred of happiness for me . . . maybe my love for you can light a dark corner for you too now and then. We have each other, and much, much more than that as well.

Smile, my love . . . and be as proud of who you are, as I am of you!!! (Star Wars is coming out again tomorrow . . . maybe we can go see it together for old-time's sake. 'May the Force be with you,' cute one, it always is, you know!!)

Take care, my darling – very, very good care! I love you with all my heart,

Mom

From then on, after he left the hospital, my heart stopped each time the phone rang. I think I knew what was coming.

But after this last attempt, Nick seemed better than he ever had been. Ever. For the first time in his life, he appeared to accept both the fact and

Nick and Beatie

Nick and Julie

With his friend, Sam Ewing

With Julie

responsibilities of his illness. We tested his lithium levels weekly to make sure he was okay after that. The band was doing splendidly, he was making CDs and videos, and going on short tours. He came to the house whenever he had time, and was in great spirits. And he looked fantastic. And he even came on vacation with the family to Hawaii for the first time in years. And it warmed my heart to see him playing with the children. Sammy the Mick and Julie came with him to keep an eye on him.

We all had a great time with Nick as he cavorted on the beach, swam with his friend 'Sammy the Mick,' and took videos of all of us. He was terrific company, and the kids and I loved having him around. It was our favorite vacation with him, and meant more to us because he hadn't come in so long. Until that year, he had really been unable to travel.

We were also safeguarding his lithium and Prozac levels as well. Whereas most people have their levels checked every three to four months at most, we were checking Nick's weekly, because the medications didn't always absorb evenly, and we could detect the slightest dip, and correct it, by checking his levels more often. It was something I had insisted on in January, for my own peace of mind. And Nick readily agreed to it. He was also seeing two psychiatrists, the same one he had seen for several years, Dr Seifried, whom we all liked so much, and one from the hospital as a backup. He had also gone to an outpatient psychiatric program for two months, but no longer had time between tours, concerts, and rehearsals. Link 80 was really getting off the ground, and Nick loved it. The sweet smell of success was in his nostrils. It was definitely coming.

They had been booked into a ten-week tour around the country that summer, and there was talk of a tour in Europe in the fall, and possibly one in Japan after Christmas. It was taxing for him, but he seemed up to it, and he loved it so much that, as long as he was well, it made no sense to interfere with it. And Julie and I were keeping close tabs on him, as were his attendants. He even went to twelve-step meetings at times, to try and bolster his resolve never to use drugs, if for some reason his lithium levels went down and he got uncomfortable, and wanted the added comfort they gave him. We were doing our part, but he was doing his as well, and it paid off. He looked and sounded terrific.

And we were all looking forward to Beatie's wedding. It was a month away, and all of her siblings were in it. The girls were going to be junior bridesmaids, Maxx the ring bearer, Zara the flower girl, and Nick, Trevor and Todd were going to be ushers. There had been some debate as to whether Nick was up to it, but in light of how well he seemed, and how in command of himself and his career he was, it seemed foolish to worry. The only thing we'd talked about, half jokingly, was what would happen if he'd get bored standing at the altar with the other ushers, and let his lack of impulse control get the best of him. But given the way he was behaving these days, that seemed unlikely.

He seemed to have finally grown up into a loving, caring, responsible young man and he even accepted willingly the responsibilities of his illness.

He was good about keeping track of it, taking his medicine, and for the first time ever, when he didn't feel right, he told Julie, and she and Nick's psychiatrist adjusted his medications. It had been three months since his last attempt to obliterate himself, and it seemed to be the furthest thing from his mind now. He was handsome, suddenly more mature, successful, and very happy. And we had never been closer.

In fact, we had such a good time together in Hawaii that we started having weekly lunches with each other, and we always had a great time together. The older he got, the more alike we were. We were similarly sensitive, compassionate, generous, foolish, and naive at times, we had soft hearts, quick minds, and the same sense of humor. Life had been tough at various times for both of us, and we had each developed a real appreciation for it when times were easy. But best of all, we had a powerful bond to each other and knew it.

I found I could talk to him about anything and everything. I confided in him about things that worried me in the family, problems I had with John, my work, and even my love life. He was still crazy about Tom and happy for me that things were going well. And I warned him about the pitfalls of celebrity, certain that one day he would have to face them. He was startled by the people who were already envious of him and at the same time trying to take advantage of him. We had a lot of wisdom to offer each other. We saw things from a similar point of view, which amused us both. And he had some astoundingly profound insights about people. It was extraordinary how close we were. How understanding and wise he was. And most of all, I was always so touched by how much he cared about me, appreciated me, and wanted me to be happy. I would never have imagined it years before, but he had grown up to be a man I loved, respected, and knew I could count on, a rarity in my life. And he knew I was always there for him, and always would be. We counted on each other to be there, and never disappointed each other. Nick was someone I could count on and sometimes even lean on, which amazed me. It was a rare gift he gave me, which I treasured.

We had lunch together about once a week, more often when we could, and between rehearsals and appointments, he'd stop by the house, sit in my office, and just chat. We made fun of people we disliked, or who took themselves too seriously, told each other bad jokes, and there was always a certain innocence about both of us, we trusted people, 'not enough, and too much,' as Nick said. We had so damn much in common, so much we not only loved, but liked and admired about each other.

After the wedding, we were all going our separate ways for a while. I was taking the kids to Europe for six weeks. Nick was going on tour for ten weeks, and was really excited about it. I was happy for him, and not even worried. His attendants were going with him, as they always did, and Julie was flying out every week to wherever he was to check on him. She had already made arrangements with hospitals along the way, to check his lithium levels. We had thought of everything, and he was intent on his music. He had never seemed in better shape, saner, or stronger. And at the very end of May, we all turned our attention to Beatie's wedding.

There was a rehearsal dinner the night before, fraught with whoopee cushions, which enchanted Nicky. Beatie looked exquisite in a lavender satin gown, and Nick looked sensational in a black suit and leopard creepers. He'd just had a terrific haircut, his hair was shiny black, and he was looking very handsome. We all had a great time, and the next day, we all posed for pictures before the wedding. Nick looked incredible in a new tuxedo.

His behavior at the ceremony was exemplary. No sign of poor impulse control anywhere, and as he promised, he walked me down the aisle, very circumspectly. And as we started down, he tucked my hand into his arm and melted my heart by telling me how much he loved me. There is a lovely photograph of us at precisely that moment. I remember when they took it.

I told him I loved him too, and that every child is a gift to their mother, but he had not only been a gift to me, but he was extra special because he had been a gift to me so many times. 'You have to be good to yourself now, Nick,' I said softly. 'I love you,' I whispered. I was nervous about walking down the aisle, and he knew it, and patted my hand. And then he said he loved me again, kissed me, left me at my pew, and went up to the altar to join the other ushers. He had never looked or seemed better to me.

He danced with me a number of times that night, but maintained his usual reputation as a Casanova. At the very end, he left the reception with one of the

At Beatie's rehearsal dinner, 23 May 1997
(The ring Nick is wearing in this photograph is one he wore every day for many years. It was given to me when he died, and I have worn it every day since then. I had it copied for the rest of the family, and now all his siblings, John, Nick's biological father, Bill, Sammy the Mick, Thea, and the Campbells all wear it. It's a bright, shining star, as he was.)

Nick and Beatie

(He wore the glasses – with no lenses – to be silly. I found them in his van long after, and they now sit on my dresser.)

Nick, DS

Zara, Trevor, Victoria, Nick, Beatie, Sam, Todd, Vanessa, Maxx

Victoria, Nick, DS

Going down the aisle at
Grace Cathedral

Maxx, Trevor, Sam, Todd, DS, Mike, Beatie, Nick,
Vanessa, Victoria, Zara

prettiest women there. She was thirty years old, and looked spectacular, particularly on Nick's arm as they left the party with Cody to drive them. Nick had never learned to drive, never wanted to, and knew that it was not something he was up to. He really didn't need to, since there was always someone with him. And Nick's problems with impulse control would have been lethal on the freeway.

It was a beautiful wedding, and one of the happiest events of our lives. It was wonderful to see the family all together. Everyone looked beautiful and had a great time and we were all happy for Beatie.

Two weeks later, after another of our lunches where we laughed all afternoon, Nick left on tour with the band, and the children and I left for Europe. I promised to call him in the van from Europe. I was going to be a lot easier to reach than he was. I was going to Paris, and the South of France, London, and a weekend at a country house in England. And Nick was going to be driving across the country, and back, wowing his audiences and adding new fans. He was so excited about it, and I was happy for him. I knew it was going to be a great summer.

18

Disastrous Summer

Just before Nick left on tour, he hurt his back. He had an inflamed disk, which worried him, given the athletic challenges of his onstage performance. He jumped, he leapt, he writhed, he twisted, not an easy thing to do if your back is hurting. Somehow he thought the tour had been booked so they would be driving no more than four or five hours a day. But Nick's notions about time had never been perfect. As it turned out, they were facing twelve to fifteen hours of driving daily between the towns and cities they were playing. Sitting in a crowded van, with nine other guys, for fifteen hours a day was going to be hard for him and he knew it. I told him to ice his back, and lie down whenever possible. And not wanting to complicate his chemistry, he didn't want to take pain medication, but he said the back was, at times, excruciating.

The musical and performance aspects of the tour went well at first but the boys were young, and strains between them were inevitable. Trapped in a van for a dozen hours a day, crowded, often hot and tired after late night performances and little sleep, they began to squabble, which surprised no one. The tour was a lot harder than any of them had expected. But Nick felt it was important for their future, and pressed onward. Sometimes, when they didn't like what was happening, they blamed him, because he managed the group, and was responsible for everything they did, and all of them, including Nick, were vocal about their displeasures and discomforts.

But I learned afterwards, from Julie, how much the other boys complaining to him upset him. It made him feel that they didn't appreciate him, or his tireless efforts. Nick felt the responsibility of the band rested almost entirely on his shoulders. And as he was the one organizing everything, working with the booking agents and concert halls, making endless phone calls, as well as writing songs, performing, and organizing rehearsals, he wasn't mistaken.

Now, in retrospect, it is easier to see that the potential was there for the tour to be disastrous for Nick. But at the time, it seemed important to all of us to let him do it. Touring with the band meant everything to him, it was the culmination of all his work, and it was what the band needed to do, if it was going to be successful. Nick himself had dropped out of junior college seven months before, because he felt that being in a potentially successful band was an opportunity that might not come his way again, and he figured he could always go back to college later. Two of the others had dropped out of college too, another band member had left high school to go on independent study. They had all made major sacrifices for it, and

Nick at eighteen

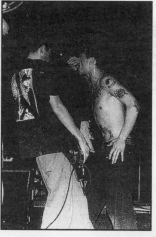

committed themselves entirely to it. And for them, the summer tour was only the beginning. They were planning to tour for a year, off and on. Eleven weeks that summer, possibly Europe in the fall, if the U.S. tour went well, and Japan after Christmas. They had a lot resting on it, and it was going to be a proving ground for Link 80.

My heart trembled a little bit when I thought of Nick touring, as did Julie's, but we all knew how much it meant to him. And if we hadn't let him do it, he might have walked out on us, and done it anyway, without our blessing and protection. And we were encouraged by the fact that he seemed healthier and saner than he ever had. It seemed the perfect time for him to do it. So, we set it up in the best way we could, to safeguard his health and protect him. An intricate schedule was set up for both Cody and Paul, his attendants, to tour with him alternately. And Julie was planning to fly and meet them once a week, travel with them for several days, and make sure Nick was holding up to the physical and psychological pressures. We thought, when they set out in June, that we had all bases covered. Julie even had a list of hospitals along the way, where he was going to be taken to have his lithium levels tested.

Usually, it was Julie who fought for independence for him. It was she who had encouraged him in his passion for the band in the first place, while I was always a little bit more hesitant, more cautious, more skeptical, and more worried. But she understood even better than I how important it was for him to have a sense of accomplishment and freedom. If I could have, I would have kept him wrapped in cotton wool all his life. But he was 'my baby.' And I knew she was right in at least giving him the illusion of independence. If he was going to live with an illness all his life, the goal for all of us was to help him lead a normal life, or as normal as possible. And the tour was part of helping him to do that. And most of all, it was what Nick so desperately wanted, and what he had worked so hard for. But as though she feared for him this time, for once Julie was more anxious than I was. I was the one this time who was sure that he could do it. And as usual, we provided a good balance. We had the same kinds of conversations about Nick's cottage.

I thought he needed to be more closely observed than he could be in a separate house, sleeping alone. His nurses left him late at night, and only returned in the morning. But Julie felt he needed privacy and freedom. He needed to feel like a grown-up. He was so surrounded and protected and so closely watched that it was oppressive for him at times, and rare for us to be able to give him the illusion of adulthood. The freestanding mother-in-law unit only inches from her front door helped foster that illusion. And he just loved it. Sometimes she was right about what she wanted for him, and sometimes I was to give in to what Nick called my 'paranoia.' He had attempted suicide once there, in the cottage, but he had done it right in Julie's house as well. And in the locked ward of a hospital. So we were both right, he needed a sense of independence, as closely as we could fashion it for him, and he also needed observation. It was always a fine line, a balancing act on the high wire with Nicky.

But it was Julie who had always been supportive of his music career, even when I wasn't. In the early days, I paid little attention to it, thinking it was a passing fad for him, and worrying that it drew him into a milieu that was unsavory and he couldn't handle. But Julie was entirely right on that one. It was the life force that kept him going, brought him into his best years, and that he lived for. I was always grateful that she had prevailed, and so was Nicky.

In any case, as he set out that summer on tour, I think Julie and I both had mixed feelings, and reservations. But for once, I was almost completely convinced he could do it. And by the time he left, so was Julie. Nick had never been better.

Cody reported in several times a day, and told us that all was going well, although the boys were complaining about the heat, the van, the food, the long drives, the usual discomforts of a road tour. Nothing seemed unusual to any of us. But ten days into the trip, Julie called me in Europe. We had already spoken several times before that, and pretty much checked in with each other on a daily basis, if not more often. It was rare for a day to go by, even when he was at home, without several phone calls between us, either confirming that things were going well, or to make adjustments, or intervene when they weren't.

When Julie called this time, she sounded worried. Nick had been sounding stressed, and was upset by some of the band members complaining to him about how things were going. But she surprised me when she said she thought the tour was too much for him, and talked about the possibility of canceling the tour and bringing him home early. But when I asked if something specific had happened to make her feel that way, it seemed to be more of an uneasy feeling on her part. And I trusted her instincts.

By the next day, Nick had actually confided to her that he was feeling stressed, and depressed, and he himself was beginning to think he couldn't do it. And listening to her, I was worried. But I also knew how mercurial his moods were. He was perfectly capable of saying he wanted out at one minute, and fighting like a cat to stay, five minutes later. I somehow thought that if we did bring him home, the full impact of what it meant to his fledgling career would hit him later, and it might destroy him. For once, I was the one who thought he should stick with it, and believed he could do it. I was afraid that if he left, he would feel like a failure and an invalid forever. It was hard to assess the potential risks of either decision.

He had asked her to come out and meet them a few days earlier than planned, and told her he was going to tell the band he was leaving. Julie flew out to meet him that night. But before she did, she made Nick promise that he would say nothing to the other band members about his thoughts of leaving until she got there. And of course, Nick promised. She wanted to help him break the news to them, if he was serious about leaving.

But the inevitable lack of impulse control made the promise, like most he made, worthless. Before her plane had taken off, he had taken matters into his own hands. And rather than exposing his illness to them, which he never did, he guarded it as a secret he shared with no one. Instead he told them that he was fed up with them, didn't like them anymore, and was leaving. And, predictably, they went ballistic. Julie had been planning to discuss it at length with Nick, and if necessary, help him to make a diplomatic and graceful exit. He would have had the perfect excuse for it, as his first suicide attempt nine months before had been so physically devastating for him that he needed continuing tests afterwards, and there had been a question just before he left as to whether he had affected his heart, and he was being tested regularly for it, right up until the day before they left, and he was scheduled for another test on the road. And so far, the tests had been normal, but Julie had been planning to announce that he had a problem with his heart, if Nick needed a graceful exit. But he never gave her the chance to do that. Instead, he insulted everyone, made them furious with him, and by the time Julie arrived, the boys had been in an eight-hour debacle, telling Nick what a creep he was for wanting to desert them. They couldn't understand his reasons, and he responded with criticism and insults.

The problem for Nick was that he wanted no one to know about his manic depression, let alone the severity of it. The boys he worked with had no idea about the daily struggle he was engaged in, the seriousness of the medications he was on, the extent to which he was dependent on them, or that Cody and Paul were in fact psychiatric attendants. He told everyone they were bodyguards, provided by his famous and very overprotective mother. And I'm not sure what they thought of Julie.

But Julie found them all in heated argument when

she arrived, and Nick privately confessed to her that he hadn't known what or how to tell them, or how to cope with his own sense of failure. It was the first time that he had actually admitted it when he didn't feel right, or had asked for help. And after the three suicide attempts of the months before, it seemed an important step in taking responsibility for managing his illness. Knowing that he was in fact upset, and talking about going home, Julie thought that it was wise for him to do so.

But without Nick, there was no tour, no band, no immediate future for Link 80. He was the central focus, the lead singer, the star, the magnet that drew the crowds and groupies, the scouts and the press agents, the reps from the major labels. They couldn't go on without him at that point, and they knew it.

But Nick was even more profoundly depressed by what they were saying to him, and he and Julie talked at length about what he should do about it. He was feeling deeply wounded by what the others had said to him, but on the other hand, he had handled it all very badly. Telling them they were jerks and he hated them was hardly a tack that was going to win their support or admiration, let alone their compassion. And they knew nothing of his illness. He was acting like a spoiled brat, to cover his own fears, and they were understandably upset about it.

Julie got everyone to calm down for the night, and the next day when Nick was asleep, she spent five hours talking to the other boys to try and explain the situation to them. It was time, she knew, to come out of the closet about Nick's illness. And she told them about Nick's manic depression. But understandably, the implications of it, and the severity of it, and the potentially disastrous risks to him, were more than they could fathom. And who could blame them? If we, after years of dealing with it, didn't fully understand how lethal it could be to him, how could they? But despite Nick's wish for the illusion of normalcy, she nonetheless told them that if things got out of hand for Nick on the trip, and got to be too much for him, it was possible that he might take drugs to alleviate his pain, or worse, attempt suicide again. It was an awesome burden. And I suspect that they thought Julie was being paranoid and overstating the case, to make excuses for him. They were teenagers, and naive, and she was describing an illness to them that, for most people, is ephemeral and confusing. They wanted him to stay in spite of it, and felt he owed it to them, and they promised to call her if Nick seemed out of sorts, or developed any problems they were aware of.

In the end, the compromise Julie offered them, and eventually Nick, was that they all take a break for two to three weeks, to give her a chance to take Nick home, keep an eye on him, adjust his medications if necessary, and give him a chance to regain his balance and good spirits. But they were unenthusiastic about her suggestion, and more than likely the booking agents wouldn't have tolerated a two to three week interruption in the trip. It would have cost them money, and hurt the band's reputation.

And by the time Nick got up, Julie had convinced them to tell Nick how much they appreciated him, which they did. And hearing that when he got up, Nick announced that he had decided he wanted to stay and continue the tour. Julie still had reservations, and told him that he should follow his instincts, and that if it was too much for him to stay, he shouldn't do it. But Nick's position had reversed entirely in the past twenty-four hours. He told Julie that if she made him leave with her, he would run away, for real this time. Nothing was going to make him leave, he said. He was going to do the tour, come hell or high water. And he flatly refused to go home with Julie.

I was talking to Julie about it every few hours, and she finally decided to stick around for a while, and watch him. And the one thing she didn't like, nor did I, was the fact that the boys had been so adamant about his not leaving, whatever the risk to Nicky. They wanted him to stay not out of any disregard for him, but because they didn't understand the risk to him, and they needed him so badly. I don't think any of us realized, not even Julie or I, or even Nick's psychiatrist, how taxing the trip would be for him psychologically, or the revelations he would have to face about his own limits, which ultimately destroyed him. Had we realized the eventual risk to Nick, he never would have been allowed to go on tour in the first place. After all we had done to that point to keep him safe, why in God's name would any of us have wanted to risk him? We didn't.

So Julie stayed and traveled with them for a while, and kept an eye on Nick, and his spirits came up again. They got busy with the business of the band, the rigors of the road, and the excitement of their concerts. The tour was going well for them, and it was a rite of passage they all knew they had to go through if they were ever going to make it big-time. And by the time Julie left again, she felt comfortable, and so did I, that he was back on track again, comfortable, and determined to continue the tour. But there was also no doubt in our minds that he was fragile. And he had promised Julie before she left that if he got depressed again, he would in fact leave the tour, and not jeopardize his well-being further.

He wasn't in his usual ebullient spirits then, but nor did he seem particularly depressed, and he and the other band members were getting on better. Now, with hindsight again, we realize that he was less sociable than usual, kept to himself more, and whenever they had some free time in the towns where they stayed, Nick was more anxious to stay in his motel and rest than to go out and have fun with the others. But he was also tired, and not long after Julie left, he broke his foot onstage during a performance. She flew out again then, and had the foot set by an orthopedist in Nashville. An incredibly nice man, Dr Greg White, whom Nick befriended. Nick maintained contact with him, I have met him since and we have become friends. And he is every bit as nice and kind and diligent as Nick had described to me when he told me about him. He gave Nick a cast that he could continue to perform in.

Julie also had his lithium levels checked when she was on the tour with him, and so far, everything seemed normal.

And all along the way, I was calling Nick in the

van, and he sounded fine to me, and happy to be touring. And from nearly every town they stopped in, he would send me funny postcards, thanking me profusely for letting him tour with the band, and supporting him in what he was doing. I kept most of the postcards he sent, and have since framed them. They are very Nicky.

In his inimitable way, Nick also took his sense of humor on tour with him. And in spite of the initial rocky start, and his broken foot, he managed to come up with some relatively innocent mischief. It was hard to keep Nick down for long, even when he was tired, and squashed in a van with nine other people. There were eight band members, Cody driving the van, Nick, and their beloved friend and roadie Stony.

Nick found a piece of cardboard on one of their stops one day, and wrote a message on it, which he thought would provide them some entertainment. He drew a simple outline of two pairs of boobs, and wrote 'SHOW US YOUR TITS!' in bold letters. The message was undeniably crude, and potentially offensive. But in typical Nicky fashion, he thought it was going to provide them hours of fun, and he wasn't mistaken.

According to Cody, he would smile at women in cars driving close to them, wave, make faces, laugh, giggle, point, and generally charm them. And as they became amused by him, trying his best to entice them from the van driving alongside their car, he would then pick up his homemade sign and hold it at the window. They must surely have been startled, some were perhaps annoyed, but what astonished Cody – and probably the others as well

– is that a number of the women who read his sign actually did what he was asking. It worked! Cody and I agreed, as he told me about it, that if anyone else tried it, they'd probably wind up in jail, or the women he'd tried it on would have been outraged. And although some probably were, others apparently thought it was funny, and Nick charming. Enough so to do what he wanted, and laugh as hard as he did. There was no malice to Nick, no evil intent, nothing even remotely sleazy. There was a childlike quality to him from beginning to end. An innocence and ingenuousness that made you want to laugh and hug him.

The sign came home from tour eventually, and amused by it, I framed it. It is an artifact of the tour, so typically Nick, and somehow strikes me funny. It hangs now on the stairs to his room, just below his microphone, which I also framed. They make me smile, just as the story did when Cody told me.

Things went on well for a while, and he sounded fine to me when I called him. I'd catch him asleep in the van between towns, God knows where, that no one had ever heard of. But it was obvious by then that he loved it. They were all tired, driving endless hours across unfamiliar terrain, but he loved the people they met, the performances they did, and was constantly enthusiastic about it. He said his back was better, though I can't imagine why, curled up in a van all day, and leaping off the stage all night. It was hardly therapy any doctor would have recommended. But he was young enough to survive it, despite his illness. Or at least I thought so.

And Julie was satisfied that things were going well too. She was flying out once a week to spend several days with him, as promised, although by then it was no easy feat for her. She had just discovered she was pregnant, and hadn't told Nick. But she knew how important it was for her to be there with him, so no matter how she felt, and often she felt ill, she flew out to meet him. She would rent a car, and have him drive alone with her, so they could talk and she could get a real sense of how he was doing.

But her reports to me were reassuring, although one of the things we were worried about was the possibility that given the long hours, the lack of sleep, and irregular eating patterns, his lithium might not absorb evenly, but so far, we saw no problems. And his weekly lithium tests were normal.

Nick complained about the cast he was wearing from time to time, and I teased him about it.

'You're falling apart!' I said, and he laughed.

'Yeah!' I could see him smile as he said it, and he inquired about my love life, which was fine for the moment. Tom and I had been talking about making plans for the future again, when we left for Europe.

I had taken the children to London and Paris, and we were in the South of France, when everything went haywire with Tom. It was one of those moments when the planets collide, and all of one's lucky stars wind up in the toilet. At least mine did. Tom and I had been traveling separately on different continents for two months, and when we got back together, things were out of synch, and suddenly felt awkward. In retrospect one can always find a lot of reasons why things happen. In truth, one never knows exactly what lights the fuse on the stick of dynamite, but it lit, and the dynamite blew our relationship right out of the water. He left the South of France suddenly, panicked by the complications of my life, convinced that the relationship was unsalvageable, and that it was over. I didn't agree with his reasons for it, but he definitely convinced me that, for him at least, it was over.

I went back to Paris from the South of France, heartbroken, and cried in all our favorite places. It was definitely a major blow, and along with our romance, and what I had hoped would be our future, went my summer. I flew back to New York with the kids, and then home, to deliver them to John for their vacation time with him, and stayed home to lick my wounds. The rest of the summer plans I'd had with Tom were canceled, but for the time being, I said nothing to Nicky.

Nick breezed through New York on the tour, and my mother and a friend of hers went to see him perform. I smiled, thinking of it, and wished I could have seen it. My mother in silk, as usual, and pearls, amongst Nick's groupies, and a thousand punk rockers. She loved the performance and her grandson. Now that he was successful, his oddities, like dyed hair, earrings, a nose ring, and tattoos, seemed more like accessories than offenses. And Nick never had a 'hard-core' look about him. He had a natural style and elegance of sorts which gave his mod looks real appeal, and only enhanced his appearance.

They got a week's break from the tour in New York, and Nick caught a bad cold. Julie was there, and his friend Thea came out to keep him company, and he had a good time, but he was feeling fairly lousy. I put him up in a decent hotel, for once, and he wrote and called endlessly to thank me. The comforts that had once seemed ordinary to him were now deeply appreciated and priceless.

He also used the time in New York to take the band to see a well-known music attorney, who was impressed by them, and agreed to represent them.

But it was after New York that things started to go sour for Nick. He was tired, he still had the cold, and the pressures of the tour were beginning to wear him down, until he began to slip slowly into a depression. They had been on tour for eight weeks, and had three more before they finished. More than anything, he seemed tired. But I think what lay beneath the fatigue and the strain was a realization that he confessed to Julie. He knew without a doubt that unless he could tour and hold up to the rigors of that life, his attempts at a career in music would be fruitless. It was something he absolutely *had* to do if he was going to make it. And what he had discovered in nearly eight weeks of tour was that he felt he couldn't. He had held up remarkably, but his spirits were slowly sinking. Like the others, he was exhausted. But unlike them, he waged a constant battle against his own limitations. The balance was just too delicate for him, and he told both Cody and Julie in those last weeks of the tour that he had come to realize that he couldn't do it. It took too much out of him, and the stresses of that lifestyle cost him too dearly. He had begun to fight a daily battle against depression. And he even told Cody that he didn't think he could tour again. It was too much for him, and

Nick at nineteen

Nick and Chris Campbell

he knew it. And what that translated to for Nick was utter failure and crushing depression.

He could no longer see himself doing the European tour, or Japan. And if he couldn't tour, he couldn't play, he couldn't live. Without being able to do what he wanted in the music world, his life was just not worth living. He was a bird with broken wings and he knew it. It was precisely the conclusion we had all prayed he would never come to. We wanted the tour to be a victory for him, but in those last exhausting weeks, it began to backfire on him. But he still insisted he could finish, and not wanting to depress him more, we agreed to let him.

Julie flew home again in those last days of the tour. She was sick from her pregnancy by then, but Nick didn't know anything about it. She had been with him for weeks, driving fifteen hours a day with him, standing around in concert halls and night-clubs, and talking endlessly with Nicky. But she and I both agreed that for the moment at least, her pregnancy had to remain a secret. Nick was always thrown off by change. And he needed so much of her time and attention that the arrival of a new baby in her life was going to present a real threat to him. We wanted him home again, rested, and settled down, before she told him. And as usual, she sacrificed herself, and her health, for his well-being. She had spent the entire summer commuting to be with him, and enduring the rigors of the tour almost as much as he did. As worried as I was about Nick, I was also worried about Julie. And with good reason, the night before Nick came home, she lost the baby, which was devastating for her. But even then, her thoughts had to turn instantly to Nicky. She had no time to recover.

The band drove to the Midwest after New York, and although Nick appeared to be okay, in fact he wasn't. He went out with the band one night, got drunk, and smoked some pot, which was potentially disastrous for him, and he knew it. The boys in the band called Paul, Nick's attendant, at the motel immediately, and told him what had happened, as they promised they would do, if Nick ever did anything he shouldn't. Paul went to pick him up, and when they got back to the motel, Nick called Julie. He was panicked by what he'd done, knowing that with him it was a sign that he was falling apart, and he knew it. She asked him if he wanted to come home, and he said he would do whatever she wanted, which knowing Nick, meant he wanted out. The fact that he had smoked pot and drank was his way of saying he couldn't do it anymore, we all knew that, and so did Nicky.

Julie said, 'What if I tell you to come home, Nick?'

'I'll come,' he said sadly. No fight, no argument. He knew then that, for him, the tour was finished. But more than that, he knew it had far greater implications for him. He knew better than anyone his own handicaps and limitations.

Nick knew he had to go home, to put himself back together, but he also knew that his agreement with the band was that if he had to leave the tour, at any point, they would fire him. That had been his deal with them, and knowing that, to spare himself the embarrassment of being fired, he told them he had to go home and was quitting Link 80. They didn't argue with him. They were exhausted by the tour, and tired of Nick's problems. They were finished with him. Nick was devastated that his three-year love affair with Link 80 was over. He had been on tour with them for nine and a half weeks by then, through thick and thin, across the country, and nearly back again. They had less than two weeks of the tour left, and without Nick, it would have to be canceled. And they were furious with him for leaving. Nick's sense of defeat was total.

Nick left them quietly, and got on a plane in Minneapolis. Julie met him when he arrived, and brought him straight home to me. We were dying to see each other, and I was desperately worried about him. I supported wholeheartedly his decision to leave. The fact that he'd allowed himself to drink, knowing how unwise it was for him, and how atypical for him, told me just what rotten shape he had to be in. And I was even more worried when I saw him. He had lost weight on tour, he was thin, and pale, and tired, still wearing a cast to his knee, and he looked mortally wounded. Despite nine and a half successful weeks on tour, the fact that he couldn't finish it made him feel like a failure. And the fact that he had quit, and they had let his decision stand and agreed with him, after all he'd done for the band for three years, nearly broke his heart. In fact, I think it may have. For the last ten days of the tour, Nick was like a fighter on his knees, not knocked out, but going down slowly, and he knew it. And when he came home finally, he was beaten. It had all gone wrong in those last two weeks, and it had been too late to stop it.

In retrospect, it's easy for all of us to say that he never should have done the tour, and I blame myself of course, for letting him do it. And yet not to let him would have been a blow of such catastrophic proportions for him that it would have broken his spirit. It would have been a way of telling him that he was an invalid and would never be able to pursue the dream he had worked so hard for. What I wanted for him was that he be able to do it because Nick himself wanted it so badly. It was what we all wanted, and we had had high hopes for him, no higher than his own. I thought the tour more of a victory for him than a defeat, and it had been an extraordinary experience for all of them, but having to leave the band had filled him with panic. The band was everything he had lived and worked for.

And although I wish they had viewed his early departure differently, and not taken as hard a stance on it, in some ways, I cannot blame them. They were fed up with him. No matter how talented he was, he brought a lot of problems with him. There was no way for them to understand the magnitude of his illness, particularly with Nick going to such great lengths to conceal it from them. He didn't want them to know how sick he was, and they didn't. Besides, asking them at their age to understand the intricacies of what it took to manage it would have been far beyond them. What Nick hoped, and what I did, when we met that night, was that they would relent when they got home, and ask him to come back to the band. I felt sure they would when they calmed down, came home, and were themselves less stressed out and more rested. For the moment, I suspected that, like Nick, they were irrational and exhausted.

I pointed out to him that they were as tired as he was, and that if you put nine people in a van, whatever age, whatever description, after nine and a half weeks of no sleep and grueling work, which the concerts were, more than likely, they'd kill each other. I was sure that once they got back, all would be forgiven.

'What if they don't take me back, Mom?' he asked, on the verge of tears, looking panicked.

'They will,' I promised. I was sure they would. I thought they'd have to be crazy not to. But then again, I loved him.

We talked about it all for a long time that night and eventually he asked about Europe. And as usual, he asked about Tom. I didn't want to tell him how badly the trip had gone, or that we had broken up. I was still hoping the rift would repair, it was still early days, it had only been a few weeks since he left me. And I figured Nick had enough on his plate, without adding my problems to his. It was odd enough that he had become my confidant, and occasional advisor. Now it was time to think of him, and not my broken romance, though I was hurting, badly. But I managed to conceal it from him, and feigned good spirits. I was far more concerned about his problems. His life was always on the line, mine wasn't.

We hugged and I made him laugh a little bit, but for the most part, he looked beaten. I told him to go home and go to bed. He did, for three weeks. By the next day, he was so depressed he couldn't move. He stayed in bed for days and weeks, sleeping and each day coming closer to the edge of destruction. We were desperately worried about him. We tried to get him to go to the hospital, but he didn't want to go this time, and the hospital said there was no legal reason to commit him. He was depressed but did not appear to be in grave danger.

The band never called him when they got back, never asked him to return. They showed up at Julie's house without warning, and wanted their equipment, which was still in our van. Nicky was so devastated he refused to come downstairs, and stayed in bed and cried. Julie and I did the same when we talked about it. There was no way for us to shield him from it. He was in despair over it, wounded, broken. He had let them down, and they had let him go. It was a natural consequence of his actions, and his illness. Those of us who loved him were desperately afraid for him. It was the greatest challenge he had ever faced, particularly given his illness. And he continued to spiral downward.

For Nick, the dream had ended. And all we could do for him was drag Nick toward the future. Julie began talking to him about starting a new band. At first Nick didn't want to hear it, but after a while the idea intrigued him. Julie kept reminding him that he could do it. As usual, she was his life preserver, his lifesaver, the driving force that would not let him drown, no matter how badly he wanted to do that.

Knowing how depressed he was, instead of waiting for him to get up to give him his meds, she began getting up and giving them to him at five A.M., rousing him only slightly to do it, in the hope that they would have begun to kick in by the time he really woke up several hours later. I'm sure that helped somewhat, but even that thoughtful gesture was not enough to work the magic that was needed.

There was no question that Nick was devastated and depressed by losing the band. But something equally dangerous had happened to him on tour that I didn't fully understand until later. Nick had come face-to-face with his own limitations and weaknesses while on tour. Cody and Julie both felt that he had seen all too clearly that he would never be able to sustain indefinitely the rigors of that lifestyle. Although he had the talent to become a megastar one day, emotionally it was too hard for him, too taxing, too demanding, too stressful, and he knew that he had come to the outer edge of his abilities and stretched them further than he should have. His success as a musician eventually would depend on his ability to tour again and again, and endure it. Being unable to do so, for him, meant never being able to do what he really had to. It was a crushing realization for him. Nick had seen at last that he would never be free of the ties that bound him. He was a proud eagle, with broken wings, destined to be earthbound. Having to face that, and what he would never be, and could never have, is perhaps what killed him. Knowing that he could not achieve his dreams, there was nothing left to live for. Julie was not even sure, nor was Nick, that the medications he relied on so totally would sustain him forever. He said nothing to any of us of his realizations or his fears, but both Cody and Julie felt that he had become more acutely aware of his limitations.

Miraculously, in the white heat of his pain, his friends stood by him. Sammy the Mick, Max, whom he had grown up with, and a boy called Chuck whom Nick had known from the music scene for some time. He was with the 'Creeps,' and they had played concerts together. Chuck came to stay in Nick's little house, to be with him night and day, and they began writing music together. But Nick was sleeping in Julie's house then. He was in no shape to sleep alone in his cottage.

And in the midst of all that, in August, it was my birthday. And in spite of our differences, Tom gave me a spectacular surprise birthday party. All my favorite people were there, faces from my past and present, even my best friend from first grade, a Swiss woman who had flown out from New York for the evening. My children were there, too, and had kept the secret. The balloons mysteriously matched my gown, a thoughtful touch even I couldn't have dreamed of. It was perfection. It was a magical evening, the only high point in an otherwise disastrous summer, but I loved it. And the only face missing was Nicky's. I learned afterwards that Tom had done everything he could to get him there, but in spite of their mutual affection, and Nick's love for me, Nick just couldn't do it. He hadn't even gotten out of bed yet. He had only been home for a week then. Scaling Everest would have been easier for him at that point. Julie didn't come either. She stayed home to keep an eye on Nicky. He was slowly struggling to his feet, enough so to become difficult at times. But his frustration was so great and his sorrow, that at times he got feisty. A week after Tom's birthday party for me, on my real birthday, just as I was about to sit down to a lunch prepared for me by the younger kids, he called and announced that he was moving out of Julie's, leaving at that precise moment. He had had enough of 'her' bullshit. He rarely made accusations like that anymore. He had grown up too much to behave that way, but he was starting to get manic. And he was leaving.

For once I didn't argue with him, reason, or cajole. I just told him he had to stay there and that was that. I also told him that I never asked him for anything and never had before, but this time I was 'asking' him to stay, hung up quickly before he could argue with me, and sat down to lunch with the children, trying not to worry about him.

We were all going out to dinner that night, at one of our favorite restaurants, a funky diner. And Nick was to meet us. He finally seemed well enough to do so, or at least I thought he was. But that night, he called just before dinner, depressed again, and said he just couldn't. He was too depressed to move, and I told him I understood completely. I did. I just wanted him to be all right. That would have been the best birthday gift of all. And that night after we got back from the restaurant, he sent me a beautiful letter by fax. It is the last one I ever got from him. One of many he wrote me, but possibly the best and the nicest. I will cherish it forever, and have read it so often to get me through these empty days, I nearly know it by heart now. It will probably keep me going for my entire lifetime, because the things he said to me recognize who I am, who I was to him, and him to me, and give me courage. It will always remind me of what a great kid Nick was, what a great son, and great human being. And his final gift to me, along with his love, was to remind me of what a great human being he thought I am. And it felt good to hear it. It was a last gift from Nick, and a very sweet one.

8/14/97 11:41 p.m.

Dear Mom,

It's still your birthday and I hope you had a wonderful time at dinner. I can't tell you how sorry I am that I'm not with you right now. I know you'll be gracious as always and quell my guilty conscience with 'the best birthday gift you can give me is to get back on the right track,' etc. Whether you mean it or not, the fact still remains that I fucked up and I'm sitting across the Bay on your birthday. I should be there with you, in good shape, having a good time. I don't know how many times I've had to say I'm sorry, but I'm saying it again. I'm sure you're just as sick of hearing it as I am of saying it. I love you so much and I want so badly to make you proud of me. I was fucked up and out of my head for so long that for a while everyone thought that was the real me. Everybody thought I was crazy. Sometimes even me. I have grown so much in the last year, especially in the last seven months, that I almost feel like a new person. Like the real me that was buried under all that bullshit was finally let out. Julie saw it. My friends saw it. I know you saw it too. You stopped being so skittish around me, and we let each other into one another's lives more than we ever have. I don't know if it was unconscious or not, but you seemed to let down a guard that had been up for a long time. You saw the true, unobstructed me that had been masked by so much turmoil for years. You enjoyed my company again. I looked forward to seeing you. We didn't fight. We called each other to see how we were doing.

I know I haven't, but I really feel like I have blown all that. I'm afraid that you think I'm back to being a crazy little shit head and you're going to step away again. Not that I'd blame you. I mean, who wants a crazy little shit head around anyway, right? And when I say 'step away,' I don't mean like you're going to abandon me. I just fear that the closeness we have shared, due a lot to the good shape I've been in, will falter. I know you love me no matter what, and I love you no matter what, and even if you treated me like a shit and called me names and stole from me and lied to me and ended up in institutions, I would still love you. I have done all those things to you and to myself and you have stood by me 100%. I know that our love for one another is totally unconditional. There is nothing you could do that would make me turn my back on you. You have demonstrated this consistently because I have done it all and you continue to be there. But regardless, I know I have let you down whether you admit it to me or not. And for that I am sorry.

For the better part of the last seven years I

have been a huge pain in your ass (I almost made a typo there and wrote 'a pain in your huge ass'), and now, slowly things seem to be improving. I just don't want you to give up on me. I'm not going to bore you or myself with all that 'I have a disease, I can't help it' crap because you've heard it all before. Okay, great, I have a disease, I will always have an obsessive compulsion, but I know I can beat this thing because we both know people who fight it successfully every day, but not you or God or Julie is going to fix me. It has to come from me. I am so fucking sick and miserable of all of it. It sucks. But there is nobody to blame except for myself. Three weeks ago I was on top of the world. I was clean and sober and feeling great. I looked great, I was in a successful band, I was seeing the country, blah blah blah. Now, I look like shit. I feel even shittier. I have no band. I know it's not the case, but I feel like a has-been. I know I have a million opportunities and I can get right back into being sober and successful, but right now at this very minute I just feel like shit. And it's my own doing.

I'm not trying to get you to feel sorry for me. I can do that good enough for the both of us. I'm just trying to express everything I feel to you. Some birthday gift, huh? This letter is probably going to end up reading like the ravings of a lunatic, and if it does, I am very sorry. My brain is mush right now with regrets and hopes and a thousand other thoughts and feelings I can't even begin to verbalize. I'm just *trying to let you in. I also drank way too much coffee so I'm going at twice my normal thought rate.*

You know, no matter who I knew I was going to hurt, it never mattered. I just didn't give a fuck. I was going to leave today and then you called me and told me you had never asked me for anything in my life, but you were asking me not to leave. You didn't even wait for my half-assed stuttering retort, you just left it at that and said good-bye. Well, I didn't leave. I don't know if that means anything, if it was you or God or me just giving up, but I'm tired of hurting you. I'm tired of hurting myself. I love you so much and I wanted to be there so much tonight, even after I was going to leave and decided to stay. I was even still contemplating going. I look like shit and I was ashamed and sick and sad, but I didn't want to disappoint you.

In the end I figured you'd be more disappointed with a sick, sad, and ugly rendition of the Nick you love than with an absent one, so I stayed home. And you know what? I knew you'd understand. It might have taken a bit, but I knew you'd understand. I personally think the reason you understand me a lot of the time, aside from the fact that you are my mom, is because you're a little crazy too. Maybe crazy on a different, higher plane, but a little cuckoo all the same. That's why Julie gets it. She's nuts! In a good way, of course. You can't be as fantastically brilliant as we are without popping a couple of minor screws loose. The human brain simply can't take all that work.

I think you and Julie should write a book together on the art of tag-team mothering. You could dress up like professional tag-team wrestlers for the cover picture. Shit. I am just rambling now. I can never articulate exactly what I want to say so I end up sounding retarded. I'm sorry. I love you. We Traina children are the luckiest people on earth to have ended up with a mother like you. Me especially. I don't think anybody would have kept faith in me like you have. One day I'll show you. I promise. I will make you prouder than you ever thought you could be. Prouder than I am of you. I am proud of your success. I am proud of the way you've handled all the hardship you've dealt with. I am proud of the way you run that household. I am proud of what a wonderful mother you are (to your children and your staff). I am proud to be your son.

I am truly my mother's son. So much of who I am, good and bad, has come from you. We have more in common than anyone would ever think. We both love small ugly dogs. We both love scrambled eggs. We both smoke too much. We are both romantics. We both have minds that could move mountains. We are perfectionists. We have hearts bigger than the sky. We both laugh when we get frustrated. Both of us have a fantastic fashion sense. We collect shoes. Our generosity has come back and bit both of us in the ass. We trust too much *yet not enough. We both want to marry everyone we fall in love with. We hate nature (bugs, dirt, etc.). There is so much we have in common.*

I hope you can make some kind of sense of this. Feel free to correct me on any misspellings or punctuation?/.' or grammar-type shit because I know it's all gone downhill. It's probably one big run-on sentence. It's no longer your birthday now and I'm sorry I missed it. My heart was there even if my body wasn't. Happy 34th birthday.

Love always,
Nick

I answered Nick immediately by fax that night, telling him again how proud of him I was, and how much I loved him. But neither Julie nor I could find the letter later.

The only thing that kept Nick going in those last grim days of August was the hope of starting a new band, with Chuck. He was beginning to catch the spark Julie had given him, and she continued to fan the flames as, night and day, he and Chuck wrote lyrics and music together. They called people they knew, rounded up other musicians, and by the end of August they had actually put something together. It was like watching a wounded thoroughbred rise slowly to his feet, a little shaky at first, but proud and tall and graceful. And once he picked up speed, as always, he really started moving. He set up bookings, booked time in a recording studio, and rented a small studio to rehearse in.

As he had with Link 80, Nick drove his band

members mercilessly. He was making up for lost time now, and the material he and Chuck had put together was terrific. I liked the songs and the music even better than his old ones. And everyone who heard them liked them. He called the new band 'Knowledge.'

He was utterly remarkable, and they played their first concert on August thirtieth. He was nervous before they went on, and they had already started taping their first recording for a new CD. It was a great night for him, a night of hope and new dreams, and finally, vindication. Link 80 came to see what the competition looked like, and after the performance, they asked Nick to come back. It was a moment that should have come sooner, but was destined not to. Nick thanked them and refused. He never went backward, he was locked into fast forward.

One of the songs he played with Knowledge that night was about his experience with Link 80, and made me so proud of him. He was one hell of a man, and as he had before, he taught me many things, about courage and hope, believing in yourself, and loving. If Nick could get back on his feet, with all the obstacles he faced and the hurdles he had to jump over, so could I, so could anyone. What right did I have to whine, if Nick could do it? And God, how I loved him for it. I was so damn proud of him, and still am. I always will be.

Still Standing
Now that I've been said and done
Fallen in the name of fun
I know I'm not the only one

But I'm still all by myself.
You overlooked my times of need
Laughed away thoughts of helping me.
I guess you thought I'd be all right
When I was the one on top.
Today I refuse to live in a hole
But a time not quite too long ago
I was wasting thoughts with my mind closed.
My heart was dead
My soul was broke.
You put off tragedy for another day.
Well, my friend, that day's today.
I hit the ground with outstretched hands.
And now I see you weren't my friends
Cuz the ones who'd helped me
Had been there all along
So I guess that I . . .
I guess that I was wrong.
You can twist it round which way you like.
It doesn't really matter who was right.
I'm here standing tall again
And now I know my real true friends
So in the end
In the end again, I turned out all right.
In the end . . .
In the end again, I turned out all right.
Turned out all right.

He sure did. He was terrific, and on his feet again.
By the first of September, Nick was up and running.

19

Scrambled eggs at midnight

Those first days of September were busy for Nick. He was constantly running, calling people, setting things up, organizing, writing, recording, rehearsing. It was as though he felt he had to make up for lost time. By the middle of September they had completed their recording, and so professionally that we are marketing it now to major labels.

By mid-September he had a band, a tape, a stack of songs, and bookings. It was unheard of. But typically Nick. And Knowledge seemed to me even better than Link 80. To my ears, it was a more grown-up sound, and I could even understand the words now. But the best of all of it was that Nick was so happy. He was up on his feet again, and he was having a great time.

As always, Nick made me feel part of it. He showed up often late at night, after rehearsal, close to midnight, and usually brought some or all of the band members with him. He had me make scrambled eggs for them. He loved the way I cooked them, soft and mushy, taken off the fire at just the right time, with melted cheese in them. He could eat a dozen eggs at one sitting, and urged the others to eat them. When they didn't finish what was on their plates, he ate theirs too, telling them what a great cook I was. I didn't want to disappoint him by telling him he was the only human on the planet who thought so. He also loved my French toast and my tacos. But scrambled eggs were his favorite. Sometimes when he was home, we'd go down to the kitchen late at night, and I'd cook for him. I always tried to give him the feeling that I'd been waiting all night to do that. And in a way that was true, it was an opportunity for us to talk, and to share things. It was when he always let his guard down, and shared his problems. I cannot even think of making scrambled eggs now without thinking of Nick. In fact, since he's been gone, I haven't had the heart to make them. I know it would make me sob to do so. I would give anything in this world to cook them for him again, to share one of those moments with him. It will be a long time before I make scrambled eggs again. I'm not even sure I could now.

I remember one night particularly, when he showed up with half a dozen friends, after a rehearsal with the new band. He was driving them hard, but he had places he wanted to get to, and he knew they could do it. I had made scrambled eggs, as usual, and a ragtag looking group of kids was sitting around my kitchen table, with tattoos, assorted pierces, funny hair, they looked like a dinner party in a bad movie, and they sat there with my flock of little pedigreed dogs at their feet, in my kitchen, discussing the virtues of pit bulls. Something about the incongruity of it struck me as hysterically funny. I just stood there and laughed. I felt as though I were running a high-end trailer park for young musicians. But it was just what I wanted and I loved it. It was all part of Nicky, and it meant so much to me that he shared it with me, and wanted to include me. I'll never forget the thrill when he would introduce 'my mom . . . over there . . . give her a hand . . .' from the stage at a concert. It made me giggle.

Anyway, he was busy in those days. So was I. The kids were back in school, and I was putting my life back together. It had been two months and some since Tom left, and I was still sad. But I was trying to get up off my ass and make the best of it, as Nick had. It had been a long hard summer, and I was glad it was over.

Nick and I met for lunch a couple of times, but he really didn't have much time, and we were supposed to meet one Friday afternoon for lunch in mid-September. It was September nineteenth, and I had kind of a tight schedule because I was going out with friends that night, and I wanted to get my hair done, which seemed frivolous but it was all part of the new me I was creating, the new life I was ready to address now. He called late that morning, and had slept late, he was feeling lazy about lunch, but something in his voice caught my attention. He sounded sad or quiet or lonely or something, or maybe he was just sleepy. I asked if he was okay, and asked him bluntly if he was lonely or sad, and he laughed and said no, and to stop worrying about him. He had come for scrambled eggs a few nights before, so I had just seen him. But he was too lazy to come across the Bay for lunch. I volunteered to cancel my plans later that afternoon, but he said not to. He promised to come to dinner with me and the kids on Sunday. It was a tradition he almost always followed. He came home for Sunday night dinner, and more often if he had the time. But in the past few weeks he had been pretty busy. He had just finished polishing up his recording in the studio two days before, and he was playing a concert that night, on Friday.

I discovered later that he had a date that afternoon with a woman he'd seen in a centerfold and had pursued. He had lunch with her instead, and I'm glad. We had said everything we needed to by then. I'm glad he had some fun, and apparently he was crazy about that woman. It was their first date, and it was a success. They made a date for the following night too, and afterwards she wrote me a long letter.

Nick had also made overtures to John recently, which he had told me at our last lunch. They were on good terms, but not immensely close, and hadn't seen each other in a while. They both had busy lives, and Nick had always been closer to me than to his father, but he spoke of John lovingly, and had made a date with him for lunch the following week. They didn't do that often, as sometimes Nick found his father harder to talk to. It wasn't for lack of love on their part, we were just more used to each other, and to baring our souls to each other. Maybe we had more in common, and our styles were similar, in opening up to people. And men so rarely seem to open up to each other. I was more a part of his daily, hourly struggles. And sometimes talking to Nick, and listening to him, was like looking in the mirror for me, with a few added splashes of color, and some ripples. But there was a deep resemblance of spirit.

In any case, we never got together that afternoon. He went off to lunch with his centerfold, and I got my hair done.

That night I came home from dinner early, and went to bed, but found I couldn't sleep, which was unusual for me. Usually I fall asleep seconds after my head hits the pillow. But that night, I tossed and turned, got up, and finally took a bath. I went back to bed at four-thirty in the morning, and fell asleep at last at five in the morning. Nick and I must have gone to sleep that night at exactly the same time, from all I could determine later. I must have been feeling him close to me, part of my soul, racked and troubled. I never knew why I couldn't sleep that night, but I feel certain that some instinctive part of me knew he was in trouble. I was thinking of him when I fell asleep. And the phone rang at nine o'clock the next morning. It was Julie.

She didn't cry. She didn't scream. Her voice sounded perfectly normal. All she said was my name in a monotone.

'Danielle.' I think I knew without knowing.

'He's dead.' The words flew out of my mouth before I could stop them.

'Yes. He's dead.' She sounded startled that I knew it, but I didn't.

'You're kidding,' was all I could say. 'You're kidding . . . you're joking . . . he's not dead . . . you're kidding.' I couldn't stop saying the same words over and over and over. I must have said them a hundred times to her, over and over, like a machine that couldn't stop spitting out all its screws

and nails going haywire, irreparably broken . . .
you're kidding . . . you're kidding . . . you're
joking . . .

'He's *dead!!*' she screamed at me finally. 'I'm
NOT kidding.' In a burst of words, she told me
what had happened. He had taken a massive overdose of morphine. They had found him on his knees
on the floor, his head bowed on his bed, the needle
beside him. He had died instantly, they said. But
Julie knew what I did. Nick knew that he had had
an anaphylactic reaction to the same substance
three times before, and they had told him without
a doubt that if he did it again, it would kill him.
From what Julie could guess, he had done roughly
twice to five times the quantity he had done before.
He wanted to be sure this time. And he was sure.
Paul had left him alone finally at four-thirty that
morning, just as I was slipping into bed after my
bath. For the first time ever, Julie had left for the
night, to go to a midnight mass in Santa Cruz. Nick
knew that this time she would not be there to stop
him. Her husband, Bill, would have checked him
the next morning between six and seven, and had,
and that was when he had found him. Nick knew
that no one was there to stop him, or save him. He
was entirely alone this time, taking a substance he
knew would kill him and enough of it to be sure it
did so. It was a method of suicide called 'Toss it to
the Fates' by the experts, like Russian Roulette. The
intent was there, but he had once again taunted the
fates to take him or save him. And this time they
had taken him.

It made no sense because things were going so
well for him, and he was so happy. The concert had

gone brilliantly the night before. Had he been secretly depressed, or had he been manic? But whatever he had been, however charming, however talented, however beautiful, however loved, however desperately we had tried to save him from himself, he was gone. He had made sure of it this time. There wasn't, and never will be, a way to know if he truly meant to do it this time, or just threw caution to the winds and decided to ride the edge one more time, a game of Russian Roulette like no other. Or did he mean to do it? Perhaps the disease had finally overcome him, that and the fact that he had been forced to face his own limitations while he was on tour and lost Link 80. But he had been so excited recently about his new band, Knowledge. What had happened that last night? What had gone on in his head? What was he thinking? Despair, or manic folly? We will never know now, and can only second-guess him. But I have learned since that manic-depressives rarely kill themselves while in the depths of depression. They wait to do it until they feel better, are slightly manic, and have the strength to do so.

He left no note, no clue as to what had gone wrong. He had called a dozen friends between three and four in the morning, and all the while I had been pacing. He could have called me, but he also knew I might have heard, I might have known, I would have tried to stop him. And he didn't want to be stopped this time. He saw to it that neither Julie, nor I, nor Paul, nor even his friend Sammy the Mick were near at hand to stop him.

I gently set down the phone, as wracking sobs enveloped me. And without reason I ran down the stairs, down . . . down . . . down . . . sobbing . . . toward nothing . . . My own words rang in my head over and over again . . . are you kidding? . . . are you kidding? . . . this time God was. The flame that had been so bright, that had lit my life for so long, had been suddenly, silently extinguished. I could not even conceive of the darkness that began to engulf me.

edge rider

riding ever
    so close
        to the edge,
            you dare feats
            that terrify
            all who
                watch you,
            you love the gasp
                of the crowd,
                the roar in the air,
                the terror
                    you cause,
                    the furor
                        you stir,
                the hysteria mounts,
                    the panic,
                    the tension,
                        the terror,
            will he fall?
                will he dare?
                    will he care?
                        will he die?
                            will he live?
                    will he make it?
                            safe?
                                sound?
                                    or gory?
            you walk the edge,
                you tease
                    the abyss,
                you taunt
                    all the fates

you risk
    our hearts
        and your life,
            and at what price
                glory?

lost boy

poor lost boy,
        you wander
            endlessly in the maze
                of your own making,
                    shaking
                        with fury,
                    terror,
                            rage,
        you dart around
        trying to point
            fingers
                at shadows
                    in the mist,
        wanting ghosts
                to take
                    the blame,
            but only
                your own name
                    echoes
                        in the darkness.

we love you

we're here
  in the dark,
    waiting for you,
      hands
          outstretched
        trying to catch you,
            trying to hold you,
      catching you
        from the limb
        as it breaks,
    trying to spare you
        endless
          heartaches,
      you thrash,
      and you scream,
          thinking
              you're falling,
                calling out
              in despair,
                but we're here,
                  Nick,
                    we care,
                  we'll catch you.
                  we'll be there.
                      we love you.

20

A sea of yellow roses

Somewhere in those first minutes after Julie's call, I called three close friends, and at some point that morning, I know they came over. They were Nick's friends and mine, Jo Schuman, Kathy Jewett, and Beverly Dreyfous. My friends Victoria Leonard and Nancy Montgomery came later. The rest is a blur of faces and sounds and agonizing memories, intense pain, and constant tears. I felt as though my heart had been sliced in half with a machete. I could not even begin to conceive of what had happened, and what it would mean to me when I came to my senses. The prospect of it, the vague reality was so horrifying as to taunt me with madness. But for my children's sake, I had to at least pretend to think straight and of what I had to do for them. I had to think of them now.

I called John with shaking hands right after Julie called, and he was so stunned he said very little. I asked him if he wanted to come and tell the children with me, but he thought it was better if I did it before he got there. He was in the country, and it would take time for him to come. He promised to come as soon as he locked up the house in Napa, and could get to town to be with us. And I suspected Nick would have wanted me to tell his siblings. But I could not bear the thought of what I had to do now. All I could look at were the tiny steps I had to take, inch by inch, by agonizing inch. I could not look beyond that. All I knew, as my three friends arrived, and I forgot how they had gotten there, or why, was that I had to tell my children. For the moment, those three women, Julie and Bill, John, and I were the only people who knew what had happened. I knew that if the children saw crying faces all around them, baby-sitters, housekeepers, any of them, all of whom had been with me for one or two decades, the children would know instantly that tragedy had struck us. Alternately hysterical and calm, I felt like a zombie, but I had to think of them now. Not even Nick. But his siblings. The rest would have to wait till later.

Two of the children had slept overnight at friends', and I had to bring them home without arousing their suspicions unduly. I called them and said they had to come home for lunch. They were furious at my imposing myself on them and interrupting their fun. But I said I wanted to have lunch with them, and they complained bitterly about it. And in the meantime, I knew I had to hide from the others.

It was noon before I had all five rounded up. Zara, the youngest, was to turn ten in a week. Maxx, eleven, Vanessa twelve, Victoria just fourteen two weeks earlier, and Sammie fifteen. Hard ages to sustain a loss as great as this. And my greatest fear was for Sam who was his soul mate.

She adored him, and he was her hero. He was a hero to all of us, and to all those who knew him. He had accomplished so much, and had so many victories, after the tough hand life had dealt him. Nick was not a loser, but a winner.

There is a small sitting room off my bedroom, a sunny room with a pretty view and yellow flowered furniture. I waited for them there, where we always have family meetings because of its size and cozy feeling. They looked annoyed as they walked in. I was being unreasonable, ruining their Saturday, and they said so. I was about to ruin it irreparably, and deliver a blow none of them would forget in their entire lifetimes. I felt like an executioner, thinking of them and not myself. And they laughed at me as I asked them to form a circle, and we put our arms around each other tightly. It was something I had never done before, but I could think of no other way to do it. I wanted to have my hands on each of them, and them touching each other, enclosed, tightly, as one, as though to remind each other that even with this mortal blow, the circle of our love would not be broken. And Nick would still be in it, as he had always been, and always would be.

They teased me and called it a group hug. Someone said it was dumb, but as they saw my face, my eyes, they must have known, and they suddenly looked frightened. With good reason. I spoke up quickly, telling them that I was going to tell them something so terrible, so awful that they would not forget it, and I hoped never to tell them anything so terrible again. Sam's eyes were directly across from mine, only inches away, and as I looked into hers I began to cry and she asked in a choked voice, 'What is it?'

'It's Nick,' I said . . .

'What . . . why . . .' Their terrified eyes all met mine at once and I cut right to it.

'He's gone,' I choked out.

'What do you mean, "gone"?' Sam looked panicked.

'Gone . . . he's gone . . . I love you . . . I love you all so much . . . just as he loved you . . . he died this morning.' There was no other way to tell them, no better way to deliver a lethal blow like that one. And as though I had stuck a knife in each of five hearts, in unison they screamed, a sound I will never forget . . . long, hideous, howling screams of pain as we all sobbed and hugged each other. I will never forget delivering that death blow to them. I knew that whatever I did from that moment on would never be forgotten, would make a difference to how each of them lived their lives, and how they got through it. It was an awesome burden.

We cried together for a long time, and I told them that whatever they did now, however they chose to face this was their choice . . . if they wanted friends with them, if they needed to go out, if they wanted to be alone, or stay with me . . . whatever they did or needed or wanted was fair and reasonable (as long as it was not dangerous to them). But I pointed out to them that there was no right way to do this, and all I asked of them was that they be loving to each other.

They moved as one body from then on, drifting from room to room, crying, sobbing, talking, holding and hugging each other. I was as stunned as they were, as unable to understand or absorb it.

The household learned the news quickly then, and everywhere around me was a sea of sobbing people. The rest of the day is a blur of faces and tears and tragedy. People came and went. I had to make plans and decisions. We were suddenly talking about his funeral, and it sounded absurd to me . . . his tie . . . his shirt . . . his skateboard . . . his dog, maybe . . . his meds . . . his nurses . . . his anything . . . but his *funeral*? That was crazy. Even now there is a ring of disbelief to it.

The bishop came and talked to me. All I did was cry. We set the day for the funeral. John arrived and made phone calls for me. I went over lists of names, spoke to no one, checked on the children, made decisions. I called Julie. Her home and her life and her heart and her children were as disrupted as mine. She was his other mother. The tag-team mothers had lost in the end. He had slipped right through our fingers, through no fault of ours. He had done it himself, just like a big boy, a grown-up. We had lost him. I still could not absorb it, or understand what it meant for our future.

I knew I wanted music at his funeral. Songs he would like. His own songs. John was still making frantic attempts to reach the older boys, and found them finally. Beatie and her husband were still missing. All I knew was that they were in Lake Tahoe for the weekend. For the first and only time in her entire life, she had forgotten to leave me a number. And I had no way to find her. All I could do was hope she'd call me.

I asked Julie to come to dinner with her family, and told her how much I loved her, how much she had given me and Nick. She was afraid that somehow I would blame her. How could I? She had given him her life, her home, opened her heart to him in every way. For five years, she had given him what no other human could have. There is no way on earth I can ever forget that, nor will I.

People were called, flowers arrived, faces appeared. It is all a blur now. I drifted in and out of my children's rooms. I sobbed much of the time, as I still do now. I went to sit in his room and could not believe it. I felt as though he would come home any minute. This was a trick, a joke. He was kidding. It was all so wrong, so crazy. How would I live from that day on?

And then, suddenly someone put a phone in my hand, and I heard an all too familiar voice. It was Tom. Someone had called him. He said he was coming. And within minutes, he was there with me, holding me, a powerful presence, a strong force to sustain me and to lean on. I was not sure then if he came out of sympathy, or something more, for Nick's sake or mine or his own, and perhaps he didn't know either at that point. Maybe he just felt he had to be there. But whatever his reasons, I was grateful for his presence. For the next week, he never left me. And whatever he had done before, whatever had happened to frighten him, whatever pain he'd caused me when he left, no longer mattered. He was there for me when it counted, when I needed him most, just as Nick always said he would be. And I know that Nick would have been grateful to him, as I was. I could just hear him say 'Take care of my mom for me.' He did, Nick, better than anyone ever could have. It washed away all the pain of the summer before. It was the only thing that kept me going. And I had to do what I could to help the others who were counting on me to be strong. Everyone was counting on me to get them through it. And for once I feared I couldn't do it, but knew I had to manage somehow.

We decided on yellow roses for the funeral. I called my niece Sasha in New York and asked her to fly out and sing the 'Ave Maria,' as she had at Beatie's wedding. Nick would have been pleased to know she was coming out to sing for him, as he was crazy about her.

We listened to tapes of his songs, to find one we could play. Other people made calls. And I called my mother's best friend in New York and asked him to tell her in person. I asked John to call Bill's parents. They had a right to know, as did he, wherever he was. Nick was his son. I wanted him to know what had happened. And John was gentle and kind when he called. And still we could not find Beatie.

There were twenty people or more at my dinner table that night, and I looked around blindly at familiar faces. My publisher and her husband, Carole and Richard Baron, were there, and Lucy, who had taken care of Nick and loved him for eighteen years, Nick's psychiatrist Dr Seifried, Julie, her husband, Bill, and their children, who were as devastated as we were. My friends, my assistant, Heather, and Tom, and seven of my children were there. The only ones missing were Nick and Beatie. And although I had asked him to stay, John had gone home for a few hours to regain his composure. I suspected it felt awkward to him to have Tom there, although after more than two years in my life, he was a familiar figure by then.

And Beatie called finally as we finished dinner. I don't think I ate. I read Nick's birthday letter to me at the table. And when I spoke to Beatie on the phone, she said she had called just to tell me how much she loved me. It was unfair beyond words to reward her loving gesture with so much pain, but I couldn't wait to tell her. The press had been calling all day, and I wanted her to know before she heard it on the news and saw it in the papers. Her screams rang out in the car just as the younger children's had. It was a familiar sound now. But for Beatie it was perhaps even worse. We had lost 'our' baby. She said they would drive home immediately, and be home in a few hours. The blur continued after that, but finally she was in it. We all cried endlessly. It was truly a nightmare, one from which I knew we would never wake up, just as Nick had chosen not to in the end, for whatever reason.

The next day we went to the funeral home, to pick caskets. John came with me, my two loyal friends Kathy and Jo, my assistant Heather, and Beatie. Without even asking me, my whole staff had chosen to work all weekend. The entire office crew came in to help make 'arrangements,' a word I had always hated. And seeing the caskets in that abysmal room in the basement of the funeral home was so ghoulish I couldn't bear it. We picked a room for him, a box for him, a suit for him at home. It became crucial to find the right tie, right shoes, and have his suit pressed. It was absurd the things one clung to. His shoes were all strewn around my dressing room so I could pick the right ones. It took me days to put them away, as though if I left them there, he would return to fill them or put them away himself.

On Monday I went to the cemetery, and looked at what they referred to as 'estates' for him. John and Beatie joined me, and as the people at the cemetery told me how much they loved Nick too, I began to feel nauseous. I thought it a miracle by then that I hadn't fainted. I looked like a small, sad black bird, in clothes that were beginning to hang on me. I hadn't eaten, and didn't care if I never did again. What was there to eat for? Nick was gone.

We all went to the funeral home for the first time that night, with the children and close friends, and I had to decide if I wanted to see him. I did. I wanted to hold him, cradle him in my arms, rock him to sleep as I had when he was a baby, hold him for a last time. But I was afraid that if I saw the truth, it would truly kill me, so feeling guilty for it, I didn't. My three oldest children did and were destroyed by it. Julie did, and a few others. The sobs coming from that room nearly undid me.

And on Tuesday, hundreds of people came as we sat with his closed casket, covered by a blanket of yellow roses. The children were there and sobbed, John, Julie and her family, familiar faces of people I have known. A few stand out in the crowd, but I think I was so deeply in shock by then that I remember very little. It is a small mercy. I am aware that Tom was always there with me, supporting me, greeting friends, and crying beside me. He loved Nick too. We all did. Tom came back into my life then, which would have pleased Nicky no end. Perhaps it was his last gift to me, to bring us back together, which was what he had wanted.

I was startled at one point at the funeral home to look up and see Bill standing there, hesitantly, with his parents. He looked well, and unchanged in many ways. He was wearing a suit, and I could see instantly that he was in good shape, and appeared to have straightened out his life. And as I looked at him, all I could think of was the bond that Nick had been between us. Nearly twenty years had passed, yet the gift he had given me so long ago had been one of the greatest of my existence. I walked toward him, we hugged, and I told him how sorry I was, and we walked to the casket together. And what had once been love, then disappointment, melted into grief, and slowly became friendship, the bond Nick had given us, and left us with in the end.

There was so much I wanted to say to him, to tell him, about Nick. I owed him so much, and he had missed it all. His lifestyle and his demons had swept him away from us, and now the tide had brought him in, too late for Nick, or for himself, and all I could feel was compassion and sadness for him, and gratitude that he had survived and returned.

Bill told me that, by chance, he had put himself in a program a month before, and cleaned up for the first time in twenty years, and had been planning to come to see Nicky. It was a cruel turn of fate that Nick had left us before he could do it.

I saw him the next day, on the steps of the church, off to one side, with his parents and a friend, as I waited for the pallbearers to come up the stairs with

Grace Cathedral, 24 September 1997. Nick's funeral

Tom and I at top of stairs. Group ascending stairs,
counterclockwise on left: Maxx, Todd, Sam Ewing, Bill
Campbell, Stony (Nick's friend and roadie with Link 80).
Clockwise on right, behind leaders: Trevor, Paul, Cody,
Max Leavitt.

the casket. I hugged him again, without words this time. We talk often now and meet from time to time. He has come to know Nick through us, and we have become loving friends. I hope that Nick is being a guardian angel to him, and will keep him safe. One tragedy is enough. He has shown me kindness and healed an old wound. But most of all he gave me a great gift in Nicky. I will always be grateful to him for it, and wish him well.

The funeral was beautiful, in a handsome cathedral, there were eleven hundred people there, Nick's friends and mine, people who knew him from the music scene, my publishers, our family and friends. Trevor and Todd were pallbearers along with Bill Campbell, both of Nick's nurses, Cody and Paul, and two of Nick's friends, Max Leavitt and Sam Ewing (Sammy the Mick), and his beloved friend and roadie Stony. Nick's little brother, Maxx, walked beside them, and as they carried Nick to the altar, I walked slowly behind him alone. Four months before to the day, he had walked me down that aisle at Beatie's wedding, and I had told him how much I loved him. He had been there for me, and now I was there for him. I did it for Nick, and I felt I owed it to him. I carried one of the animals he had slept with all his life, a small shaggy character named Gizmo. He sits on my desk now, along with the other, a little white lamb Nick called Lambie. (I put duplicates of them that I had kept over the years in his casket with him the next day, and kept his old ones.)

My niece Sasha sang the 'Ave Maria,' we played one of Nick's songs, 'I Am All Alone,' which demolished everyone, and Trevor, Todd, Beatrix, and Max Leavitt delivered eulogies while the children and I and eleven hundred people sobbed as we listened.

And at the end, Val Diamond sang 'Wind Beneath My Wings' from *Beaches* that said everything I felt about him. 'Did you ever know that you're my hero? . . . I was the one with all the glory, while you were the one with all the strength . . .' And everywhere I looked around me there was a sea of yellow roses. From now on, yellow roses will always remind me of Nicky.

When we left the church and walked down the steps behind Nick, I turned when we reached the bottom, and looking up, I saw more than a thousand faces as people stood still, without moving a hair, silent, respectful, row after row after row of them, like statues, mourning with us, as the church bells tolled in the steeple.

Three hundred people came to the house afterwards, and then it was over. Almost. We had to bury him the next day, or leave him at the cemetery at least. I was awake all night the night before, but came up with an idea around six A.M. I couldn't bear seeing my children in their sad little black dresses again, and knew they had had all the pain they could take. The formalities no longer mattered. It was only going to be the family and a handful of friends at the chapel at the cemetery. I called everyone at the crack of dawn and told them we were celebrating 'Bad Taste Day' in honor of Nicky. Since he had had the bad taste to leave us in the lurch, we had to dress in a way that would be truly embarrassing to him. The truth was he would have loved it. It was just his brand of humor, and I was doing it to help the children.

Everyone showed up in the worst outfits I have ever seen, in sparkles, sequins, tie-dyed shirts, flowered combat boots, and rock star glasses. John outdid himself in Versace, and although I have worn nothing but black since, I wore something colorful that day. The kids loved it, and we kept it brief. A musician friend played show tunes and things from *Sesame Street*, there were brightly colored roses in the tiny chapel, two priests said a quick prayer, and outside a fleet of motorcycle cops waited. The mayor had provided a motorcade for us, to keep the press away. There were no dry eyes amongst the policemen when I shook their hands before we went into the chapel.

I suppose we were meant to say good-bye to Nicky there, but I can't see why. I did not leave him there. I took him away with me in my heart. He will be ever next to me in a thousand ways. He is a part of the very fiber of my being. I cannot lose that, or pry it from me, or give it away. He belongs to me, as I belong to him, because of the hearts we gave each other, the years, the tears, the defeats, the victories, the endless joys we shared. I can't ever lose that, or him. Ever.

But loving Nick wasn't about losing. It was about winning. It was about hoping and believing, and trying, finding new avenues and racing down them, and then trying others when they failed. Nick taught me a thousand valuable lessons, how to love foremost among them. How to give your heart until it breaks, or you die, whichever comes first. The lessons Nick taught me were too valuable to forget, or throw away, or walk away from.

What is my life like now without him? At times, it seems intolerably empty. He has left a hole in my heart the size of Texas. Bigger than that. Much bigger. The size of Nicky.

I still can't believe that he is gone. I do things to fill the days, and nights, sometimes frantically, sometimes quietly. I sort through albums and look at his pictures. I copy them for other members of the family. I have organized his videos, read all his journals. I call the lawyer in New York to see about releasing his last recording. I have worked on this book. And organized a memorial concert with the bands he loved, and a foundation.

I want his memory to live on forever. I want people to remember him, to know him, to love him, to know how important he was to me, how much I loved him, and how much he loved me, how much we all loved him. I want them to know what an extraordinary person he was, how much he laughed, how much joy he brought us, how talented he was, how brilliant and loving. Will that fill the void? I doubt it. I suspect that nothing will. There will be a hole in my heart forever, like a doughnut. The years that I gave him, with so much passion and energy, were his, and he took them with him. There is nothing that can replace them or ever will.

I have eight other wonderful children to love and care for, and keep me company, each one of them as infinitely precious as Nick. My life belongs to them now, as it always has. And I know, or at least I hope, that in time we will laugh again, live again. I hope that wonderful things will happen to us, and when they do, I know I will want to tell Nick about it, and I will miss him more than ever. It is a cycle of longing for him that will not be easily broken. Nick became not only my son, but my best friend. His life was not only a bright light for all of us, but a symbol of love and hope for all those who loved him and all those he met.

His room is still intact. I have tidied it up, straightened it as though he will come home again. I cannot bear the thought of taking it apart, or giving his things away, although perhaps we will some day. But I prefer to think it will always be there, forever. I have not gone to see his little house at Julie's. It will be much too painful for me, or is for now at least. I will go there in time. As I do here, Julie tidies it, and sits there peacefully sometimes. It is the house, the room, the place where he died. A memory and a visual I cannot bear to think of. Someone said in one of the condolence letters that one day we will think of him as someone who lived, not someone who died. And I like that. He lived well and hard and with endless love and passion and excitement. Life to him was one long concert, full of leaps and jumps and noise and lights and music. That is who Nicky was, and who he will always remain.

As for the rest of us left here, we remember, we think about him, we talk about him, more and more with laughter as time passes. There are endless stories about him. And without him now, some days are better than others. It's hard to believe that he's gone. Sometimes, for an instant, I still forget, or want to. Others dream of him, and think they see him. And I always seem to feel him near me. I have no experience with these things, and can't decide if he is truly nearby, watching me, or if it is simply wishful thinking. I would like to think that he can see us, that he is in fact near, and that he is at peace now. I hope more than anything that he is happy. He deserves it, as we do.

This has been infinitely hard for us, harder still to find a blessing in it, a gift, a victory, yet they are there, if one is willing to see them. His life was a victory in the end, he accomplished so much in so little time, and he was a gift to so many. He gave us all so much. He gave as good as he got.

In some ways, Nick's greatest gift to me was one of healing. In losing so much when I lost him, I faced my own worst fears and greatest demon. It was loss that I feared most all my life, and that Nick made me face with the kind of courage he always expected of me. He gave me no choice but to live with his decision, the risk he took, the choice he made, and to accept it. I still fight it sometimes, and on bad days, I whimper to myself that I can't do this. But I can, and I have to, just as he did. I cannot escape the pain, or the loss, or the memories, or the fact that I miss him so unbearably at times. I must learn to live with it, and make our lives not only good, but whole again.

Joy will come again, and has in many ways, with time, and through the people we love and who love us, and the children. We will share happy times again, and we have each other. We are beginning to laugh again, and I see the children smiling. And the Campbells will have a new baby a year after Nick died. Hope has come to each of us, in different ways, like final gifts from Nick. Spring will come, and many summers, and there will be holidays without him, when we will remember all too clearly when he was with us. But the memories linger, the sweet perfume of all he brought. He left each of us something, a gift, a dream, a memory, a little more courage than we had before, a bigger dream than we might have had without him.

Life is about dreams, and hope, and courage. The courage to go on, even after those we love have left us. And in our hearts, Nick isn't gone. He dances on, as dazzling as ever, smiling and laughing and singing. A shooting star we will cherish and re-member forever. He gave me joy enough for ten lifetimes. That will never leave me.

I love you, Nick. Thank you, and God Bless you. I'll see you again one day.

'Don't Give Up'

Just when I don't think I can take no more
Been disappointed too many times
One of my crew puts their arm around me
and says if I
don't give up, then I'll be fine.
At times in life, I've done so well,
I've spent time on the top.
I've also been in ruins
demoralized and dropped.
That's just the way things are,
You can never expect more,
Half the time you're winning,
And the rest you're on the floor.
This world's as full of beauty
as it is of hate,

That's just the way it is,
Some things won't ever change.
Focus on the positive, and use your mind.
Don't ever give up, and you'll be just fine.
Some of dem like drugs,
and some of dem like to fight.
Negativity inspired somewhere
every single night.
Got to set examples for
the weak of mind.
Don't stop spreading knowledge
till the end of time.
So many hateful people,
so many are deranged.
It can take its toll on you,
when life gets rearranged.
It's a proven fact that you
get what you give,
and you can make an impact
in the way your life is lived.

Nick Traina

Afterword

Time has passed since I first wrote this book about Nicky. It has been nineteen months since he left us. Long months, hard months. Like a dog on a leash being dragged across the sidewalk, I resist the passage of time. It happens anyway. In some ways, it seems an eternity, in others a very short time. I dread what it will feel like when I say he has been gone for ten years or twenty, or twenty-five. Such a long, long time. Now it isn't very long, in relation to a lifetime, yet time marches on. His brothers and sisters are getting older. Things happen and change. Right now, there are still many things in our lives that he was a part of, we still do the same things and go to the same places we did with Nick. One day that won't be so. His brothers and sisters will grow up and move on, marry, have children of their own. But not yet. He still seems almost within our grasp.

Both Nick's room and cottage are still intact, neat, clean, orderly. His clothes still hang in the closet. His toothbrush still sits on the bathroom shelf, with the rest of his things. The room still smells vaguely, though less, of him. I go into it less often, but stop in from time to time, look around. Nothing has changed, and yet something is different. A few months ago, I looked into the room and thought it had the look and feel of a fallen leaf, still green, but drying around the edges, fading slowly. One senses rather than sees that he is gone. I could not bring myself to pack up his things, and doubt that I ever will. I imagine myself sitting in that room when I am old, thinking of him. He will eternally be a teenager, even long after his siblings are grown. They will grow old, have jobs, get wrinkles, have children. Nick never will. He will forever bounce into my mind, wearing funny cut-off pants, suspenders, a tee shirt, and sneakers, with that eternally contagious grin.

I feel him close to me. We all do. He remains part of conversation, the center of funny stories and cherished memories. 'Remember when Nick . . .' or 'Nick used to like that too.' His brother Maxx has begun to look like him, yet is even more handsome, and very much his own person. But there is an air of family. Once in a while, there is a move, a gesture, a way of leaping over something or running that makes me stop and look. But it is Maxx, not Nick. Nick was who he was, the others are who they are and will be. The echo of things Nick said stays with me. I remember his being horrified at the prospect of turning twenty. 'I want to be a teenager forever', he said, and so he will be.

Our first Christmas without him was agonizing. The second one was better. I suspect holidays will always be hard for all of us. Nick left a hole that will not fill. We have a large old house, which was built with a ballroom. We use it for storage, for celebrations, for the kids to play in, for parties. We open our Christmas presents there and as there are so many of us, we each have our designated 'spots' where our presents are, and we open them while talking and laughing with each other around them. I wrestled with Nick's spot both years. What to do? Put someone else's gifts there? Who could bear that awful feeling of trying to stand where Nick once stood? I mulled over moving everyone over a little, to kind of blend Nick's old spot into others until it disappeared. But that didn't feel right either. So the spot stands empty now during our celebrations. It reminds us of Nick. No one mentions it, but our eyes drift there as we open our gifts, remembering when he was laughing and shouting and cavorting, throwing torn gift wrap over his shoulder, and bouncing around the room like a kangaroo. You don't forget someone like Nick, or replace them, or move them out of your life or your head. He has stayed an enormous presence to all who knew him, and even in memory, he remains very much Nick.

I received thousands of letters about him, and still get new ones from time to time, from friends, from strangers, telling me funny stories about Nick. Each of those letters comes to me as a gift.

And we have been busy in his absence, particularly in that first year. We gathered photographs, tapes, films, mementoes. I have dozens of hours of tape of him in concert. We made a video for the family, of Nick in concert, and Nick amidst the family, with the background music of his last CD, some still photographs. For a long time, I could not bear seeing him on film, he was so alive, so vibrant. But now, I take comfort from those videos of him. I do not watch them often, but when I do, I miss him, but can smile. The house is filled with photographs of him. We put together a leather bound album of his funeral service, and sent it to the people who had been there.

I read his journals, pored over his notebooks, poetry and lyrics, and wrote the book, and I am so very glad I did. It was a way of honoring Nick, of bundling the many memories of his life, linking them together, and keeping them in one place for all to see. I think he would have loved it, and the response to the book has been enormous. It has been read by laymen, psychiatrists, parents, friends, strangers, people who knew him, and others who wish that they had. It has been a wonderful thing, and has gained Nick a huge amount of love, appreciation and respect. He fought a hard fight, and so did we, and whatever the outcome, we all did the best we could, even and most especially Nick. I wanted people to know that about him, and now they do.

We gave a memorial rock concert for him, a 'tribute show', eight months after he died, which was amazing, and fun actually. Eight bands performed, his old band Link 80, with his close friend Stony standing in for him as lead singer. The band has been doing well, and still speaks lovingly of him. The other bands were either bands he had performed with, toured with, or loved and respected. They came from all over the country to be in it, and the performances were terrific. It was an extra-ordinary evening, filled with admiration, love, and respect for us and for Nick, especially for Nick. He truly would have loved it. Kids lined up for hours outside the theater to get in, tickets were sold out weeks before. Eight hundred people saw it, and the room was filled with love and music. We showed the tribute video, and there was total silence, as tears slid silently down everyone's cheeks. And at the end of the evening, there was endless hugging, loving, no one wanted to leave. It ended finally at three a.m. and just about everyone who had ever mattered to Nick, in or out of his music world, was there. It was a night none of us will ever forget, and in my heart, I knew that Nick was there.

Nick's last CD was released, which did very well, and is what Nick would have wanted. His last band, Knowledge, was forced to disband, but the CD will keep the memory of them alive, along with Nick's. Two final music videos were made and shown on TV.

I did a television interview with Barbara Walters on 20/20, to talk about Nick, manic-depression, and the book. And the TV show he had been on at fourteen, 'First Cut', a news show for and by teenagers, did a special on him. Nick was certainly not forgotten, and did not go out in silence. He has become the focal point for attention on manic-depression and young people. I hope that lives will be saved and people will be helped because of him.

There have been numerous articles in psychiatric journals, and some impressive changes have come about, not necessarily because of him specifically, but because of so many others like him, and the voices that have been raised along with mine. It is becoming more and more common to diagnose teenagers with manic-depression, and to prescribe the appropriate medications, often lithium, sometimes Depakote sometimes others. I would like to think that the spotlight on Nick, and others like him, has encouraged psychiatrists and physicians to diagnose manic-depression and offer medication earlier than they have in recent years. Even more exciting is the more recent news that psychiatrists have begun diagnosing what they now call 'baby bi-polar', diagnosing children as young as 5 or 6, and medicating them then. There is some belief now that medicating too late, or beginning with inappropriate or inadequate medications can diminish the effectiveness of drugs like lithium once they're administered later on, whereas starting with the right medications early on can increase their positive impact on bi-polar disease. So there is hope. The light begins to dawn. And more lives will be saved. I feel now that Nicky was fully manic by the time he was four, and only wish they had been talking about, and medicating, 'baby bi-polar' then. It might have made a life-saving difference to Nick.

To mark the anniversary of Nick's death, a grim day for us, we held a memorial celebration, and unveiled the monument we had built for Nick. It is a large park-like plot in a local cemetery, with four big trees on it, surrounded by cypress trees, standing close together, to block out the view of the cemetery. It is a sunny spot, and Nick's monument itself is a large black granite disk, and engraved on it are messages from each member of the family, and the Campbells, poems, letters, whatever they wanted to say. It is surrounded by white marble benches, and the black granite disk itself is at 'coffee table height' so people can sit on it if they want to. Nick rests under it. There is a low bounded black granite wall in the background, with four white marble columns. And a 'hoaky' touch Nick would have loved is a long glass case on a marble stand. In it are teddy bears, letters, a menorah, a Buddha, rosary beads, Star Wars figures, toys, candy, cigarettes, every kind of imaginable memorabilia that people leave for him. And each time I go there, people have left more for him. At Christmas, I put up and decorated a big Christmas tree for him. I couldn't imagine Nicky not having a tree. It makes me sad to go there, but it is peaceful and pretty, another of the many tributes we made to him.

We brought him to that final resting place on a sunny September day, driven in the van he toured in with his band. The van, covered in miscellaneous graffiti, where he had spent so many hours with his friends, seemed like a suitable last ride for him.

After much thought and consultation, we have decided to celebrate his birthdays. His doctors, nurses, psychiatrists, bands, friends, family, and people who loved him gather forty or fifty strong to talk and laugh and cry and sit and tell stories about him. It is a happy opportunity for all of us to gather and celebrate, rather than staying home and being sad on our own. We just celebrated his twenty-first birthday. It was a hard day, but it was better spent amongst those who loved him, than separately, alone.

We also set up the Nick Traina Foundation, with the proceeds from the book, and donations people have made. We have made a lot of donations to non profit organizations involved with manic-depression, mental illness, child abuse, and some to organizations helping musicians with mental health needs. The foundation is growing, and is something I believe Nick would have loved, as he was of a very charitable bent.

Paul and Cody, Nick's nurses, are still with us. Cody works for the foundation and in my office. Paul works in security. It is comforting to see their familiar faces every day. They have become part of our family. The Campbells are doing well. They had a baby, Sofia, who was born almost exactly a year after Nick left, and she is a joy to all of us.

His friends still call often and come to visit. His friend Sam Ewing comes to dinner at least once a week, and is also part of our family. Nick's biological father, Bill, is well, has remained a much valued friend and visits us regularly. Through us, he has come to know Nick.

As for us, the immediate family, there are good days and bad days, hard times and sad ones, and happy ones. We draw on the millions of memories we have of Nick, and derive strength from each other. We all still miss him terribly. Our lives are forever changed, but we have grown too. Sammie is flourishing, and growing into a wonderful young woman, as are her sisters Victoria, Vanessa and Zara. Maxx is a teenager now. Beatie has struggled long and hard with losing the boy who was 'her baby' too. We all think about what life would be like if Nick were still with us. But in so many ways he still is.

I feel Nick with me constantly, daily. I see him in my head, always with his big smile, and sense him close to me. I cannot lose him, leave him, he is and always will be a part of me. He was one of life's greatest gifts. No book, no words, no description, no song, no illness can confine him or describe him adequately. He was larger than life, bigger than my heart and soul, and his own. He lived, he loved, he laughed, he gave us all gifts beyond measure. And now, precious child of my heart, he is free.

> With my love to all of you
> who read about him.
> D.S.
> 18 May 1999